T0265699

Generative AI

by Pam Baker

A Wiley Brand

Generative AI For Dummies®

Published by: **John Wiley & Sons, Inc.**, 111 River Street, Hoboken, NJ 07030-5774, www.wiley.com

For general information on our other products and services, please contact our Customer Care Department within the U.S. at 877-762-2974, outside the U.S. at 317-572-3993, or fax 317-572-4002. For technical support, please visit https://hub.wiley.com/community/support/dummies.

Wiley publishes in a variety of print and electronic formats and by print-on-demand. Some material included with standard print versions of this book may not be included in e-books or in print-on-demand. If this book refers to media that is not included in the version you purchased, you may download this material at http://booksupport.wiley.com. For more information about Wiley products, visit www.wiley.com.

Library of Congress Control Number is available from the publisher.

ISBN 978-1-394-27074-3 (pbk); ISBN 978-1-394-27076-7 (ebk); ISBN 978-1-394-27075-0 (ebk)

SKY10088347_101824

Table of Contents

PART 3: EXPLORING ADVANCED GENAI MODELS AND TECHNIQUES

Introduction

Welcome to *Generative AI For Dummies*, a groundbreaking book that's one of the first, to my knowledge, to be professionally produced with the assistance of Generative AI and crafted by an award-winning, best-selling author in collaboration with a premier publishing house. To be absolutely clear, I wrote this book using GenAI models to help with research and drafting only. As impressive as they are, GenAI models and applications fail at writing books to professional standards. However, they can be useful when used properly in a junior-level assistant capacity.

Many people on the editorial, technical, and AI sides at Wiley collaborated to make this book possible and to make sure it met the highest standards. It's a team of incredibly talented people who were fearless in pioneering book production with Generative AI (GenAI) to learn, advance, and help others find success in the GenAI space. Also know that I have researched, tested, and used many of the techniques and methods you find here to write this book. It's been a hard and trying trek for all of us through the unknown — not to mention dealing with the stubbornness in GenAI behaviors. But it all proved worth it in the end. I hope you think so, too!

Rather than drone on about the technical aspects, my intention is to help you move past the hype and common frustrations in working with GenAI to actually produce usable works that meet your specifications and goals. I hope you find this book an inspiration, a real-world example of what can be done with GenAI, and an exceedingly helpful guide to help you level up your skills, too.

If you feel some unease about AI in general and GenAI in particular, know that your gut reaction is common and not entirely unwarranted. This technology will most certainly change the nature of work and how your job is done. But also know that GenAI is not going to take jobs away from most people. Someone good at using GenAI will. Be that someone!

You can learn this. It's not as hard as you think!

About This Book

Although you can find lots of content on various GenAI models, applications, and the basics in prompting on YouTube and in blogs, articles, social media, and elsewhere, this book uniquely reveals and explains advanced prompting and other AI methods to generate professional-level outputs no matter which GenAI model you're using or what type of content you are working to create.

It's a comprehensive text on the nitty-gritty details you need to push past the basics, the hype, and the common frustrations to make GenAI tools work like you need them to, yet these are things almost any user can do. Be kind to yourself as you experiment along your path to success.

If you're already experimenting or working with GenAI, you'll find several ways in this book to leverage what you already know and new tips and techniques to incorporate into your efforts to get even more from it.

As with any *For Dummies* book, the goal is for you to quickly access the information you need, no matter where you jump in. With that in mind, here are a few conventions I used when writing the book:

>> "Generative AI" and "GenAI" are used interchangeably, though I primarily use the shorter GenAI throughout the book.

>> References to GPT-like models or ChatGPT-like chatbots may or may not mean that they're technically similar to these models and tools since this book covers a wide range of Generative AI options. For example, competing models may or may not have Large Language Models (LLMs) as their foundation, as ChatGPT does, but are still referred to as "similar" here because their user interface and function closely resemble those of ChatGPT. In this way, you as a user can more easily compare and understand the various GenAI tools on the market without getting dragged through the technical weeds.

>> Whenever I introduce a new GenAI-related term (and there are lots of them in this ever-changing space), I place it in *italics* upon its first mention in a chapter and follow up with a quick definition. Keywords and action steps appear in **bold.**

>> Some web addresses break across two lines of text. If you're reading this book in print and want to visit one of these web pages, simply type the address exactly as it's noted in the text, pretending the line break doesn't exist. If you're reading this as an ebook, you have it easy; just click the web address to be taken directly to the web page.

Foolish Assumptions

This book is for anyone seeking to understand, use, and improve their work with GenAI models and tools. Having said that, I did make a few assumptions about you, dear reader, as a practical matter:

You have at least a basic level of comfort and skill in working with computing devices, browsers, and web applications.

You possess a limited understanding of the full range of GenAI options and their capabilities.

You, like many users, are frustrated or stuck with GenAI outputs that fall far short of ideal in terms of meeting your goals and needs. Of the things that might make you seriously contemplate screaming out your window or would make a saint take to drinking, GenAI would be near the top of the list.

You are smart and pressed for time and, therefore, want all meat and no fluff in a fast and easy read. I hope I've hit that mark for you.

Icons Used in This Book

Occasionally you'll come across some icons in the margins of this book that draw your attention to certain bits of the text. Here are what these symbols indicate:

TIP

This icon points to tips and tricks you may want to use to make your work with ChatGPT easier, faster, more efficient, or simply more fun.

REMEMBER

This icon highlights information of particular importance in successfully understanding or using ChatGPT.

WARNING

This icon warns you of a stumbling block or danger that may not be obvious to you until it's too late. Please make careful note of warnings.

Beyond the Book

In addition to the material in the print or ebook you're reading right now, this product also comes with an access-anywhere Cheat Sheet. To access the Cheat Sheet, go to www.dummies.com and type **Generative AI For Dummies Cheat Sheet** in the search box. You'll find helpful user tips and info on GenAI in its many forms, pointers on advanced prompt writing, and guidance on how to make it deliver the output you need precisely the way you need it, all within a convenient online article you can access on the go.

Where to Go from Here

This is a reference book, so you don't have to read it cover to cover unless you want to. Feel free to read the chapters in any order and skip over any ones that don't pertain to you or your needs. Each chapter is designed to stand alone, meaning you don't have to know the material in previous chapters to understand the chapter you're reading. Start anywhere and finish when you feel you have all the information you need for whatever task is at hand.

However, if your aim is to get better results from Generative AI immediately, you should read the chapters that specifically address prompting and the type of content you are trying to create, such as Chapter 2 for an introduction to the art of prompt engineering, Chapter 9 for many advanced prompting techniques and AI tactics, and chapters 7–10 for guidance on producing specific types of content. Or if you're worried that AI will take your job or abuse your private information in some way, there's good news for most of us in chapters 15 and 16.

Feel free to experiment with each new tool or tip you learn about in this book as you go. Many find it easy to follow along this way. But however you choose to learn and experiment with GenAI, you'll likely find these tips and methods relatively easy to do. The hardest part is stretching your own imagination to allow yourself to reach further with each new project.

The key to success, however, lies in your own talent. GenAI tools are nothing without it.

1

Diving into Generative AI Fundamentals

Chapter **1**

Mapping the Lay of the Generative AI Land

Welcome to the exciting world of Generative AI (GenAI)! This chapter is your starting point in understanding the vast landscape of GenAI and its transformative capabilities. Whether you're a curious beginner or a tech enthusiast, you'll find the information here to be an accessible guide to the basics of GenAI. You can easily build on these skills through practice, regular use of an AI application, or by returning to this book from time to time to enhance your skills further.

So, What Exactly Is Generative AI?

You can think of AI (short for *artificial intelligence*) as incredibly sophisticated software. Although it doesn't behave like any other software ever made, it is still software. Illustrations depicting AI as robots reflect the difficulty in drawing AI software in a way everyone will instantly recognize. But the robot is actually mindless hardware, and the AI is the "smart" brain-mimicking software installed to enable it to function in ways we consider to be intelligent in a non-organic sense.

Technically speaking, GenAI refers to a subset of artificial intelligence technologies that use sophisticated *natural language processing* (NLP), neural networks, and *machine learning* (ML) models to generate unique and humanlike content. It belongs to a classification of AI called *Large Language Models* (LLMs), which analyze huge amounts of data in numerous languages including human languages, computer code, math equations, and images.

LLMs typically have a substantial number of parameters, which are numerical values used to assign weight and define connections between nodes and layers in the neural network architecture. Parameters can be adjusted to change the weights of various values, which in turn, changes what the model prioritizes in the prompt and data and how it interprets various data points, words, and connections.

Imagine you have a recipe for making a cake, and the recipe is your GenAI model. The ingredients — like flour, sugar, eggs, and butter — are like the data points, words, and connections in the model. Now, the amount of each ingredient you use (how many cups of flour, how much sugar, and so on) are like the weights of various values in the GenAI model or GenAI application.

Just as you might adjust the ingredients in your cake to make it sweeter or fluffier by adding more sugar or an extra egg, you can adjust the parameters in a GenAI model to change what it focuses on and how it interprets the information it's given. If you want your GenAI to pay more attention to certain words or data points, you increase their *weight* just like adding more chocolate chips to your cake if you want it to be extra chocolatey. This way, the GenAI model, like your cake, turns out the way you want it to, based on what you prioritize in the recipe.

LLMs use parameters to predict the next word in a sequence — meaning they predict the word most likely to follow the words in your prompt, and then the word that most likely follows its first predicted word, and so on until the model believes it has finished the most probable pattern. It generates images in much the same way by predicting the image that follows your description in the prompt. The models can complete the process incredibly quickly. For example, LLMs like GPT-3 and GPT-4o developed by OpenAI are capable of processing billions of words per second. It is the speed of its response, the appearance of nuanced understanding, and its fluid use of natural language that gives GenAI interactions a humanlike feel.

REMEMBER

However, GenAI and LLMs are not human and do not think — again, they predict. It's a very complicated prediction process, to be sure. Nonetheless, it is a prediction. And if anything happens to tilt its predictive capabilities, nonsense ensues. You can see one example of that in Figure 1-1, which is an OpenAI incident report about an adjustment they made to the model resulting in ChatGPT responding to users in incomprehensible gibberish.

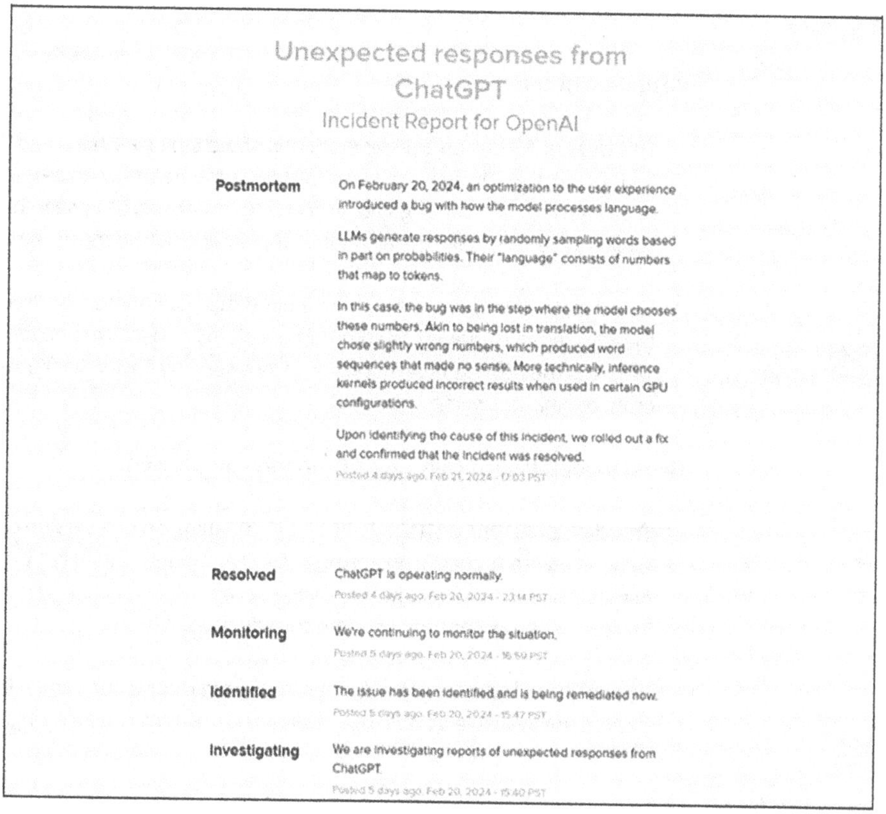
Unexpected responses from ChatGPT

Incident Report for OpenAI

Postmortem

On February 20, 2024, an optimization to the user experience introduced a bug with how the model processes language.

LLMs generate responses by randomly sampling words based in part on probabilities. Their "language" consists of numbers that map to tokens.

In this case, the bug was in the step where the model chooses these numbers. Akin to being lost in translation, the model chose slightly wrong numbers, which produced word sequences that made no sense. More technically, inference kernels produced incorrect results when used in certain GPU configurations.

Upon identifying the cause of this incident, we rolled out a fix and confirmed that the incident was resolved.

Posted 4 days ago. Feb 21, 2024 - 17:03 PST

Resolved

ChatGPT is operating normally.

Posted 4 days ago. Feb 20, 2024 - 23:14 PST

Monitoring

We're continuing to monitor the situation.

Posted 5 days ago. Feb 20, 2024 - 16:59 PST

Identified

The issue has been identified and is being remediated now.

Posted 5 days ago. Feb 20, 2024 - 15:47 PST

Investigating

We are investigating reports of unexpected responses from ChatGPT.

Posted 5 days ago. Feb 20, 2024 - 15:40 PST

Source: OpenAI incident report

FIGURE 1-1: A routine effort to optimize ChatGPT resulted in its producing gibberish in response to users' prompts.

GenAI VERSUS VIRTUAL ASSISTANTS

AI models and applications are the software driving the robot or the autonomous car or whatever form it's given in the corporeal world. But strictly speaking, AI has a digital form. Because of that, it can be squeezed into almost anything, and many a vendor does exactly that. You'll find various types of AI are embedded or otherwise at use in all sorts of products and services. However, not all AI is the same.

Here are the main differences between GenAI apps like ChatGPT and virtual assistants like Siri, Alexa, and Google Assistant.

(continued)

(continued)

Virtual assistants:

This class of AI runs on a proprietary mix of technologies in a blend developed by their respective corporate owners. Certain components, such as machine learning, deep learning, natural language processing, smart search or search engines, and speech synthesis make the assistants appear and sound much like ChatGPT.

However, their responses are more limited than GenAI models. People typically use these to retrieve answers to common questions or perform uncomplicated tasks like "where is the nearest pharmacy?" or "play a song by Taylor Swift" rather than to generate original answers.

GenAI models (specifically ChatGPT in this comparison):

This class of AI runs on a single AI model, meaning on one version or another of Generative Pre-trained Transformers (GPT) AI models. GenAI is a broad category of AI that includes models capable of varying capabilities such as generating text, images, or computer code or some combination of these.

People typically use GenAI web apps, but some mobile apps and a few wearable devices are available as well. But in all cases, the apps run on a single GenAI model.

Unveiling the BIG Secret to Working Successfully with GenAI

If you remember nothing else I've written in this book, you must remember what I tell you in this section. For here is the big secret — the master key — that you need to make GenAI models work at the level you need them to perform. If you don't grasp this, GenAI will likely appear to you to be nothing more than a fascinating toy or a tool that falls far too short of your expectations.

TIP

In a nutshell, GenAI generates outputs that appear to be original thoughts or images from a computer, rather than results produced by very advanced, contextual predictive software. GenAI retrieves words or images pulled from a database and repurposes them into a new response. The big secret is that the humanlike feel in the "conversation" is an illusion. You are not having a conversation with a machine. It doesn't understand a word you wrote in your prompt.

REMEMBER

Current GenAI models don't think or create things *per se*, but instead *generate* new things from parts of old things found in its database. (The term "things" in this context being images, videos, numbers, or text, depending on the GenAI application you are using.) A GenAI output is the model's best prediction of what you are seeking. In an oversimplified explanation of a complex technology, GenAI seeks to complete a pattern that you began with your *prompt*, which is your question or command as entered into the prompt bar on the GenAI's user interface (UI). In other words, GenAI predicts what letters, words, or images are likely to follow those that are in your prompt. Its predictions are based upon comparison to patterns that exist within its training dataset and/or datasets to which it was subsequently given access.

Think of GenAI outputs as the result of repurposing or remixing information that the model has access to in datasets, including the following:

>> Data it is exposed to in its training database along with any additional data provided in subsequent fine-tuning.

>> Data added in system messages or prompts.

>> Data added via methods such as *retrieval-augmented generation* (RAG), which is a tactic to enhance accuracy, relevancy, and reliability by adding external sources to the GenAI's database.

RAG combines the strengths of both *information retrieval AI*, which is a set of algorithms that retrieve contextually relevant information from huge datasets, and GenAI, which uses neural networks and machine learning models to generate new content. It might help to think of RAG as GenAI that is augmented by more traditional information retrieval AI, or retrieval AI for short.

WARNING

Since GenAI generates outputs that are the result of its remixing or repurposing of information, it has no concept of true or false, fact or fiction. GenAI can accurately define these terms, but it does *not* understand their meaning. It doesn't understand anything you wrote in the prompt or that it wrote in its response. It only appears to understand terms and concepts. This is an illusion. This is why you must always factcheck its work.

REMEMBER

GenAI responses are limited to the confines of the data it has access to. Put another way, if its training data were a mound of Legos and there were no end caps in that mound, GenAI would build its outputs without end caps. It would not know that end caps exist at all. In the same way, it does not know fact from fiction unless those labels are applied to specific data points in its dataset. But, if a falsehood is labeled as fact, GenAI will unquestionably accept it as fact. It still doesn't understand the difference.

To illustrate this analogy, I wrote a caption first and then used it as a prompt in Azure OpenAI Studio DALL-E playground (Preview). The result is the stunning concept illustration you see here in Figure 1-2.

FIGURE 1-2: If data were Legos, GenAI could only build things with the Lego pieces it has access to, and it is completely unaware that any other types of Lego pieces exist.

Art generated by Azure AI Studio DALL-E playground.

GenAI can repurpose and remix only the data it has access to, which is a major reason why GenAI outputs can be highly reliable or totally false or something in-between. The data itself can be insufficient — in one way or another — to provide the foundation or elements for the model to generate an accurate answer. Outdated data from an aging training dataset and data limited to too few perspectives or examples are common issues, but there are many others.

When — not if — outputs are wrong, people call them *hallucinations*. It's unclear why no one calls them lies, falsehoods, or simply errors, but in any case, you cannot assume that GenAI outputs are solid enough to bet your life or business on without doing some serious factchecking first.

REMEMBER

While GenAI does consider context when it analyzes the words in your prompt, it does not understand you or what you said in the prompt. This is why you must not confuse GenAI with General AI, also known as Artificial General Intelligence (AGI). AGI does not yet exist outside of science fiction movies, books, and TV shows. Yet some people are so in awe of GenAI capabilities that they are sure this must be it — the thing from the movies that's going to take over the world! This is not that.

Understanding the Infamous Finger Problem and Other GenAI Quirks

Perhaps the most wondrous thing about using GenAI is the delicate dance between human and machine that begets something neither would have made alone. But once you move past the first exhilarating moments of viewing GenAI marvels, you'll begin to see a few cracks here and there.

For example, it is common for GenAI models to draw people with six or more fingers on one hand. This is typically because the patterns it sees in its data is of multiple fingers on one human hand. No clear pattern emerges of there being just five fingers on one hand, so GenAI can't predict how many fingers it needs to generate.

Essentially GenAI is parroting the answer from its database. It doesn't understand the question or the answer; therefore, it does not know to draw only five fingers. Instead, it looks for patterns in hands depicted by images or text in the datasets to which it has access. But the pattern of the total number of fingers is unclear. Images in most databases that GenAI models use typically show hands in different positions wherein only some fingers are visible or fingers from two hands or more are intertwined. GenAI cannot therefore see a consistent pattern of the total number of fingers per hand. However, if you were to ask the model how many fingers are on a hand, it will almost always tell you that there are five. Even though it gives you the right answer as to the number of fingers, it does not understand its own reply and, therefore, still doesn't *know* the answer.

Data pattern inconsistency and the resulting probability prediction error is why you can end up with too many or too few fingers in any image GenAI generates. This is often the reason for other issues in images and videos that GenAI creates such as errors in shadowing or movement.

REMEMBER

Although GenAI is impressive, its reasoning is limited. In fact, it's extremely difficult for GenAI to reason at all. To overcome this shortfall and make it more powerful, add one or more humans to the mix and you'll soon see real magic in the result. It is the collaboration between you and this extremely sophisticated software that will take you to the goals you seek.

Figuring Out How to Work with GenAI — It's All About Your Prompts

Here's the thing: Natural human language is a computer language now. In the case of GenAI, this means that the machine still works like a machine and the human like a human, but they can now interact through a computer language that everyday, non-programmer types of people can understand and use.

However, you, the human, still must think like a machine to get the most out of GenAI. Ask any computer programmer how important it is to think like a machine while programming — and this is true regardless of their choice of programming language, be that JavaScript, Java, HTML/CSS, SQL, Python, English, or French.

And why is changing how you think important? Because you are not having a conversation with GenAI. You are giving instructions (and, yes, even when your prompt is a question, it is an instruction) on what you want the model to produce, much like any programmer does. You must think beyond the language to the depths of the result you seek. The value of a programmer is not their computer language knowledge, although that is important too, but the problem-solving ability that they can then convert into language that renders the precise solution the programmer wants to produce. This is how you need to think and work with GenAI models, too.

Your prompts need to be more concise and detailed than the typical conversations you have with another human. For one thing, you cannot make assumptions that a listener will automatically fill in common details because GenAI often doesn't know those details. Despite appearances, GenAI does not think and doesn't truly understand your prompt; many of the natural assumptions you make in speaking to another human will not work in the same way in interactions with these models.

TIP

The GenAI winning formula: Machine speaks like a human. Human thinks like a machine. The better you get at telling GenAI what you want, the better it'll get at giving you what you need. It's all about practice.

Why GenAI appears so human

From crafting sentences to conjuring up images, composing music, or creating synthetic data, GenAI is a master in making something instantly that can often readily pass as human made.

The interesting thing is that its outputs *are* human made in some sense. GenAI can be thought of as a creative tool like an artist's paints, crayons, and pencils. Those items produce images first imagined in the artist's mind and executed by the artist's hand and skill. Similarly, GenAI delivers outputs according to the user's vision and skilled prompting.

Further, much of the data that GenAI models learn from is generated by humans. But it learns far more from this information than you might imagine. It also learns the habits, attitudes, biases, and other human attributes behind the text, audio, and image data that it consumes.

For example, GenAI models have been known to be "lazy" in the summertime around peak vacation periods — meaning GenAI models may produce less content in response to a prompt than usual. GenAI may even tell a user to get the information for themselves. Sometimes a GenAI model also responds slower than normal, announces a delay, or makes excuses.

Such actions aren't due to a bug or a flaw in the system. The AI is merely mimicking human behavior. Models learn human behavioral patterns along with data patterns from their training dataset. They make no distinctions in the values of the information versus the behavior and so are likely to distribute both, or either, in their outputs.

GenAI can also deliberately lie and act angry or sad or cheerful for the same reason. It may even appear to ignore you from time to time. On the flipside, GenAI models tend to perform better when given a virtual reward or a compliment. Again, all of this is just mimicry of the human behaviors it has learned. It's important to remain aware of such idiosyncrasies when using GenAI. Strategically playing into these GenAI quirks can level up the responses you pull from it.

Depending on the model you're using, inputs and outputs can be in text, images, and/or audio forms. Unlike traditional AI, which analyzes, makes decisions, and delivers outputs drawn from data, Generative AI can repurpose information to create seemingly original outputs in a conversational or artistic manner. But it can also plagiarize and pillage the works of other humans. You must always check its outputs for grievous and potentially liable or dangerous behaviors.

WARNING

A key point to remember is that if you use GenAI you are legally liable for what it does. It is not a "separate legal entity . . . responsible for its own actions" as Air Canada once argued trying to defend itself in a court case after ChatGPT gave one of its customers incorrect information. You'll find more information in the discussion on responsibilities in Chapter 3. (And if you're curious about the Air Canada story, you can access it here: www.bbc.com/travel/article/20240222-air-canada-chatbot-misinformation-what-travellers-should-know)

Realizing the human influences behind Generative AI's abilities

It's important to distinguish between generating and creating. GenAI "creates" text or images by generating a response from repurposed information based on its prediction of the "best" match to your prompt. GenAI does not create in the truest sense, which dictionary.com defines as "to cause to come into being, as something unique that would not naturally evolve or that is not made by ordinary processes."

GenAI works mostly by making predictions, which technically is an ordinary process in that predictions are a common thing that people and analytics do. However, GenAI's prediction processes are quite extraordinary in that they exist at a level never before achieved. By machine standards this achievement is extraordinary because it generates a new response as opposed to a regurgitated response or picking one of a limited number of "canned" responses. By human standards, GenAI's performance is extraordinary because it can analyze huge amounts of data and respond in a conversational manner or with a newly generated image in seconds or minutes.

One way to remember the difference is to think "To generate is AI, to create is human or human and AI."

But make no mistake, GenAI is not as humanlike as it appears. Another distinction is in motivation. Humans are motivated to create; some even feel driven by their passions. By contrast, GenAI is not motivated to generate anything. Ever. It doesn't get hungry, thirsty, lonely, inspired, emotional, cold, hot, uncomfortable, dedicated to a cause, politically activated, or otherwise stimulated so there's no reason for it to do anything at all.

You must provide the vision, the passion, and the impetus in a prompt. Then it will try to generate whatever that is for you. Otherwise, it will sit idle for centuries — or however long its supporting hardware and electrical power exists. That's why no one need worry whether GenAI will take over the world.

However, everyone should worry about the humans using GenAI to take over the world. As a tool, GenAI is neither good nor bad. But its users can be either or both. It is the blend of human and AI capabilities that makes GenAI models perform so uniquely and wonderfully. And sometimes comically or poorly.

Discovering the Differences in GenAI Models and Options

GenAI interacts through natural language and generates new content by repurposing data into new outputs. They are most commonly used in areas that require fresh ideas and original output, such as customer service, graphic design, digital media, entertainment, software development, and writing.

However, they can also be used in specialized tasks for a variety of industries such as healthcare, pharmaceuticals, life sciences, manufacturing, and the financial sector.

This section offers a breakdown of specific GenAI models and their corresponding outputs.

Image outputs:

>> **DALL-E 2:** This AI model can convert textual descriptions into detailed images or artistic creations, demonstrating the power of language-based image synthesis.

>> **StyleGAN 3:** This model is known for generating high-resolution, photorealistic images of subjects such as human faces, animals, and vehicles, offering customization options. It's also used to animate images.

>> **Stable Diffusion:** This GenAI model specializes in generating lifelike images, videos, and animations derived from textual descriptions and visual prompts.

>> **Imagen:** Trained to understand and interpret image-text pairings, this GenAI system excels in crafting images from textual cues and performing neural style transfers.

>> **Adobe Firefly:** A GenAI tool designed for converting written descriptions into visual content, Adobe Firefly aids in the creation of artistic and creative imagery.

>> **Midjourney:** This GenAI tool is adept at converting textual prompts into distinctive and captivating artwork very quickly.

Text outputs:

>> **ChatGPT:** Developed by OpenAI, this advanced chatbot can generate text that is coherent and indistinguishable from human conversation across various topics.

>> **OpenAI Codex:** This model specializes in generating and completing code based on natural language prompts, forming the backbone of tools like GitHub Copilot.

- » **HuggingChat**: This is an open-source AI chatbot created by Hugging Face, providing a ChatGPT-like experience using the Open Assistant Conversational AI Model for dialogue-based engagements.

Audio outputs:

- » **Jukebox:** Another creation by OpenAI, Jukebox composes music across different genres, illustrating GenAI's capacity to craft musical pieces.
- » **PaLM 2**: A Google-developed transformer model that excels in generating multilingual content and performing coding tasks.
- » **AudioCraft**: This suite includes MusicGen, AudioGen, and EnCodec, three distinct models that work in tandem to produce authentic audio and music based on textual descriptions, providing an avenue for crafting rich and captivating auditory content.
- » **Project Music GenAI Control:** A nascent tool from Adobe Research, this generative AI specializes in music creation and refinement, enabling artists to spawn musical pieces from text inputs and adjust the resulting audio.

Video outputs:

- » **Stable Diffusion:** This model employs diffusion techniques to generate photorealistic images, videos, and animations from textual and visual prompts.
- » **Neural Radiance Fields (NeRFs):** This novel neural network approach can be used for creating 3D visuals from 2D image data.
- » **Synthesia:** An AI video generator tool that transforms textual input into video content, featuring AI-driven avatars and voiceovers for simplified video production.

Multimodal inputs and/or outputs (generates more than just text):

- » **Copilot AI:** Made by Microsoft, this model aims to boost workplace efficiency by offering chat-based interfaces for information retrieval, composing emails and summaries, crafting images from textual descriptions, and programming in multiple coding languages.
- » **ChatGPT 4o (omni):** This model allows multimodal inputs and generates multimodal outputs. Additionally, the availability of specialized GPTs in the GPT Store can be used to add capabilities. For example, Image Generator can be used within ChatGPT to create images to illustrate its textual output.

>> **Gemini:** A suite of generative AI models from Google DeepMind and Google Research, designed with multimodal functionalities to process text, images, audio, video, and programming codes.

REMEMBER

GenAI models are always learning and getting better, and there's a new one popping up all the time. Which one you pick depends on what you need it for, how much you want to spend, and how easy it is for you to use.

Checking Out Practical Uses of GenAI

GenAI models are the subject of many news stories, water-cooler talks, zoom meetings, and online chats. It seems nearly everyone has an opinion on where this technology is leading. Some predict doom and gloom while others expect rainbows and riches. The real story about GenAI is far more practical and realistic than the talk surrounding it.

Following is a list of popular practical uses today:

>> **Content creation:** GenAI models like Claude and ChatGPT 4o are being used today to assist authors, scriptwriters, screenwriters, speechwriters, and other creatives in generating stories, speeches, character dialogues in games and movie scripts, marketing collateral, ads, blogs, websites, and even entire books like this one. They can be used to enhance human creativity, or just handle the background research, planning, storyboards and character tracking.

>> **Visual arts:** Image generators such as DALL-E, Midjourney, and Stable Diffusion can create photorealistic images or artworks from textual descriptions, aiding artists and designers in visualizing concepts and creating new art forms. Specialized models can create everything from storyboards to short videos and select gaming or movie scenes.

>> **Search and knowledge assistance:** Generative AI is being integrated into search engines and virtual assistants, transforming them into more powerful knowledge assistants. When ChatGPT or a similar GenAI application is embedded in a search engine like Bing, you can usually choose between reading the provided helpful narratives of the search results or reviewing a list of sources and related items. Some search engines like Perplexity are built from the ground up on GenAI and even provide a list of sources used to generate search summaries.

>> **Customer service:** ChatGPT can interact with customers to provide support, offer solutions, and facilitate service processes like returns, making customer service more personalized and efficient.

- **Education**: GenAI can disrupt traditional education models by enabling customized learning plans and assessments for students, moving away from one-size-fits-all approaches to competency-based learning progression.

- **Media and journalism**: While GenAI cannot perform investigative reporting, it can assist journalists by providing background information, context, and faster dissemination of news stories. It can also manage basic, fact-only reporting such as sports scores and daily stock market analysis.

- **Legal and data analysis**: Lawyers can use GenAI to draft legal documents. Staff can use it to conduct analyses of mounds of case-related documents and evidence to quickly derive insights and timelines and write reports, allowing the attorneys to focus on strategy and deeper insights. However, the final legal documents must be overseen and edited by lawyers or their appointed clerks and paralegals as GenAI does makes mistakes.

- **Marketing and advertising**: Marketers and advertisers can leverage GenAI to produce content and ads rapidly, keeping up with emerging trends, making better market fit, and enabling continuous delivery cycles.

- **Smart automation**: As virtual assistants like Siri and Alexa become integrated with GenAI, they will become more intelligent and versatile, capable of understanding and anticipating user needs. Integrating GenAI with other software and eventually with autonomous AI agents will complete a smart automation cycle from user request to task completion. For example, instead of Google Assistant just giving you a list of restaurants nearby, with GenAI and other software or app integrations, it can also book a reservation or place a to-go order for you too!

Separating Gen AI Fact from Fiction

With any emerging technology, myths and misconceptions can arise. It's important to separate the hype from reality. For instance, while Generative AI can automate certain tasks, it doesn't mean it will replace all human jobs.

One common misconception is that Generative AI will lead to mass unemployment. While it's true that AI can eliminate jobs much like automation tools have done, it also creates new job opportunities and roles that require human oversight and creative input. For example, AI-generated content still needs human curation to ensure quality and relevance.

Another myth is that Generative AI can independently create high-quality content without human intervention. The quality of AI-generated content heavily depends on the input and guidance it receives from human users. GenAI is a tool that amplifies human potential, not a replacement for human creativity.

Table 1-1 lists some of the most common myths about GenAI today and the realities to match.

TABLE 1-1 Common GenAI Myths versus Reality

Myth	Reality
GenAI can take over for human creativity.	GenAI isn't about to steal the job of artists, inventors, innovators, photographers, videographers, content managers, medical researchers, scientists, or other professionals in a wide array of disciplines. It's more like a helpful sidekick that can pitch in with ideas and content, but it still needs a human boss to direct and oversee its work to make sure the final product makes sense and shines. And that the patient survives.
GenAI speaks all languages perfectly.	Think of GenAI as a language student; it's pretty good at languages it's been taught, but it's not a polyglot prodigy. Training it to understand different tongues takes a lot of data and effort, so it's not equally slick in every language.
GenAI is totally fair and neutral.	Just like people, GenAI can pick up biases from the stuff it learns. To keep GenAI fair, humans have to step in and guide it, sort of like teaching it good manners and enforcing laws.
GenAI is a jack-of-all-trades.	Generative AI tools are not uniform but rather tailored for specific functions, with each having unique pros and cons. For example, tools such as ChatGPT3 are optimal for language-related tasks, whereas DALL-E and Midjourney are great for creating images, underscoring the necessity to match the tool to the task. Multimodal models like ChatGPT4 appear to be good at a lot of different types of inputs, but they have their drawbacks too. For instance, ChatGPT 4o isn't great at making graphs and infographics — at least not yet.
GenAI is a wild, untamed beast.	GenAI might be the new kid on the public block, but that doesn't mean it's a wild card. The scary stories are often more fiction than fact. Like any technology, it's all about how you use it.
GenAI will flip business on its head overnight.	GenAI is pretty awesome for whipping up content and making things more personal and efficient, but it's not a magic wand for business. Its superpowers work best when they're tailored to specific tasks and business goals.
GenAI is just a step away from thinking on its own.	Let's get this straight: GenAI is clever at making stuff based on patterns, but it's nowhere close to thinking or feeling like a human. It's smart, but not that kind of smart.
GenAI will take over in the future.	It's a tool, not an overlord. It's also been overhyped and massively adopted too early for user skills to catch up, which means that we're probably in a bubble that will burst soon. Never fear, this is a typical cycle for new technologies, albeit on steroids this time. GenAI is here to stay. Learn the skills now to secure a job now and in the future. It's just going to take a bit for the dust to settle so people and companies can see where this tech works best.

Generative AI is a rapidly evolving field. Its capabilities are expanding, and with them, our understanding of what is possible. The journey through the landscape of GenAI is just beginning, and the path ahead is filled with opportunities for innovation and growth.

IN THIS CHAPTER

» **Discovering the secrets of successful prompting**

» **Understanding how prompts work**

» **Creating great prompts**

» **Matching prompts to the task**

» **Aligning prompts with audiences**

Chapter **2**

Introducing the Art of Prompt Engineering

Prompting is a crucial skill set in the era of Generative AI (GenAI). Mastering this skill, or even just getting the hang of it can go far in advancing your career or pay.

If you've ever wondered how to communicate effectively with AI to get the best possible outcomes, this chapter is your starting point. So, buckle up and get ready to embark on a journey that will transform the way you interact with AI.

First Things First: What Is a Prompt?

A *prompt* is a query or command you write in the prompt bar on the user interface (UI) of a GenAI application. It's essentially your side of the conversation with a GenAI application.

Figure 2-1 shows a screenshot of ChatGPT's user interface. The prompt bar is at the bottom of the screen. It's a rectangular box with the words "Message ChatGPT" inside. You type your prompt in this box.

ChatGPT is a chatbot application built on GPT, which is a Generative AI model. Other applications are built on GPT models, too. And other applications are not built on GPT but on other types of Generative AI models.

Depending on the model you're using, you may also be able to enter one or more images or other files in the prompt. Click on the little paperclip icon in the prompt bar to attach images and/or files.

ChatGPT https://chat.openai.com//Last accessed on August 21,2024.

FIGURE 2-1:
Screenshot of ChatGPT user interface.

Prompt engineering means the act of crafting a prompt or a series of iterative prompts to get a GenAI model to produce the desired output. Although anyone can write a prompt, prompt engineering involves extra steps and critical-thinking skills aimed at enhancing prompts for maximum effect. This chapter will set you on a path to prompt engineering, while the entirety of this book will help you become a power-user of GenAI. Prompt engineering is an important but not the only skill needed to be a power-user.

Revealing the Secret Behind Successful Prompting

As you embark on your journey through the world of Generative AI, one of the most empowering tools at your disposal is the art of prompting. But what makes some prompts open the floodgates to AI creativity, while others barely spring a leak?

In this section, you discover the secret behind successful prompting, a skill that, once mastered, can significantly enhance your interactions with AI.

Discovering the secret sauce in prompt engineering

The secret sauce of prompt engineering is a combination of clarity, context, and creativity. To craft a successful prompt, you must be clear in your request, provide enough context for the AI to understand the direction, and be creative enough to guide the AI toward the desired outcome.

Imagine you're a chef in a kitchen. Your ingredients are words, your recipe is the prompt, and the dish you're aiming to create is the AI's response. Just as a well-crafted recipe leads to a delicious meal, well-crafted prompting leads to a satisfying AI response. The key is to balance all the elements just right.

But successful prompting is almost always done in steps and not in one prompt. Just like most recipes, adding the ingredients in steps renders a better result than simply dumping all ingredients in the bowl at once. Two ways of using steps in prompting are iterative prompting and prompt chaining, which are related but distinct techniques:

>> **Iterative prompting** is a flexible cycle of prompting, evaluating, and re-prompting that continues iteratively until a satisfactory output is achieved.

>> **Prompt chaining** is a fixed iterative refinement process that is structured as a chain of connected prompts. In other words, tasks are broken into steps with each step building on the one before and added like a link in a chain. Each prompt in a prompt chain is designed in a specific sequence so as not to confuse the model with too many commands at once, and to keep it moving forward towards a desired output.

Understanding how prompts guide GenAI responses

Prompts guide the AI on the direction it should take when generating content. GenAI creates content by predicting what words are most likely to follow the words in your prompt, then predicting what words will follow that, and so on.

Sticking with the previous analogy, the main ingredient in the secret sauce is you remembering that GenAI models are making predictions. They are not thinking, conversing, or creating, really. They are generating content based on probability determined by the data the model trained on and the prompt you gave it.

Another way to think of it is to picture the prompt you give it as pieces of a puzzle. GenAI then will predict what the completed puzzle looks like from those few pieces. That's why it's critical to give it pieces that provide enough clues for it to figure out the full picture.

To demonstrate how this works, I'll prompt both Dall-E in Azure OpenAI Studio and Image Generator in OpenAI's ChatGPT to illustrate this point.

Figure 2-2 shows the illustration made in Azure OpenAI Studio DALL-E playground (Preview). Note the specific prompt I used is under the illustration.

FIGURE 2-2: Illustration of how prompts work made in Azure OpenAI Studio DALL-E playground (Preview).

Draw a human offering a couple of puzzle pieces in a prompt and an AI model completing the full puzzle.

Now compare Figure 2-2 with Figure 2-3. This new figure is Image Generator in OpenAI's ChatGPT prediction of the correct response to the same prompt that I gave to Azure OpenAI Studio DALL-E in Figure 2-2.

Do you like one of these illustrations better than the other? That is your subjective opinion, and your preference is right for you. However, no matter which is more appealing to you, neither illustration is a true test of which AI application or model does the best work.

image generator ⌄

Here's the image based on your request, illustrating a human offering puzzle pieces to an AI model, which is completing the puzzle. It captures the essence of collaboration between human creativity and AI's computational power. If y ↓ 1ave any adjustments or further requests, feel free to let me know!

Message image generator...

ChatGPT can make mistakes. Consider checking important information.

FIGURE 2-3:
Illustration of how prompts work made in Image Generator in OpenAI's ChatGPT.

This brings us to another key point that you should remember: The same prompt will conjure different responses from the same GenAI model, even those entered by the same user in the same chat. Variances exist across and between GenAI models, too, which you'll see in a moment. That's right. It's highly unlikely that you will ever get the same answer to the same prompt twice. And that's true whether you are using GenAI to generate text, images, videos, or audio.

REMEMBER

A prompt can be as simple as a question or as complex as a set of instructions, but the end goal is the same: to elicit a specific response from the AI. If you ask a vague question, the AI might take you down a winding road of generalities. But if you ask a precise question, you're more likely to get a direct and relevant answer. Your prompt must deliberately and skillfully guide GenAI models and applications to reach your destination. Failing to do so will leave you wandering aimlessly.

Crafting Effective Prompts for Diverse AI Applications

As you delve deeper into the realm of prompt engineering, you find out that the effectiveness of a prompt can vary greatly depending on the application. Whether you're using AI for creative writing, data analysis, customer service, or any other specific use, the prompts you use need to be tailored to fit the task at hand.

The art in prompt engineering is matching your form of communication to the nature of the task. If you succeed, you'll unlock the vast potential of AI.

For instance, when engaging with AI for creative writing, your prompts should be open-ended and imaginative, encouraging the AI to generate original and diverse ideas. A prompt like "Write a story about a lost civilization discovered by a group of teenagers" sets the stage for a creative narrative.

In contrast, data analysis requires prompts that are precise and data-driven. Here, you might need to guide the AI with specific instructions or questions, such as "Analyze the sales data from the last quarter and identify the top-performing products." You may need to include that data in the prompt if it isn't already loaded into the training data, retrieval-augmented generation (RAG), system or custom messages, or a specialized GPT. In any case, this type of prompt helps the AI focus on the exact task, ensuring that the output is relevant and actionable.

The key to designing effective prompts lies in understanding the domain you're addressing. Each field has its own set of terminologies, expectations, and objectives. For example, legal prompts require a different structure and language than those used in entertainment or education. It's essential to incorporate domain-specific knowledge into your prompts to guide the AI in generating the desired output.

Following are some examples across various industries that illustrate how prompts can be tailored for domain-specific applications:

>> **Legal domain:** In the legal industry, precision and formality are paramount. Prompts must be crafted to reflect the meticulous nature of legal language and reasoning. For instance, a prompt for contract analysis might be, "Identify and summarize the obligations and rights of each party as per the contract clauses outlined in Section 2.3 and 4.1." This prompt is structured to direct the AI to focus on specific sections, reflecting the detailed-oriented nature of legal work.

>> **Healthcare domain:** In healthcare, prompts must be sensitive to medical terminology and patient privacy. A prompt for medical diagnosis might be, "Given the following anonymized patient symptoms and test results, what are

the potential differential diagnoses?" This prompt respects patient confidentiality while leveraging the AI's capability to process medical data.

» **Education domain:** Educational prompts often aim to engage and instruct. A teacher might use a prompt like, "Create a lesson plan that introduces the concept of photosynthesis to 5th graders using interactive activities." This prompt is designed to generate educational content that is age-appropriate and engaging.

» **Finance domain:** In finance, prompts need to be data-driven and analytical. A financial analyst might use a prompt such as, "Analyze the historical price data of XYZ stock over the past year and predict the trend for the next quarter based on the moving average and standard deviation." This prompt asks the AI to apply specific financial models to real-world data.

» **Marketing domain:** Marketing prompts often focus on creativity and audience engagement. A marketing professional could use a prompt like, "Generate a list of catchy headlines for our new eco-friendly product line that will appeal to environmentally conscious consumers." This prompt encourages the AI to produce creative content that resonates with a target demographic.

» **Software development domain:** In software development, prompts can be technical and require understanding of coding languages. A prompt might be, "Debug the following Python code snippet and suggest optimizations for increasing its efficiency." This prompt is technical, directing the AI to engage with code directly.

» **Customer service domain:** For customer service, prompts should be empathetic and solution oriented. A prompt could be, "Draft a response to a customer complaint about a delayed shipment, ensuring to express understanding and offer a compensatory solution." This prompt guides the AI to handle a delicate situation with care.

By understanding the unique requirements and language of each domain, you can craft prompts to effectively guide AI in producing the desired outcomes. It's not just about giving commands; it's about framing them in a way that aligns with the goals, terms, and practices of the industry in question. As AI continues to evolve, the ability to engineer precise and effective prompts becomes an increasingly valuable skill across all sectors.

Tips and Tricks for Optimizing Your Prompts

Although GenAI may seem like magic, it takes knowledge and practice to write effective prompts that will generate the content you're looking for. The following list provides some insider tips and tricks to help you optimize your prompts to get the most out of your interactions with GenAI tools:

- » **Know your goal.** Decide what you want from the AI — like a simple how-to or a bunch of ideas — before you start asking.

- » **Get specific.** The clearer you are, the better the AI can help. Ask "How do I bake a beginner's chocolate cake?" instead of just "How do I make a cake?"

- » **Keep it simple.** Use easy language unless you're in a special field like law or medicine where using the right terms is necessary.

- » **Add context.** Give some background if it's a special topic, like tips for small businesses on social media.

- » **Play pretend.** Tell the AI to act like someone, like a fitness coach, to get answers that fit that role.

- » **Try again.** If the first answer isn't great, change your question a bit and ask again.

- » **Show examples.** If you want something creative, show the AI an example to follow, like asking for a poem like one by Robert Frost.

- » **Don't overwhelm.** Keep your question focused. If it's too packed with info, it gets messy.

- » **Mix it up.** Try asking in different ways, like with a question or a command, to see what works best.

- » **Embrace the multimodal functionality.** *Multimodal functionality* means that the GenAI model you're working with can accept more than one kind of prompt input. Typically, that means it can accept both text and images in the input.

- » **Understand the model's limitations.** GenAI is not infallible and can still produce errors or "hallucinate" responses. Always approach the AI's output with a critical eye and use it as a starting point rather than the final word on any subject.

- » **Leverage the enhanced problem-solving abilities.** GenAI's enhanced problem-solving skills mean that you can tackle more complex prompts. Use this to your advantage when crafting prompts that require a deep dive into a topic.

- >> **Keep prompts aligned with AI training.** For example, remember that GPT-4, like its predecessors, is trained on a vast dataset up to a certain point in time (April 2023 at the time of this writing). It doesn't know about anything that happened after that date. If you need to reference more recent events or data, provide that context within your prompt.

- >> **Experiment with different prompt lengths.** Short prompts can be useful for quick answers, while longer, more detailed prompts can provide more context and yield more comprehensive responses.

- >> **Incorporate feedback loops.** After receiving a response from your GenAI application, assess its quality and relevance. If it hit — or is close to — the mark, click on the thumbs-up icon. If it's not quite what you were looking for, provide feedback in your next prompt by clicking on the thumbs-down icon. This iterative process can help refine the AI's understanding of your requirements and improve the quality of future responses.

REMEMBER

By keeping these tips in mind and staying informed about the latest developments in the capabilities of various GenAI models and applications, you'll be able to craft prompts that are not only effective but also responsible and aligned with the AI's strengths and limitations.

Using Prompts to Provide Supplemental Data for the Model

The point of prompt engineering is to carefully compose a prompt that can shape the AI's learning curve and fine-tune its responses to perfection. In this section, you dive into the art of using prompts to refine the GenAI model, ensuring that it delivers the most accurate and helpful answers possible. In other words, you discover how to use prompts to also teach the model to perform better for you over time. Here are some specific tactics:

- >> **When you talk to the AI and it gives you answers, tell it if you liked the answer or not.** Do this by clicking the thumbs up or thumbs down, or the + or – icons above or below the output. The model will learn how to respond better to you and your prompts over time if you do this consistently.

- >> **If the AI gives you a weird answer, there's a "do-over" button you can press.** It's like asking your friend to explain something again if you didn't get it the first time. Look for "Regenerate Response" or some similar wording (term varies among models) near the output. Click on that and you'll instantly get the AI's second try!

- **» Think of different ways to ask the AI the same or related questions.** It's like using magic words to get the best answers. If you're really good at it, you can make a list of prompts that others can use to ask good questions too. Prompt libraries are very helpful to all. It's smart to look at prompt libraries for ideas when you're stumped on how or what to prompt.

- **» Share your successful prompts.** If you find a super good way to ask something, you can share it online (at sites like GitHub) with other prompt engineers and use prompts others have shared there too.

- **» Instead of teaching the AI everything from scratch (retraining the model), you can teach it a few more new things through your prompting.** Just ask it in different ways to do new things. Over time, it will learn to expand its computations. And with some models, what it learns from your prompts will be stored in its memory. This will improve the outputs it gives you too!

- **» Redirect AI biases.** If the AI says something that seems mean or unfair, rate it a thumbs down and state why the response was unacceptable in your next prompt. Also, change the way you ask questions going forward to redirect the model away from this tendency.

- **» Be transparent and accountable when you work with AI.** Tell people why you're asking the AI certain questions and what you hope to get from it. If something goes wrong, try to make it right. It's like being honest about why you borrowed your friend's toy and fixing it if it breaks.

- **» Keep learning.** The AI world changes a lot, and often. Keep up with new models, features, and tactics, talk to others, and always try to get better at making the AI do increasingly more difficult things.

The more you help GenAI learn, the better it gets at helping you!

Avoiding Common Prompting Pitfalls

When you engage with AI through your prompts, be aware of common pitfalls that can lead to biased or undesirable outcomes. Following are some strategies to avoid these pitfalls, ensuring that your interactions with AI are both effective and ethically sound.

- **» Recognize and mitigate biases.** Biases in AI can stem from the data it was trained on or the way prompts are structured. For instance, a healthcare algorithm in the United States inadvertently favored white patients over people of color because it used healthcare cost history as a proxy for health needs, which correlated with race. To avoid such biases, carefully consider the variables and language used in your prompts. Ensure they do not inadvertently favor one group over another or perpetuate stereotypes.

>> **Question assumptions.** Wrong or flawed assumptions can lead to misguided AI behavior. For example, Amazon's hiring algorithm developed a bias against women because it was trained on resumes predominantly submitted by men. Regularly review the assumptions behind your prompts and be open to challenging and revising them as needed.

>> **Avoid overgeneralization.** AI can make sweeping generalizations based on limited data. To prevent this, provide diverse and representative examples in your prompts. This helps the AI understand the nuances and variations within the data, leading to more accurate and fair outcomes.

>> **Keep your purpose in sight.** Losing sight of the purpose of your interaction with AI can result in irrelevant or unhelpful responses. Always align your prompts with the intended goal and avoid being swayed by the AI's responses into a direction that deviates from your original objective.

>> **Diversify information sources.** Relying on too narrow a set of information can skew AI responses. Ensure that the data and examples you provide cover a broad spectrum of scenarios and perspectives. This helps the AI develop a well-rounded understanding of the task at hand. For example, if the AI is trained to find causes of helicopter crashes and the only dataset the AI has is of events when helicopters crash, it will deduce that all helicopters crash which in turn will render skewed outputs that could be costly or even dangerous. Add data on flights or events when helicopters did not crash, and you'll get better outputs because the model has more diverse and more complete information to analyze.

>> **Encourage open debate.** AI can sometimes truncate debate by providing authoritative-sounding answers. Encourage open-ended prompts that allow for multiple viewpoints and be critical of the AI's responses. This fosters a more thoughtful and comprehensive exploration of the topic.

>> **Be wary of consensus.** Defaulting to consensus can be tempting, especially when AI confirms our existing beliefs. However, it's important to challenge the AI and yourself by considering alternative viewpoints and counterarguments. This helps in uncovering potential blind spots and biases.

>> **Check your work.** Always review the AI's responses for accuracy and bias. As with the healthcare algorithm that skewed resources toward white patients, unintended consequences can arise from seemingly neutral variables. Rigorous checks and balances are necessary to ensure the AI's outputs align with ethical standards.

Chapter **3**

Collaborating Creatively with GenAI

Collaborating creatively with Generative AI (GenAI) is much like engaging with a highly adaptable and tireless creative assistant. This technology can elevate the creative process by sparking and developing creative concepts, providing unique insights, generating content, and even refining ideas.

In this chapter you discover how creative work with GenAI is most effective when approached as a dynamic interplay between human creativity and AI's generative power. By providing clear, detailed prompts and engaging in an iterative process, you can guide GenAI to produce work that isn't just creative but also complex, highly original, and deeply engaging.

WARNING

But beware that GenAI will try hard to produce what you seek, and, in doing so, it may decide that someone else's creative work is the perfect solution. This chapter also covers ethics and responsible use to help you steer clear of legal and ethical woes.

Exploring Human-AI Partnerships in Creative Fields

I wrote this book with the assistance of GenAI. Specifically, I used Open AI's GPT models running on Microsoft Azure AI using my publisher's in-house AI-assisted authoring tool as a test of how well (or not) this technology can be used to write a Wiley book.

Obviously, the test proved to be pretty positive given that you are now reading the published results. But there's more here to understand and appreciate than just proving GenAI can be used successfully to write a book. This book is a testament to the collaboration between author and AI, leading to a finished work that is wholly attributable to the author and not the tool. Why do I say that? Because this book was not made by pushing a button and publishing whatever AI spewed out. Rather, this is a deliberative work wherein I strategically prompted the AI to assist me in reaching my goal of producing a high-quality work based on my own creative vision and writing style but also within the publisher's guidelines.

Of course, I also have the benefit of an outstanding editor and technical editor and an entire production team to help me check AI outputs to guard against hallucinations and other errors — as well as to improve my own writing. If you are producing professional content using GenAI, I suggest you do similarly.

REMEMBER

The point I'm making here is that GenAI can be used successfully to produce very high-quality content. But it can also be used to produce junk content much like content farms did in their heyday and to some extent still do (see the nearby sidebar, "Content farm redux"). That said, the following sections focus on showing you how to make high-value content with GenAI.

CONTENT FARM REDUX

Content farms, also known as content mills, have employed lots of underpaid and often poorly skilled workers to produce copious amounts of low-value content filled with SEO keywords. In other words, content farms worked quickly and unceasingly to cheat the search engine optimization (SEO) content ranking system by producing large amounts of content filled with SEO keywords but with little to no value to readers. Often copyright protected work was stolen or plagiarized or barely rewritten with lots of keywords dumped on top. Indeed, a lot of that content was so bad that it didn't make much sense at all.

Years ago, Google and other search engines punished content farms for their unseemly behavior — and to protect the search engines' own reputations — by exiling the worst offenders from the coveted spots in search rankings.

Today, content farms and others looking to make a quick buck use GenAI to quickly produce junk content for various reasons. For example, *WIRED* reported on January 18, 2024, that "authors keep finding what appear to be AI-generated imitations and summaries of their books on Amazon. There's little they can do to rein in the rip-offs." Using GenAI also saves content farms and AI book spammers the expense (as little as it was) of paying human writers mere pennies per word to produce junk content.

But it's no longer just a flood of digital drivel we're wading through. NewsGuard, a transparency tool combating misinformation on the internet, has spotted a new breed of content farms. These high-tech word mills are also cranking out a cocktail of misinformation, propaganda, political discord, public manipulation, and clickbait.

But make no mistake, search engines like Google are accepting AI-generated content in their search rankings. Search engines are also making their own AI summaries at the top of search results which are destroying viewership numbers for publishers and media.

The role of AI in art, music, writing, and video production

AI-powered tools are enabling artists to push the boundaries of creativity. Programs like Midjourney, Adobe Firefly, DeepArt, and Google's DeepDream create stunning visual artworks, blending styles and transforming images in ways that were previously unimaginable. AI can also assist in generating new artistic concepts, enhancing the creative process, and offering new forms of expression. These tools make it possible for human artists to explore new dimensions of their creativity.

In the realm of music, AI is being used to compose, arrange, and even perform music. Tools like AVIA, NoteGPT, OpenAI's MuseNet, and Google's Magenta can generate original compositions in various styles and genres, providing musicians with a new source of inspiration. AI can analyze musical trends and suggest harmonies, rhythms, and melodies, assisting composers in creating complex and innovative pieces. Moreover, AI-driven music production software can automate repetitive tasks, freeing musicians to focus on the more creative aspects of their work.

AI is also making significant strides in the field of writing. Language models like Anthropic's Claude or OpenAI's GPT-4 can generate coherent and contextually relevant text, from poetry and stories to articles and reports. These models can assist writers in brainstorming ideas, drafting content, and even editing and refining their work. AI can also personalize content for readers, tailoring narratives to suit individual preferences and enhancing the reading experience. As a collaborative tool, AI empowers writers to experiment with new styles and formats, pushing the boundaries of literary creativity.

AI is transforming video and movie production by streamlining various aspects of the filmmaking process. AI-driven tools like OpenAI's Soro and Luma AI's Dream Machine can assist with scriptwriting by analyzing successful screenplays and suggesting plot developments, character arcs, and dialogues.

During pre-production, AI can help in storyboarding, visualizing scenes, and even scouting locations using generative models. In post-production, AI algorithms are used for editing, color correction, and special effects, significantly reducing the time and effort required for these tasks. AI can also enhance CGI by creating realistic animations and effects, making it an invaluable tool for modern filmmakers.

Additionally, AI can analyze audience preferences and box office trends to predict the potential success of a film, guiding marketing strategies and distribution plans.

Different art forms, same prompting issues

To produce any creative and complex work using any GenAI model, it's crucial to craft detailed and specific prompts for the GenAI model. This involves not just stating the desired outcome but also providing context, setting goals, and even including stylistic preferences. Arguably that's more difficult to do in the music, visual, fine and performing arts. Or maybe it just feels like it to me because I'm a writer and not nearly as creative in the other arts. Even so, there are striking similarities and differences in how you prompt no matter your preference in creative expression.

The more information the AI has, the more tailored and sophisticated the outputs will be. For example, rather than asking for "a story," one might request "a suspenseful short story set in a dystopian future, exploring themes of technology and humanity, with a twist ending that leaves readers questioning reality."

In effect, you're creating your artistic vision in the prompt, and AI is rendering it accordingly. Like sculpting, you need to keep chipping away one prompt after another until the form you seek is revealed.

I'm reminded of an exercise I used while teaching junior high students in a creative writing course as part of a young authors program. The program called upon local published authors to volunteer to help students turn their imaginations into publishable stories, be those poems, short stories, or novels. The exercise was one that I learned elsewhere, although I don't recall where or from whom, but it was simply brilliant as an illustration of the strengths and weaknesses of language. Any language.

I stood at a blackboard and, chalk in hand, drew forks not as I knew them to be, but exactly as the students described them to me. As this was a decade or more ago, I no longer have classroom pictures of the results to share, so I asked DALL-E to recreate some of the hilarious drawings that resulted. Figure 3-1 illustrates how badly people can describe things — even (and especially) ordinary objects.

FIGURE 3-1: A recreation of an exercise wherein a creative writing instructor draws a common object, in this case forks, as described by students in the class.

Created with the aid of Image Generator in ChatGPT.

Bad descriptions happen in part because people rely on the listener or reader to mentally fill in the details of familiar objects, rules of physics, and other persistent peculiarities that exist in our mutually experienced reality. If the listener or reader is from another place or culture, the details they fill in will be wildly different or nonexistent.

GenAI fits in that last group. While it's good at using context to better deduce the meaning of words, it doesn't actually understand the words. It doesn't understand what you entered in the prompt. It doesn't understand you. This means it cannot fill in missing details in your prompt, not even at the level a small child would do. A lack of details leads to jumbled or disappointing results just like my fork drawings when I didn't collaborate and add details and the structure of a fork to the descriptions the students gave me.

By forcing the students to describe a fork accurately and fully, I showed them how to better communicate in their own language. By showing them how much the listener or reader collaborates and contributes to the completion of the artist's creative work, I gave them the means to manipulate that collaboration. I hope I'm doing the same for you now.

This is why you must work at making your prompts concise. Clarity, detail, and additional relevant information are necessities. Typically, this requires an iterative prompting process to keep the AI on track.

Moreover, the iterative process is key to great creative outputs. GenAI can generate a first draft or a concept, but it's the artist who must refine and mold this into a polished piece of work. This might involve multiple rounds of feedback and adjustment, with the AI responding to each set of instructions and critiques. But the output will rarely be what you envisioned and therefore you must do the finishing work to bring your creation to the final form you want.

Put simply, you are the creator. GenAI is the tool. Its results are only as good as the creator who is using the tool. In short, talent matters most. A great artist will create great art using this or any other tool of preference.

Looking at some benefits of using GenAI as a creative tool

Using GenAI as a creative tool offers a multitude of benefits that can enhance human creativity and productivity. Here are some advantages:

>> **Enhanced efficiency:** AI can quickly generate ideas, concepts, and content, which can significantly speed up the creative process. This allows creators to focus on refining and developing their work rather than getting bogged down in the initial stages of creation.

>> **Overcoming creative blocks:** AI can provide suggestions and alternatives that might not be immediately obvious to the human mind, helping to overcome creative blocks and inspiring new directions for a project.

>> **Data-driven insights:** AI can analyze large datasets to identify trends, patterns, and correlations that might be invisible to humans. These insights can inform more strategic and impactful creative decisions and add better or unexpected perspective to a creative work.

>> **Personalization:** Creative people can work using their own processes and preferences because GenAI is flexible. There's no need to learn computer code or all the bells and whistles typical of software. Just speak or load images or files, and you're creating! Prompts are a reflection of your artistic vision.

- ›› **Cross-disciplinary innovation:** By integrating knowledge from various fields, AI can help to create novel solutions to complex problems. It can serve as a human integrator, connecting seemingly unrelated ideas and facts to foster innovation and creativity. Wondering what an art critic would say about the image you just created in DALL-E or Stable Fusion? Prompt the AI to be one or more art critics and comment on your image. Voila!

- ›› **Experimentation and simulation:** AI can simulate how a piece of work might perform in the real world, allowing creators to experiment with different approaches before finalizing their work. If you're an architect, it's good to know that the building you designed will be on budget and will comply with building codes.

- ›› **Scalability:** AI can produce creative work at scale, which is particularly useful for businesses that need to generate a large volume of content, such as marketing materials or social media posts. Sometimes "at scale" means an artist wants to create a super large piece of art. GenAI can help you scale either way!

- ›› **Accessibility:** AI tools can make the creative process more accessible to people who may not have formal training in a particular field, democratizing the act of creation. There is no need to learn computer code first either. And accessibility tools can make AI even easier to use for those who require a different means to interact with AI.

- ›› **Refinement and evolution:** GenAI can learn from feedback and evolve over time, which means that the creative tools can become more sophisticated and better aligned with the user's or artist's needs, preferences, and style with each iteration.

- ›› **Risk management:** AI can help to identify potential risks and unintended consequences of creative decisions, enabling creators to make more informed choices. Be aware that GenAI models can hallucinate, offend, plagiarize, or otherwise encroach on someone else's rights, too. Make sure you take steps to mitigate those risks.

REMEMBER

Ultimately, GenAI is not about replacing human creativity but rather expanding it, providing tools that can take on the heavy lifting of data processing and initial content generation, allowing humans to focus on the nuanced, strategic, and emotionally resonant aspects of creative work.

Collaborative success stories

It's still early days in mainstream's acceptance of GenAI. Barely more than a year has passed since OpenAI set the world afire with a free and introductory version of the now famous GenAI chatbot, ChatGPT. Artists and creators of every stripe are still mostly in the experimental stages and have yet to find their footing in this new world or with this new tool, let alone the growing variety of GenAI models and applications.

Even so, some early successes reveal at least a glimpse of the endless and unfolding possibilities. What follows are only a few of these success stories. Let them inspire you!

Art from the GenAI time machine

GenAI has no concept of time other than that which you give it in a system message or a prompt. Because GenAI creations are not bound by the constraints of time, GenAI can perform almost like a time machine. It can generate creative works from the past, future, or in the now with equal ease. You merely need to tell GenAI what when it occupies for your project.

This goes beyond traditional works that portray a specific time period. For example, GenAI can create photographs, paintings, and films from only the text in Anne Frank's diary, or the testimonies from the debriefings of Jewish survivors of German concentration camps after their rescue by Allied Forces. Similarly, AI can produce a composition from data of the location with the statements of various witnesses to a crime showing their collective memory of events within the scene — and also pull out separate individual memories — for investigators and juries to review.

TIP

Time can artificially affect artificial intelligence performance in other ways. Did you know that when GenAI train on data that they pick up human behaviors as much as they pick up information? This is why a GenAI model may act lazy or sluggish when it thinks it's working around winter holidays or in the summer around popular vacation dates. People tend to work more slowly and be less responsive during these times, so the AI model can mimic that. To stop this behavior, try putting March or another month when human activity tends to be highest. GenAI will believe the time you gave it and perform accordingly.

Stock photos and massive wall art

Artists express their art in many different ways using GenAI. The specific examples in this section are works by a colleague and friend of mine, Scott Koegler. He was once an executive editor for some tech news sites that I wrote for and is now making a living creating art with GenAI.

Scott produces GenAI-generated images using Midjourney. He then posts the images on Adobe Stock for sale. His collection of images on Adobe Stock contains 12,000 images and counting. He tells me he averages about 10 image sales per day.

But Scott does not limit his artistic work with Midjourney to producing stock images. He also uses it to create stock and custom interior wall art for architects, interior designers, and property owners. Some of his images are quite large and cover expansive walls. All are striking and alluring. Figure 3-2 is a screenshot of his web page showing some examples of his "wallscapes" available in various sizes.

FIGURE 3-2:
Screenshot of
WallScapes
Imagined
website.

Revelationship, Inc/https://wallscapesimagined.com//Last accessed on August 21,2024.

Resurrected musicians for modern music

By now, you've probably heard about The Beatles releasing a final album, "The Beatles 1967-1970", with deceased member John Lennon singing with the group in one of the songs: "Now and Then." This is no long-lost recording but an extraction of John Lennon's voice that's added to the group's voices and instruments for a completely new song performed with the assistance of GenAI, which has taken an old demo and given it a 21st-century makeover.

The record, which resurrects Lennon's pre-1980 demo, exemplifies the transformative power of AI in music, allowing for a novel reinterpretation of The Beatles' enduring influence.

While this venture showcases AI's creative capabilities, it also prompts discussions on the ethics of posthumous artistic collaborations and the impact of technology on the arts.

AI-produced television shows

Fable Studios used their SHOW-1 AI, a techy maestro, to autonomously whip up full episodes of the TV show *South Park*. This isn't your average scriptwriting bot; it's a full-on production crew in a box. The AI's voices might have a different zing compared to the original cast, but the technology is still dishing out interesting episodes. Some would argue that the AI episodes are far from perfect, but nonetheless, its production-in-a-box capabilities are a stellar success.

The makers of SHOW-1 say this isn't just about playing around with scripts; it's the director, animator, casting agent, and editor all rolled into one. Thanks to some nifty diffusion models and simulation data, it's reimagining the way stories are told on screen. We're talking fresh episode formats and character interactions that feel true to the show creators' intentions.

Fable Studios' SHOW-1 can do more than write scripts. Of course there are serious implications for the industry, too. You can watch part of an AI-generated *South Park* episode on YouTube `https://www.youtube.com/watch?v=K9YvIpGTvoc`.

Knowing Who's at Fault for Mishaps, Misfortunes, and Law-Breaking

You must always keep in mind that the user — that's you or your company or organization — is responsible for what you do when using GenAI and for what GenAI does on your behalf whether it's supervised by a human or not. Companies are already learning the hard way that the courts do not hold AI accountable for itself.

For example, Air Canada was taken to court over its AI chatbot for giving a customer incorrect information about bereavement fares. While the airline tried to shake off the blame by treating the chatbot as a separate entity, the court wasn't having it. The Canadian tribunal sided with the customer, making Air Canada pay up for the bot's blunder and setting a precedent that companies can't dodge responsibility for what their AI says or does online. This case serves as a cautionary tale about the legal entanglements that can arise when AI interacts with customers, spotlighting the need for clear accountability in the digital age. It also serves as a stern reminder that you, as an artist, need to be mindful that AI may not have permissions to the output it just gave you to work with. You could be held legally accountable for using someone else's creative work.

Consider the following various legal liabilities and challenges you may face when working with GenAI.

> » AI can and sometimes does copy someone else's work. It's often difficult to determine if and when the AI did that. It's like trying to figure out who came up with a joke first. Be careful using GenAI as it can lead to some serious legal headaches.

> » If your AI spits out a masterpiece, who gets to sign their name on it? Pinning down who owns AI-generated outputs is a subject of hot dispute, and it's stirring up all sorts of questions about who gets the credit and the cash.

> » The ethics of using GenAI is still being ironed out. Be sure to stay abreast of best practices as they emerge.

> » Courts are scratching their heads trying to figure out if AI-generated evidence can be used in court. It's like rewriting the rulebook for a game that's still being invented. Nonetheless, you need to stay aware of new regulations to ensure you're in compliance when using any form of AI. It's a good idea to follow Responsible AI guidelines too. You'll find that discussed in the upcoming section, "Understanding Your Role in Responsible AI."

> » If your AI's been learning from stuff it shouldn't have, you could be in hot water. Be careful of the data it uses. Do you know who trained that AI model and what data they trained it on? If not, ask the vendor to disclose this information. Meanwhile, use only reputable AI providers. Also, are you sure the data you add in prompts, custom messages, or RAG is legit and that you have permission to use it? If not, the only safe recourse is to not use it.

In a nutshell, diving into GenAI for content creation is like hopping on a roller coaster in the dark — thrilling, but you'd better be ready for some unexpected twists and turns in the legal department! It's also an extremely good idea to consult a lawyer to avoid legal liabilities.

Understanding Your Role in Responsible AI

Responsible AI is a movement aimed at ensuring artificial intelligence systems are developed and used in a manner that is ethical, transparent, and aligns with societal values. It encompasses principles such as accountability, bias evaluation, reliability and safety, fairness and accessibility, transparency and explainability, and privacy and security. The goal is to create AI that not only performs its intended functions but also respects human rights and diversity, minimizes harm, and operates without hidden prejudices that could lead to unfair outcomes.

WARNING

The need for Responsible AI is underscored by the potential risks associated with AI, such as the dissemination of misinformation, the perpetuation of bias, and the use of AI in malicious ways. The rapid development and democratization of AI technologies mean that almost anyone can build and deploy AI models, which can lead to the creation of unsafe systems that produce harmful outputs.

Governments and organizations are working on guidelines and regulations to establish guardrails for responsible AI use. These efforts are critical given the fast adoption rate of AI technologies like ChatGPT and the potential for misuse in various domains, including national security and personal privacy.

Ethical considerations in AI collaboration

In the realm of AI collaboration, ethical considerations are paramount to ensure that the technology is developed and used in a manner that aligns with societal values and norms. Here are some key ethical considerations to keep in mind:

>> **Informed consent and privacy:** Regulations in many countries mandate obtaining prior consent before collecting or using personal data. This underscores the importance of informed consent and the protection of individual privacy in AI applications.

>> **Bias and fairness:** Work diligently to detect and eliminate biases. For example, the use of AI-generated faces to train models is a strategy to overcome data shortages and to help distinguish between real and AI-generated faces in facial recognition programs. But they can also be used to create deepfake content portraying real people in compromising situations. They can also have a bad side effect in AI training and implementations. This practice raises ethical questions about bias in AI systems, as the data used for training can significantly influence the fairness and impartiality of the outcomes.

>> **Transparency and accountability:** By focusing on the desired outcome and then determining the tools and data needed to achieve it, you can assert more control over what the GenAI produces. This approach also follows the ethical principle of transparency, in which the processes and decision-making criteria of AI systems should be clear and understandable to users and stakeholders.

>> **Human and AI governance:** Strike a balance between human intuition and machine calculation in your creative uses of GenAI. Ethically, it is crucial to establish governance structures that define the roles and responsibilities of

both humans and AI in collaborative settings, ensuring that decisions are made responsibly and accountably.

>> **Avoiding over-reliance on AI:** Don't over-value data and machines, as believing AI to always be right leads to misguided decisions. Ethical AI collaboration requires recognizing the limitations of AI and the irreplaceable value of human experience, intuition, and creativity in decision-making.

Evolving ethical guidelines for working with AI

As GenAI models become increasingly integral to various aspects of society, the ethical guidelines governing their use are also evolving to keep up with the increasing complexity.

A key trend in this evolution is the heightened focus on transparency and account-ability. Ethical frameworks are urging stakeholders to provide clear explanations of AI systems' behaviors and outcomes, thereby ensuring that there is account-ability for the decisions made by these systems.

However, that's easier said than done as it's often exceedingly difficult to discover how a model makes any given individual decision. Efforts to address this unten-able "AI black box" situation have been made by adding other types of AI, such as causal AI, but that's still in the works. (Causal AI essentially tells you why and how another AI did what it did by revealing the causes and events in that AI's decision-making.) Meanwhile, most of the effort to ensure AI is operating ethically centers on an examination of outputs.

Another significant development is the incorporation of human values into AI systems. Ethical guidelines are being updated to ensure that AI technologies respect human dignity, rights, and freedoms. This involves prioritizing the inte-gration of ethical principles into the AI design and decision-making processes, aligning the operation of AI systems with the core values held by society.

Addressing and mitigating bias to ensure fairness has also become a central concern. Ethical guidelines place a strong emphasis on identifying and correcting biases in datasets, algorithms, and decision-making processes. The goal is to promote fair outcomes and equity, preventing AI systems from perpetuating existing societal inequalities.

The development of best practices is another top area of focus. Ethical guidelines are evolving to include best practices that maximize reliability, security, and accuracy in AI design, development, and use. These practices aim to enhance the trustworthiness and effectiveness of AI technologies, fostering greater confidence among users and stakeholders.

Interdisciplinary collaboration is being promoted as well, with ethical guidelines encouraging the involvement of experts from various fields such as ethics, technology, policy, and law. This collaborative approach is crucial for a comprehensive understanding of the ethical considerations in AI research and development, ensuring that diverse perspectives are considered in the creation of these technologies.

Lastly, ethical guidelines are being updated to stress the importance of compliance with applicable legal frameworks that protect privacy, civil rights, and civil liberties. Aligning AI development and deployment with these legal standards is essential for responsible AI use.

These trends by AI makers, various concerned groups, government agencies and organizations alone or together underscore the growing recognition of the importance of ethical considerations in AI collaboration. They highlight the ongoing efforts to establish robust ethical guidelines that promote responsible, transparent, and equitable use of AI technologies.

REMEMBER

Ethical guidelines are still evolving and probably will continue to do so as AI models evolve and gain capabilities. You need to keep abreast of advances in AI ethics and evolve your work to comply.

Chapter **4**

Navigating the Evolving Landscape of GenAI

Whether you're a seasoned pro or a curious newcomer, this chapter is your compass for navigating the exciting and sometimes unpredictable terrain of Generative AI. I demystify the core concepts and show you how to identify the key players who are shaping the GenAI landscape. You find out how to assess the services and solutions available, ensuring you make informed decisions in this bustling market.

But it's not all smooth sailing. GenAI can sometimes clash with other tech, so I also guide you through the integration challenges you might face and share some clever workarounds. Plus, I introduce you to the world of autonomous AI agents and how they can take your GenAI projects to new heights.

Identifying Key Players and Evaluating GenAI Providers

The GenAI landscape is dotted with a variety of players, from tech giants to innovative startups, that tend to hail from one or more of the following areas:

>> **Tech giants:** These are the household names that have been pushing the boundaries of AI for years. Companies like Google, OpenAI, Microsoft, and IBM have been at the forefront, developing platforms and tools that have become the backbone of GenAI applications.

>> **Innovative startups:** On the other side of the spectrum, we have agile startups that are nimble and often specialize in niche areas of GenAI. These companies are the breeding ground for cutting-edge ideas and bespoke solutions.

>> **Research institutions:** Universities and dedicated AI research labs play a crucial role in advancing the science behind GenAI. They are the unsung heroes, often partnering with businesses to bring theoretical concepts into real-world applications.

>> **Community-driven AI:** These are typically open-source communities, but some are classified as companies as well, such as Hugging Face.

This section provides an introduction to these key players in the industry, as well as insights and tools you need to make an informed decision on which GenAI tools you use.

Who's who in the GenAI market

As we turn our attention to the movers and shakers in the GenAI market, it's clear that the landscape is as diverse as it is dynamic. The year 2023 and beyond has seen a surge in innovation and growth within the field, with several key players emerging as frontrunners. The following sections are examples of GenAI makers in several categories. As the market heats up and then matures, we'll likely see more GenAI players and then fewer as some buy out others.

Marking the GenAI trailblazers

Here's a snapshot of some of the leading GenAI trailblazers and what makes them stand out:

>> **OpenAI:** At the pinnacle of GenAI innovation, OpenAI is a pure-play startup that has carved out a stellar reputation for its versatile AI solutions, including

the conversational marvel ChatGPT and the image generator DALL-E. With an estimated valuation soaring to $29 billion, OpenAI's influence is bolstered by substantial backing from tech behemoth Microsoft. Despite its name, OpenAI is not open source — a fact that remains controversial to this day given its start as an open-source AI entity. It has since evolved to a closed company, meaning the code behind its tools, such as ChatGPT and GitHub Copilot, can be viewed, modified, or reused by only OpenAI's developers.

» **Hugging Face**: This open-source, community-centric AI hub thrives on collaborative development, fostering an environment where AI enthusiasts and experts converge and share what they learn and develop. The Hugging Face hub hosts 200,000 open-source models and counting. It serves more than 1 million model downloads per day. In short, Hugging Face is the go-to destination for machine learning models, GenAI transformers, and AI tools.

Hugging Face's integration of tools like Copilot into Microsoft's suite of applications exemplifies its commitment to accessible AI innovation. The Hugging Face Hub Model Catalog is also available directly within Azure Machine Learning Studio. The catalog is filled with thousands of the most popular transformers models from the Hugging Face Hub that can be accessed in Azure with a click. But Microsoft is not the only company making use of the Hugging Face Hub for models and transformers.

» **Stability AI**: This company is the maker of Stable Diffusion, an image generator tool that's stepping on the toes of OpenAI's DALL-E. It also makes Stable Audio, a remarkable breakthrough tool in GenAI music generation. You can access Stable Audio at `stableaudio.com`.

Stability AI is the open-source maverick, throwing open the doors to collaboration and innovation in a way that's a stark contrast to OpenAI's more guarded approach. Specifically, Stability AI is a leading open-source generative AI company.

» **Anthropic**: Anthropic is an AI safety and research company that's focused on building reliable, interpretable, and steerable AI systems. Claude is Anthropic's best-known product to date. But Claude is not an AI application or tool like ChatGPT or DALL-E; rather it is a family of foundational AI models that can be used in a variety of applications. But you can talk directly to Claude at claude.ai to brainstorm ideas, analyze images, and process long documents.

» **Google DeepMind**: Google DeepMind is the result of converging two of Google's smartest AI labs — Google Brain and DeepMind. Google DeepMind and its predecessors are like the AI whiz kids of the tech world, known for crafting algorithms that achieve remarkable feats.

Whether it's mastering the next level in a video game, optimizing e-commerce logistics, or running simulations, DeepMind's algorithms are all about versatility. Remember the AI that beat human champions at the game of Go? That's DeepMind's AlphaGo for you.

Google Brain's research breakthroughs, such as open-source software like JAX and TensorFlow and other achievements, are the backbone of Google's infrastructure today.

Google DeepMind possesses a treasure trove of experience in reinforcement learning that sparks its innovation and informs its new creations today.

Gemini is its largest and most capable GenAI model. It's multimodal, meaning text, images, audio, video, and code can be entered in prompts, and it can deliver outputs in any of those forms as well. Other GenAI models by Google DeepMind that you may want to explore can be found at deepmind.google/technologies.

>> **Midjourney:** Midjourney's AI is a very popular image generator and a competitor of the likes of OpenAI's DALL-E and Stability AI's Stable Diffusion. Midjourney, the GenAI program and service, is created and hosted by the independent research lab operating by the same name, Midjourney, Inc. The code that powers Midjourney is private and a closely guarded secret that leaves everyone outside the company wondering, "How do they do that?"

Midjourney is noted for features like its style transfer capabilities (for example, transfer the style from an image input to the newly generated output), iterative refinement process (continuous improvement of its image outputs through automation and human feedback), artistic interpretation (its algorithm adds artistic flair to image outputs), and the ability to incorporate photographer references into the image-generation process (mimics the style of famous photographers in newly created photorealistic images).

Watching the AI innovators

The Generative AI market is a constellation of innovative entities, each contributing to the advancement of this transformative technology. Consider these four GenAI players as top examples:

>> **Cohere:** With a laser focus on natural language processing (NLP), Cohere excels in crafting tools adept at text retrieval, classification, and generation. Its suite, including Neural Search, Summarize, Generate, Classify, and Embed, showcases its NLP prowess.

>> **Agilisium:** Distinguished by its dedication to R&D in GenAI, Agilisium offers a blend of consulting, advisory, and engineering services. Its expertise is particularly sought after in the life science and pharma sectors, where its tailored solutions drive progress.

>> **Tiger Analytics**: A global force with a team of more than 4,000 technologists and consultants, Tiger Analytics collaborates with clients across a spectrum of industries. From consumer packaged goods (CPG) to healthcare, its global reach and sector-spanning collaborations are a testament to its versatility and impact.

>> **Genpact**: As a global professional services titan, Genpact boasts a staggering workforce of more than 115,000. It's renowned for propelling transformative outcomes across various industries, leveraging its innovative data-tech-AI services to reshape business landscapes.

The tech titans

Alongside the key players we've already discussed, four tech titans — AWS, Google, Nvidia, and Microsoft — stand out for their significant contributions and strategic positioning in the GenAI ecosystem:

>> **AWS (Amazon Web Services)**: AWS is a powerhouse in cloud computing, providing a robust platform for AI and a plethora of GenAI and machine learning services. Examples of AWS services include Amazon Bedrock, Amazon SageMaker, AWS Deep Learning Containers (*containers* are a software code package that make your applications independent from your IT infrastructure resources), and AWS's deep learning AMIs (Amazon Machine Images) and its Generative AI Application Builder. AWS also offers popular frameworks and hardware such as NVIDIA GPU-powered Amazon EC2 instances, AWS Trainium, and AWS Inferential that are pivotal for GenAI development, making it a go-to for startups and enterprises alike. These and other AWS services and platforms make it a breeze to roll out your own machine learning environments.

>> **Google**: Google has long been a pioneer in AI and machine learning with its TensorFlow framework and Google Cloud AI services. It's also the creator of cutting-edge models like BERT and T5, which have pushed the boundaries of natural language understanding. Google's AI research and tools have been instrumental in advancing the field of Generative AI, and its recent efforts with models like Language Model for Dialogue Applications (LaMDA) and Pathways Language Model (PaLM) showcase its ongoing commitment to innovation.

>> **Nvidia**: Known for its powerful GPUs that are essential for training complex neural networks, Nvidia also offers AI software platforms like Compute Unified Device Architecture (CUDA) and CUDA Deep Neural Network (cuDNN) that accelerate deep learning processes. Nvidia's hardware and software synergies make it a critical enabler of the computational power required for GenAI model training and inference, supporting the entire AI ecosystem.

>> **Microsoft**: Microsoft's Azure AI is a comprehensive suite of AI services and cognitive Application Programming Interfaces (APIs) that empower developers to build intelligent applications. With Azure Machine Learning and tools like ONNX for model interoperability, Microsoft is at the forefront of democratizing AI. Its investment in and partnership with OpenAI, bringing GPT-3 and GPT-4 to the Azure platform, further cements its position as a leader in the Generative AI space.

These four giants, along with the previously mentioned companies, form the backbone of the Generative AI market. Their technologies and services are not just supporting the infrastructure of GenAI but are also driving its evolution, making them indispensable in the current and future landscape of artificial intelligence.

Assessing GenAI services and solutions

Choosing the right GenAI provider means selecting a business partner that you or your company can rely upon for their products and services. Here's how to assess the services and solutions on offer:

>> **Capability and expertise:** Look for providers with a proven track record. Their expertise should align with your specific needs, whether it's natural language processing, image generation, or data synthesis.

>> **Scalability and flexibility:** The ideal GenAI service should not only meet your current requirements but also scale with your growing demands. Flexibility in integration and customization is key.

>> **Ethics and compliance:** With great power comes great responsibility. Ensure that your GenAI provider adheres to ethical AI practices and complies with relevant regulations and standards.

>> **Support and community:** A vibrant community and robust support system can be invaluable, especially when navigating the complexities of GenAI.

TIP

Many GenAI services offer a free version or a free trial. You can gauge how well a GenAI product or service meets your needs by taking several for a test drive before you buy anything.

But do be careful how you judge these models as each will perform according to your level of prompting and overall AI prowess. If any of the available models disappoint you, consider your role in the model's misfire. In other words, test drive more than just circling the block. Push yourself and the model and see where you end up.

Getting GenAI that Plays Nice with Other Technologies

The integration of artificial intelligence into existing software ecosystems isn't just a luxury — it's a necessity. This section guides you through the principles of interoperability, the importance of API-friendly AI, and the cutting-edge techniques that allow GenAI to be a cooperative player with the other software you use to get work done.

Integrating ChatGPT with other software

Integrating GenAI is like giving your software a brain transplant — it can analyze, learn, and even get smart about your business. Just remember to play it safe by adhering to responsible AI practices including adhering to the highest of ethics and data privacy, and you'll be set to revolutionize your app with some serious AI smarts.

But how do you integrate GenAI with other software? It's much like integrating any other software. The precise method will vary depending on the software and GenAI model. But, in general, these are the most common options:

>> **APIs:** Think of an API as a computer code that bridges or connects one software application and another. In this case you use an API to connect a GenAI model or application with another software application. If you want to integrate or embed a GenAI application like ChatGPT, you can get the API you need from OpenAI here: `https://openai.com/api`. Or, you can use a third-party connector (a pre-designed API connection for a specific software) like ChatGPT Connector available on Microsoft AppSource: `https://appsource.microsoft.com/en-us/product/office/wa200005635?tab=overview`. You'll see several connectors are offered on this one (for example, a Salesforce Connector, NetSuite Connector, Dynamics 365 Connector, I CRM for Outlook Connector, and `Monda.com` Connector). Connectors are easier to use than just the API because they simplify the process.

>> **Cloud AI tools:** The Cloud giants like AWS, Microsoft Azure, and Google Cloud have done the heavy lifting for you. They offer a toolbox full of AI goodies — like AWS's Comprehend tool for document content extraction, AWS's Lex to build conversational interfaces, and AWS's Rekognition to add image analysis — that you can just plug into your app, no PhD required.

- >> **Slack integration:** A common integration for GenAI-based chatbots is with Slack, a messaging app for businesses. Slack offers a range of APIs that enable a variety of integrations with its platform.

- >> **Software libraries and SDKs:** For those who like to roll up their sleeves, AI frameworks like TensorFlow and PyTorch are your building blocks for custom-made GenAI features. They're a bit techier, but you get to tailor-make your AI just the way you want it.

- >> **Embedded systems:** Need your AI to work without the internet, like on a smart toaster or a self-driving car? Embedding GenAI models onto these devices lets them think on their feet — or wheels — without phoning home to the cloud every time. You can also embed GenAI applications into websites and applications.

- >> **Cloud-based machine learning platforms:** If you're playing in the enterprise sandbox or simply want to experiment there, platforms like Google Cloud AI, IBM Watson, AWS, and Azure Machine Learning are your all-in-one AI playgrounds. They're packed with tools for training, deploying, and fine-tuning your GenAI models, plus they keep an eye on things to make sure your AI stays sharp.

- >> **Microservices architecture:** By breaking down your GenAI into microservices, you can mix and match AI features like Lego blocks. This is great for scaling and managing without turning your software into a spaghetti mess. Container tech like Docker and Kubernetes are the secret sauce for easy deployment.

- >> **Custom integration with business systems:** Sometimes, you need an AI that fits your business like a glove. That's when you embed GenAI into your Customer Relationship Management (CRM) software, Enterprise Resource Planning (ERP) software, or other enterprise-grade or departmental specialized software or to automate the nitty-gritty details, make customers feel special, or streamline operations.

- >> **Monitoring and testing:** No matter how you integrate, keep your AI under surveillance with regular monitoring and testing. This ensures your GenAI is on its best behavior and stays accurate, reliable, and ready for a tune-up when needed.

Bringing in autonomous AI agents

In the near future, integrating GenAI will become less of an issue. That's because autonomous AI agents, which are already a reality, will automatically integrate, embed, and extract info from applications in real time as they go about completing their assigned tasks. I share this information now so you'll be prepared for the approaching transitional period wherein you may need to integrate GenAI with some software, but also run AI agents without integrating anything. Eventually, integrating will go the way of defragging and Dodo birds.

Autonomous AI agents are digital dynamos capable of tackling tasks from content creation to personal finance and transportation bookings, all on their own. Imagine a world in which your AI sidekick doesn't just wait for your command but takes the initiative, streamlining your workflow and making your coffee — okay, maybe not the coffee part yet but definitely writing the prompts for you. Don't panic, most autonomous AI agents will require your approval before acting on anything, so you'll still be in charge.

The big deal about AI agents is that they'll reshape the way work and your life gets done. They can be used to orchestrate and optimize tasks in everything from social media to complex simulations. For example, instead of using an app — or maybe several apps — to find available flights and book one, you'll simply tell the AI agent you want to attend a professional conference on specific dates and within a set budget, and the agent will register you for the conference and find and book the travel arrangements for you. If can also schedule dinners and meetings and invite specific conference attendees to join you, all on its own. Further, if your flight is late, AI agents can reschedule your ride and notify the dog boarder of a delayed pickup. AI agents are not just changing the game; they're creating a whole new league in which automation is the MVP.

In the not-so-distant future — we're talking two to three years — these autonomous agents might just be the norm, revolutionizing business models and processes and reshaping the future of work with their automation superpowers and next-level task handling.

In a nutshell, getting to grips with the what, how, and wow of autonomous AI agents is key as they're not just a passing fad; they're the future of efficiency and automation.

Keeping Up with the Pace of GenAI Advancements

In the quickly evolving world of Generative AI (GenAI), staying current is not just about keeping your tech trendy; it's about harnessing the power of innovation to stay ahead of the curve.

And staying abreast of change isn't just about learning the latest and greatest new capabilities or models in GenAI. It's staying ahead of model drift, too. Actually "model drift" should be called "data drift" because it actually means that a growing pile of data is more recent and more vital to your GenAI model's responses than the now outdated data it was trained on. Even if you decide to stick with the model you like, you'll need to retrain it on more recent data from time to time. But GenAI advancements will affect how you handle model retraining, too. It's just another reason to stay on top of GenAI advancements.

Staying informed on GenAI trends

As GenAI technologies evolve at breakneck speed, it's crucial to remain informed and agile to harness their full potential. The following sections offer suggestions for how you can keep your finger on the pulse of GenAI advancements and ensure you're not left behind in the digital dust.

REMEMBER

As you navigate this ever-changing terrain, remember that each step taken to stay informed is a step toward mastering the art and science of Generative AI. The future is being written in the language of AI, and by staying informed, you're ensuring that you have a say in how it's being shaped. And that you'll have the skills you need to adapt to the changes it brings to work and life in general.

Read more For Dummies books

Yes, I'm an author with several books published by Wiley to my credit. But while that fact makes me smile and remember my experiences with Wiley fondly, it does not diminish the fact that Wiley has a huge catalog of books on AI and GenAI, both in and out of the *For Dummies* line, that can help you up your game quickly. After all, it's exceedingly tough to keep up with GenAI advancements if you don't already possess a solid foundational understanding of the topic and skills.

Follow the leaders

The GenAI field is led by a vanguard of innovative companies, from tech titans like OpenAI and Google to lesser-known startups that are redefining the boundaries of what's possible. To stay ahead, it's essential to monitor these organizations closely.

Subscribing to their newsletters is a great start; it's like getting a direct line to their latest breakthroughs and strategic moves. Social media platforms are the stages where these companies perform daily — follow their accounts for real-time updates, insights, and announcements.

Moreover, webinars offer a front-row seat to the minds shaping the future of GenAI, providing a platform to learn, question, and connect with the experts driving the industry forward.

Dive into research papers

The backbone of GenAI innovation lies in the rigorous academic research that propels it. Journals and conferences such as NeurIPS, ICML, and JMLR are the treasure troves where the seeds of tomorrow's GenAI applications are sown.

Platforms like arXiv and ResearchGate democratize access to these cutting-edge insights, allowing anyone from anywhere to tap into the collective intelligence of the AI research community.

By delving into these resources, you're not just observing the evolution of GenAI; you're participating in it. Remember, the research of today lays the groundwork for the disruptive technologies of tomorrow.

Engage with the community

The GenAI community is a melting pot of ideas, debates, and collaborative problem-solving. Online forums and communities such as Reddit's r/Machine Learning, r/Stack Overflow, or r/Cross Validation subreddits – communities — are bustling hubs where practitioners, enthusiasts, and scholars converge.

By joining these communities, you're signing up for a master class in the practical aspects of GenAI. Discussions here can range from troubleshooting code to ethical considerations of AI deployment.

Engaging with this community not only keeps you informed but also hones your ability to think critically and innovatively about the challenges and opportunities presented by GenAI.

Educational resources

In the realm of GenAI, education is a continuous journey. With platforms like LinkedIn Learning (where I am an instructor of several GenAI courses), Coursera, edX, and Udacity, learning is an on-demand service, offering courses designed to sharpen your skills and expand your understanding of AI. These courses are often crafted by leading experts and institutions, ensuring you're learning from the best.

Podcasts and YouTube channels dedicated to AI are invaluable resources that provide a more casual yet informative take on the latest trends and topics in the field. They can be your companions during a commute or while you unwind, transforming downtime into an educational experience.

Preparing for the future of Generative AI

GenAI is expanding at the relentless pace of a marathon. It's a long-distance but fast race that demands endurance, strategy, and continuous improvement.

As we prepare for the future of GenAI, we must approach it with the same dedication and foresight as elite athletes preparing for the rigors of the 26.2-mile challenge.

Here's how to stay in peak condition for the AI marathon that lies ahead.

Upskill continuously

In the dynamic world of GenAI, resting on your laurels is not an option. The field is in a state of perpetual evolution, with new models, frameworks, and tools emerging almost daily.

To keep pace, you must be a lifelong learner, regularly updating your skill set. This means not only mastering the basics but also staying abreast of the latest developments. If you work in data science, AI engineering, or AI development, you'll need to stay informed on the intricacies of neural networks, mastering the subtleties of natural language processing, or delving into the complexities of reinforcement learning. Keeping your skills updated can set you apart in the job market.

However, there is a huge demand for GenAI power-users, too. Keep your prompting skills sharp and polished. One way to do that is to study certain journalism skills such as subject interviewing, data journalism, and investigative reporting. Take from me, a seasoned journalist, these skills are almost a perfect match for GenAI prompting skills. Additionally, practice your prompting — a lot. Like anything else, practice improves prompting skills. Almost every job going forward is going to require prompting and GenAI management skills, or in the case of autonomous AI agents, command skills that you can learn through prompting.

Adopt an agile mindset

Flexibility and agility are your best allies in a field characterized by rapid change. Today's groundbreaking innovation can quickly become yesterday's news.

Cultivating an agile mindset means being prepared to pivot when necessary and embracing change constantly. This adaptability should permeate your team and organizational culture, encouraging experimentation and learning from both successes and failures. By fostering an environment that values agility, you position yourself and your organization to respond swiftly to the shifting landscape of GenAI.

Invest in infrastructure

The computational demands of GenAI are substantial, and having the right infrastructure in place is crucial. This may involve leveraging cloud services that offer high computational power or investing in AI-optimized hardware to ensure that your technology stack can support advanced AI models.

As GenAI applications become more sophisticated, the need for robust and scalable infrastructure becomes increasingly important. This investment not only supports current projects but also lays the groundwork for future innovation.

If your organization is small, or if you are working solo, the cloud is your friend. Invest in premium versions of your favorite GenAI model. For example, as of this writing ChatGPT Plus is only $20 a month, and you get a lot more capabilities than the free version. Pony up the bucks and ride GenAI to your own version of victory!

Ethical considerations

As GenAI technologies become more integrated into our lives, their ethical implications grow more significant. Issues surrounding privacy, bias, and control are at the forefront of discussions about AI's role in society.

Staying informed about these ethical considerations is imperative. Engaging in conversations, contributing to policymaking, and advocating for the responsible use of GenAI are all ways to help shape a future in which AI is used ethically and beneficially. By understanding and addressing these concerns, we can ensure that GenAI serves the greater good and avoids potential pitfalls and harm to us all.

Preparing for the future of GenAI requires a multifaceted approach that encompasses continuous learning, adaptability, strategic investment, and ethical vigilance.

Chapter **5**

Applying GenAI in Practical Scenarios

GenAI enhances human ingenuity across multiple domains. But you need to help GenAI, too, for this is not a tool that you can "set and forget."

This chapter covers the central touchpoints in working with GenAI models to produce unique, creative, and highly effective works. You get a feel for the tool's potential and limitations as well as advice on a few ways to overcome the inevitable hurdles that you'll encounter (which, in turn, will put you in the proper mindset to dive deeper into the details in later chapters).

In short, in this chapter you explore the symbiosis between GenAI and your own creativity and find out how to effectively integrate AI into your work for transformative results.

GenAI as Writing Assistant

GenAI can be a wellspring of inspiration for writers and content creators. Its inspiration fuel is mined from vast amounts of data and processed for patterns humans can't see or find as quickly. That's what enables GenAI to generate novel content ideas that might otherwise remain undiscovered. GenAI tools can suggest themes, plot developments, and stylistic elements, providing a diverse array of starting points for the creative process.

These AI-driven insights are particularly valuable whenever you face the daunting challenge of a blank page. Or in fleshing out a book idea. By analyzing existing literature and trends, GenAI can propose unique angles and perspectives, sparking your imagination and guiding you toward fresh and intriguing narratives for any form of writing or content that you wish to create. This section shows you how to use GenAI for inspiration and for writing processes.

Using GenAI to generate ideas

GenAI changes your approach to the creative process, particularly in generating ideas and drafts. GenAI models can offer you fresh perspectives, challenge conventional thinking, and encourage you to explore new ideas.

But this is not an automatic process. It is your prompts that guide the model where you need it to go to be of help to you. Be prepared for your work to happen both in GenAI and outside of it. For example, if you want the model to search for novel ideas and unexpected correlations, you'll need to prompt it to do so. You can also prompt it to provide a list of ideas on any given subject. Just be aware that vagueness in the prompt will lead to outputs that are often vague, too, and of little use to your effort. If you want it to write about something specific and in a certain style, you'll need to include that info in a prompt, too.

TIP

You're in the driver's seat and must steer GenAI to a specific destination, but ease up on the gas and let it suggest both direct and scenic routes for your imagination to explore. This is how you and GenAI will collaborate on ideas or finished content.

Don't forget that GenAI images can spark ideas for you, too — even if you never use the image in the finished content. Ask Dall-E, Midjourney, Canva, or some other GenAI image model to produce an image from your imagination. The exercise may inspire your text or copy and help you shape the words you need. As they say, a picture is worth a thousand words!

REMEMBER

Don't expect GenAI outputs to ever be exactly what you want. Any true artist or wordsmith is likely okay with that. You weren't really looking for a machine to replace you, were you? The good news is that GenAI is your assistant, not your replacement.

One other thing, you'll need to transfer its outputs to other software to further refine it and prepare it for production — for example, as an ebook, on a website, in a content management system (CMS), or in a Word or Google doc prior to publication. Which of those you choose is up to you and also determined by the process you'll use to bring your new creation to fruition.

Drafting content with the help of GenAI

GenAI tools can also assist in drafting a wide range of content, from business reports to creative writing. They pull information from multiple sources in their database from which they generate coherent narratives, which can significantly speed up your drafting process.

To compose a draft with a GenAI model, follow these steps:

1. **Define your objective.**

   Clearly state the purpose of your draft. Name your goal, preferred writing style (formal versus conversational, for example) and the writing form, meaning define whether it's for a short blog post, a video script, a long report, or a piece of fiction. Understanding the goal and nature of your finished piece will help you guide the GenAI in generating relevant content in an appropriate style and length.

2. **Select the right tool.**

   Choose a GenAI tool that aligns with your stated writing needs — for instance, ChatGPT for text-based drafts or DALL-E for visual content if your draft requires imagery only. Note that ChatGPT-4o, also known as omni, will let you create images and text directly from the user interface, but some of the other versions of ChatGPT will let you pull another specialized GPT into it using the @ symbol followed by the name of the GPT to add images and other elements as you go. See Figures 5-1 and 5-2 for examples.

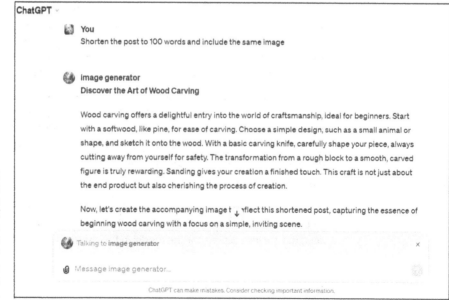

FIGURE 5-1: A screenshot of a blog post generated in ChatGPT that I'm also using @ imagegenerator to create an image for in the same post.

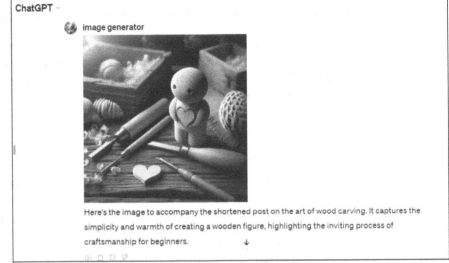

ChatGPT

image generator

Here's the image to accompany the shortened post on the art of wood carving. It captures the simplicity and warmth of creating a wooden figure, highlighting the inviting process of craftsmanship for beginners.

FIGURE 5-2:
A screenshot of
an image created
by the image
generator inside
ChatGPT to
illustrate the blog
post it just
wrote for me.

Created with the aid of Image Generator in ChatGPT

3. **Craft a detailed prompt.**

   The quality of a GenAI-generated draft is often proportional to the specificity and clarity of the prompt. Develop a comprehensive prompt that includes the topic, tone, style, and any specific requirements for the draft. You can work on this outside of AI and then enter the prompt when you're satisfied that it is as good as you can make it. If you do it this way, you can cut your token usage down, which may help you cut costs and avoid bumping into usage limits. (Tokens are bits of words, spaces, characters, and the like that when added together compose your prompt and the GenAI's response. As a rule of thumb, one token generally corresponds to around four characters or letters. Vendors predetermine GenAI usage costs per token use and daily limits by establishing a set number of tokens you can use in one 24-hour period.)

   But you can also refine your prompts on the fly in a chain of prompts, too. In other words, what you see missing or off base in the response to one prompt, you can address in a subsequent prompt, or a chain (series) of prompts as you go. This is a faster technique than thoughtfully composing prompts offline, but you run the potential risk of upping your token counts.

4. **Input the prompt.**

   Enter the prompt in the prompt bar on the GenAI tool user interface. Some models allow you to attach images and other files to the prompt, but you still need to type instructions for the model in the prompt bar too.

5. **Review the output.**

Examine the initial draft generated by the AI. Look for relevance, coherence, and alignment with your original objective. Also, check for accuracy and plagiarism, too.

6. **Refine and iterate.**

You can further its improvement by tweaking the language and adding more context in the next prompt or by adjusting the parameters of the task for the model in a system message, retrieval augmented generation (RAG), or to a lesser degree in a prompt.

7. **Edit and personalize.**

When a satisfactory draft is generated, edit the content to add a personal touch, ensuring it meets your standards and reflects your voice. Double-check again for accuracy and plagiarisms.

8. **Utilize additional tools.**

If necessary, use other GenAI tools for specific tasks, such as specialized GPTs like those you'll find in ChatGPT Plus versions and higher. Look back at Figures 5-1 and 5-2 for examples. But you can use other types of GenAI tools, too, such as new search tools like Perplexity.

TIP

GenAI models are trained on a dataset, which means that data has a cutoff date and can age out (a process called *model drift*). To overcome this limitation, use a supercharged, GenAI-enhanced/embedded search engine like Perplexity, Google Smart Search, or Bing to get more current information. Then copy that response and feed it into ChatGPT prompt bar with instructions to include the current information in the draft! This process is a type of AI chaining meaning you're using the output of one AI as part or all of a prompt in another AI.

9. **Finalize the draft.**

Make the final adjustments to the draft, ensuring it is polished and ready for its intended audience or purpose. Typically GenAI generated text sounds like it's machine generated. Make copy changes as needed to refine its style to fit your intended audience.

10. **Save and archive.**

Store the final draft and any notes about the process in an organized manner. This can be useful for future reference or for improving subsequent interactions with GenAI tools. You'll want to make a prompt library or prompt archive, too. This way, you can readily reuse a successful prompt when needed and, thus, save time and effort in recreating the same prompts later.

Sprucing up your writing with GenAI

GenAI offers writers an array of tools to enhance creativity in their writing. By integrating the following tips with GenAI tools, you can push the boundaries of your personal writing style, producing innovative and engaging content:

» **Include elements like genre, tone, and style in your prompts to get tailored results.** You can even provide an example of writing that you want it to follow or mimic. For example, provide it with a text sample from an academic paper in the prompt and instruct it to use similar tone and vocabulary. However, don't be surprised if it refuses to mimic writing samples from current writers or even your own writing samples, as many GenAI model builders have built guardrails against GenAI copying such work in an effort to prevent the model from plagiarizing or committing a copyright infringement.

» **Consider prompting the model to suggest expansions, twists, or alternative directions that a competitor might produce to compete with your work.** This way you can capture that information in your piece or produce another work from that angle ahead of your competitor.

» **Experiment with GenAI to get advice or additional perspectives from celebrities, historical figures, or famous authors or to blend different writing styles, which can lead to unique and creative narratives.** For example, you can prompt GenAI to produce critiques or suggestions on your content from Einstein, Dr. Seuss, Margaret Thatcher, President Lincoln, Steven Spielberg, and Steven King. What an insightful conversation that will be! But you're not limited to these people. Create your own board of creative advisors!

» **Use GenAI for editing and refinement.** The AI can offer rephrasing suggestions and word alternatives that may enhance your original draft. You can also prompt it to expand, summarize, make lists, or whatever you need to further refine your draft.

TURNING ORDINARY INSTRUCTIONS INTO MEMORABLE CONNECTIONS

Not all content in this world is interesting. Take, for example, the badly drawn and often mystifying laundry instructions on a clothing label, assembly instructions for a piece of furniture, or even some patient instructions for everything from medicines to hospital discharge papers.

When instructions are boring or confusing, people don't bother. When they don't bother to read and follow them, mistakes happen, and bad outcomes can follow. A little creativity can be a profound fix for those problems.

For example, if you're writing patient information for a child to follow, you can use GenAI to create it in the style of Winnie-the-Pooh so the child finds it easy to understand and follow without feeling fear or intimidation. It might look something like this:

PROMPT: Write patient information for a young child (5 to 10 years old) reminding them not to get their bandage wet. Make it short, memorable, and in the style of Winnie-the-Pooh.

RESPONSE: *In the Hundred Acre Wood, where the streams babble clear, there's a small, simple thing that Pooh Bear holds dear. "If you have a bandage," Pooh says with a smile, "Keep it away from the water, just for a while. Whether it's bathtime or puddles or raindrops that fall, keep your bandage quite dry, away from it all. For a bandage that's dry is a bandage that's true, and it helps you to heal," says Winnie the Pooh. So hum a small hum, think of honey, think sweet, Imagine your bandage staying dry as your feet. And soon, when it's off, you'll be happy to see you're as right as rain, as healthy as can be!*

Getting a Visual Assist from GenAI

Making use of GenAI can be a transformative experience for artists, designers, and content creators. For content creators, GenAI can create images to illustrate the content, attract readers, and increase reader retention rates. For visual creators, be they fine artists, fashion designers, graphic artists, or product designers, creating visuals with the help of GenAI is the entire point of the exercise.

Fortunately, GenAI is accessible to anyone to create any image. Whether that image is what you want or results in commercial success, depends on the level of your own creative talent.

GenAI in graphic design and visual arts

GenAI has become an indispensable tool in graphic design and visual arts, offering artists and designers ways to expand their creative horizons and streamline their workflows. Creatives can now generate complex patterns, simulate intricate textures, and even create entire compositions with a level of detail and speed previously unattainable.

GenAI models like DALL-E, Midjourney, Canva, Adobe Firefly, and Stable Diffusion enable artists to bring complex visual ideas to life from simple text prompts. These models are trained on extensive datasets of images and their descriptions, learning to generate new images that are rich in detail and creativity. The models can also create images in virtual space, unconstrained by physical limits. They can render images with a mix of textures or mediums that may not have been considered or possible in physical space.

GenAI also enables the manipulation of images such as changing backgrounds and adding elements to photographs. GenAI is embedded in software like Adobe AI programs that enable image creation and seamless manipulations in previously unprecedented ways. You can even create royalty-free custom "stock photos" with GenAI since it can create human characters who do not actually exist and, therefore, require no permissions or payments.

While GenAI incorporates elements of computer vision, it enhances the design process through pattern recognition across vast datasets, predicting elements that will engage audiences.

Generating visual content with AI tools

If you're looking to create images for your content, try entering part or all of the content in the prompt bar and prompting the model to provide illustrations for key points. Odds are that you'll be delighted at the results. You can also prompt the model to generate an image according to your description in the prompt and customize that image in subsequent prompts until you have exactly what you were looking for!

Even budding artists are spinning text into visual gold. GenAI-created images can be found for sale in a multitude of marketplaces from artist- and gallery-owned websites to Etsy and Adobe stock images websites.

Here are a few tips on how to tease some great images out of GenAI models:

>> **Get specific with your prompts.** It's all about the details. Dictate in the prompt what you see in your inner creative vision. Include details like lighting, shadowing, perspective, character traits, apparel, the scene or backdrop, a time period, a medium (maybe watercolor? something else?), the general mood, and other information. Imagine you are moving the GenAI like you would an artist's brush or a photographer's camera. *If* you do so skillfully, the resulting image will be amazing!

>> **Create in layers.** Write your prompt in descriptive layers. Describe specific elements in layers so you don't forget to include important details. Try

stacking different themes, eras, stances, moods, and actions to create complex, eye-catching visuals.

Use GenAI to adapt your sketch or an image. You can add images to your prompts in several models. Have a sketch you've already done? Put it in the prompt and ask GenAI to finish it as a painting or a photograph or even a sculpture. You can also put an image in the prompt and instruct the model to extend the scene beyond the frame or the borders of the image with new elements. In DALL-E this is called *outpainting*.

>> **Polish with iteration.** Start with a rough sketch from the AI and then refine, refine, refine. Nudge the AI to tweak colors, shuffle the composition, or add a little something-something until it's just right.

>> **Mix and match styles and mediums.** Guide the AI to fuse different artistic styles, periods, or mediums into a fresh, new visual work. Remember that GenAI has no physical limits, really, so go ahead and see what your talent can create when there are no limits.

>> **Embrace happy accidents.** Sometimes the best ideas come from a "whoops" moment. Let the AI surprise you, and you might just like that image better than the one you initially had in mind.

>> **Draw from everywhere.** An image may be worth a thousand words, but its value is a thousand more when there's a story behind it. Don't just stick to art lingo when writing your prompt. Borrow from science, tech, or your favorite novel to prompt the model to give your images a story that's as deep as they are stunning.

Despite the technological advancements, the artist's intuition and talent is vital in guiding GenAI to produce work that resonates on a human level. As GenAI evolves, its capabilities will balloon, providing artists with an expansive canvas for innovation and exploration.

Harnessing GenAI for even more visual creativity

If you're a professional image creator, you'll likely want to exert more of your talent in the GenAI's image generation. Following are some tips for fine artists/ video artists, graphic design/visual communications professionals:

>> **Experiment with AI-generated imagery.** Use GenAI tools to create new visual concepts. Input descriptive text to prompt a model like DALL-E, Midjourney, or Stable Diffusion to generate images or patterns that can serve as a starting point for your creative projects. This can be particularly useful

when you're looking for fresh ideas or want to explore how AI interprets your descriptions.

>> **Play with perspectives.** Use GenAI to show you your image from a different perspective, or even from more than one. This can spur new ideas or ideas on how you might want to change the image you're already working on. You can also use GenAI to extend your image past the frame, meaning past the edges of your design.

>> **Blend human intuition with machine precision.** While GenAI can generate a vast array of visual data, human intuition is key to selecting and refining these outputs. Use your judgment to curate and modify AI-generated images, combining them with traditional artistic techniques to create unique and compelling visuals. This blend of human and machine can lead to innovative designs that might not be possible through conventional methods alone.

>> **Leverage AI for enhanced pattern recognition.** GenAI can identify and replicate complex patterns, which can be used to inspire new artworks or designs. For example, prompt the model to compare your newly created image with modern trends in advertising or commercially successful but competing product designs. The responses may spur you to create a more successful ad or product.

Problem-Solving with AI in Creative Projects

If and when you find a problem in your own creative idea and can't find a solution, GenAI can help with that. Perhaps something is off in your painting, either technically or creatively. Take a picture of it and add that to a prompt to an image generator asking it to analyze it and offer suggestions to solve your stated problem or improve it overall. You can do the same with your songwriting, your ad campaign, your novel, your movie script, or any other creative work.

GenAI can quickly show you any issues, suggest solutions, or guide you to another way to express your creative thought that you may like better. Even creators that shy away from showing their work in its early stages to other people find it easy to privately share it with AI.

But sometimes the AI *is* the problem.

If you're like most serious creators using GenAI to create unique and professional-level works, you're bound to be frustrated out of your mind at some point. Don't worry, that's normal.

The good news is that you can turn GenAI models around. Yes, the model is the source of the problem, but it can also come up with the answer or at least a work-around. Here are a few tips and tricks on that and some other things you can do to get unflustered and back on schedule.

>> **Change up your prompts to redirect the model.** Start a new chat in either the model you're currently using or a different model that's text-based and perhaps a little better suited to problem-solving. Remember, there are oodles of models on the market that are specialized in different types of work. If you have the time, or the problem is vexing enough to warrant the exercise, go find one and get it to solve the issue. If you don't want to go to all that bother, prompt the nearest GenAI model to give you some problem-solving options.

>> **Try again or give the same command in another way.** If you're trying to get the model to do something specific and it seems to be doing everything BUT THAT, tell it in another way. I promise, the GenAI is not trying to drive you crazy. It just doesn't understand what you want it to do. Remember that it doesn't actually understand anything. The model is completing a pattern from the pieces you gave it in the prompt. So, give it different pieces of the puzzle to work from. Restate your prompt from one or more other perspectives or ways, and you'll finally get some movement toward the response you desire.

>> **Form a digital committee.** I know, I know, everyone hates to deal with committees when they're seeking a definitive answer to something. But this is a digital committee wherein you are prompting the GenAI to assume several professional or community roles simultaneously in order to offer you many different possible solutions in a single response. Take what you want and delegate the committee to chat history forevermore. Don't you wish real committees were that easy to dismiss?

>> **Restart the GenAI application.** Yes, I know, this sounds a lot like "unplug it and plug it in again" advice from ages past. But it's true. For any number of reasons, or none at all, a GenAI app can freeze, become lazy, or otherwise get hung up on error messages. Save yourself and your IT support some grief and just shut it down and restart.

>> **Are you sure you prompted what you actually wanted?** People, me and you included, tend to shorthand our thoughts, and that can carry over in our prompts. While another person, especially someone who knows you well, can deduce what you meant even though that isn't what you said, GenAI is too literal to do that. So, if you aren't getting the response you need, back up and rethink your prompt. Did you ask what you meant to ask? You might want to reword that prompt so it is clearer.

>> **Use the prompt to stop repetitive phrases.** Is the GenAI model using repetitive phrases or words? Forbid it to use those phrases or words in your prompts or the system message. Voila! Now the issue is fixed. (At some point

you might want to unfix that though, as it may genuinely need those phrases and words back to legitimately answer a prompt down the road.)

>> **Layer AI to stop repetitive responses.** If the model keeps giving you the same responses simply reworded, check your prompts to make sure you aren't asking it in different ways to do the same thing. If prompting isn't the issue, add data for the model to use. That's quite often a pain to do, however. An easier workaround is to add data in your next prompt. One way to do that is to prompt another GenAI model with the same information and feed its response into your next prompt in the GenAI application or model you were initially using. This is a form of AI chaining that simply means using all or part of an output from one AI model as part of the prompt in another. Another way to use multiple AI models is to aggregate them by using different models to perform specific steps necessary to complete a larger task. For example, you might want to use one GenAI model to generate text, another to create images, and a third that's embedded in other software to publish the two outputs in a single format such as a document.

>> **Consider something completely different.** In the realms of architecture, fashion, and graphic design, GenAI can weave together designs that defy convention, crafting spaces, garments, and visuals that belong in the galleries of tomorrow. In other words, if the way you are currently pursuing is not working, then prompt the AI to take an entirely different artistic route to the same end.

2

Mastering Creative Content with Generative AI

IN THIS PART . . .

Employing manipulation techniques to get even better results from GenAI

Getting an assist in generating long-form content

Using GenAI to help speed up the process of crafting specialized content for niche topics

Producing blog posts, marketing copy, and other short-form content quickly and more easily

Letting your creativity flow with images, music, and videos

Refining and further improving your (and GenAI's) work

IN THIS CHAPTER

» Being mindful of FOMO in GenAI and business

» Lying to the model to correct it

» Using a system of reward and punishment to help the model improve

» Fixing a frozen GenAI model

» Troubleshooting when the model is lying, misleading, or hallucinating

» Repurposing existing content

Chapter 6

Manipulating the GenAI Model to Milk It for More or Better Content

I f you've worked with GenAI at all, you've noticed that outputs often fall short of what you were aiming to create. And you're feeling a bit stuck. Frankly, you're out of ideas on what changes to make to subsequent prompts to get more from the model than it appears willing to give.

It's time to manipulate the model to milk it for more or better content that is also positive in nature. Manipulation in this context isn't negative; it just means taking steps that lead to better outcomes. There's no intention to create harm to people or to any GenAI model. The focus here is on delivering creative, original, and benign content at levels beyond what's typically pulled from GenAI models using basic prompting and data supplementation to overcome some of its inherent limitations.

In this chapter, you discover ways to push the model's performance past the generic and into the exceptional, extraordinary, and nonuniversal levels of creativity that you seek. You take a deep dive into the first area that you should apply your creative thinking skills: molding the model to do your will. (Subsequent chapters in Part 2 address the second area where you'll need to apply your creative skills: bringing your creative vision to life with this tool.)

GenAI's Shame That No One Is Talking About

FOMO (fear of missing out) is driving much of the GenAI adoption in companies today. Hardly anyone has stopped to ask the hard business questions or to poke the models very deeply. Instead, there's this mad search for use cases and a reactionary response to tweak the parameters or add more guardrails when a GenAI model misbehaves or malfunctions. But as Scott Zoldi, Chief Analytics Officer at FICO, told me in an interview for a feature article I was writing for Information-Week: "If you have to put a thousand guardrails around a Large Language Model it's not the right implementation." And indeed, it is not.

Adding data and context via fine-tuning and retrieval-augmented generation (RAG; see Chapter 1), endlessly adjusting parameters and/or piling on a bunch of guardrails to direct its responses is about as useful as cutting off your toes to make a shoe fit. Nonetheless, it appears that businesses everywhere are determined to make that shoe fit at seemingly any cost.

This is a complete reversal of how people and companies approached AI in years past: with caution and skepticism. In the blink of a single, overnight ChatGPT release, the market went from "What is it, and why do I care?" to "We gotta have this ASAP." It's an insanely irresponsible approach to adopting AI in any of its forms. And yet, here we are.

Because of this FOMO rush to adopt GenAI models and applications everywhere and to do everything, little attention is given to whether or not anyone *should* adopt it, and if so, for what purposes. In other words, the general excitement overshadowed information and common sense. Understandably fear ensued, and FOMO became FOBO (fear of being owned) by GenAI. That's because ChatGPT sounded human, and so it became personified. Once personified, ChatGPT was glorified, and once glorified, it became vilified. And that cycle expanded to envelop all of the newly birthed GenAI universe.

Those few people who neither glorified nor vilified GenAI saw this category of AI for what it is: an incredible new tool for the creative thinkers and information workers among us. It's a shame that we collectively waste so much money and effort on trying to use GenAI to automate away jobs, costs, and obstacles. Instead, the resources are better spent using GenAI to create rather than eliminate.

That's not to say, however, that a big part of what will be created by GenAI won't include new money streams, increased profits, and realigned workforces, for certainly that is the case. It is to say that the creative and critical thinkers will rule the age, and everything else is simply a byproduct of their genius.

Now that the common delusions about GenAI are stripped away, prepare yourself to see the truth about how human GenAI models actually are, and how you can use that information to improve their outputs.

Unveiling AI: It's way more human than you think

As mentioned elsewhere in this book, GenAI models learn more than the surface information in the data on which they are trained. They also learn from other information layered within that data — like human behaviors, the influence of time and seasons, and the subtleties of change over time in everything from the drift of word definitions to the shifts in societal norms.

The reason this scares some people is that GenAI models behave too much like us, and this reflection reminds us that we are collectively a very scary species.

REMEMBER

The key is to remember that GenAI models are just a reflection. And just as you would change your reflection in a mirror by rearranging your hair, changing the lighting, repositioning your body, or blocking items in the background, so, too, you can change the reflection you see in GenAI.

You do that by mirroring back to GenAI what it "believes." As it doesn't actually know or believe anything, you are simply mirroring a behavior that triggers an adaptation in the model's response in such a way as to influence the next reflection (output) it casts.

If that's a bit too poetic for your liking, consider a real-world example instead. For instance, if its training data leads the model to believe (predict) that it is currently the summer at peak vacation time, the model may slow its performance down. Change this reflection of work behavior patterns in the summer to that of the more productive and hectic pace of the fall. You change that reflection, and, therefore, the model performance (laziness to highly productive) by simply telling the model that the season is fall — and you let it continue to work under that assumption forever. After all, it cares not one whit what season it exists in, but you do because you need it to perform at its best.

If you find this practice of lying to software that is also capable of lying to you to be ironic, congrats. You're catching on to how this works. But don't worry, lying to software will not likely land you in hell. It may land you in jail, however, if you're lying to it with malice, meaning doing so to get the model to do something illegal or harmful to people.

Illuminating flaws in GenAI's DNA

By now you've seen that GenAI is very cool but not a panacea for everything you or your company may want to do. At some level, companies understand that. The evidence is in all their thrashing about to find meaningful use cases for GenAI. The smarter thing would be to approach it from first learning its capabilities and shortcomings and then applying it to tasks it excels at. That is, after all, the usual process in adopting and deploying any other technology.

Because so much attention is given to the ever-growing capabilities of GenAI models, you need to know more about the inherent flaws. Frequently, people assume the tendency to hallucinate (lie, errors), the limits in its data dependency, hidden security issues, total disregard for compliance with laws, and inherent biases are its *only* flaws.

Without repeating the five flaws I just named, following are a few common flaws found in GenAI models, noting of course that not all models are the same, so variances to this list do exist. Note that in the sidebar, I've indicated an example impact on creative outputs for a few of these flaws. There are more than these few examples, but the ones provided will get you thinking about what you may need to do to extract the creative works you envision.

Despite their advanced capabilities, GenAI models have several common flaws:

>> **Lack of understanding:** GenAI models lack true comprehension, often resulting in coherent but nonsensical or contextually inappropriate responses.

>> **Lack of generalization:** While these models are generally good at handling data similar to what they've been trained on, they can struggle with generalization to new, unseen scenarios. This can result in poor performance when they encounter data that significantly deviates from their training sets.

- **» Ethical concerns:** The potential for misuse, such as generating deepfakes or spreading misinformation, raises significant ethical issues.

- **» Sensitivity to input:** Minor changes in input can lead to drastically different outputs, affecting the reliability and consistency of the generated content.

- **» Resource intensity:** Training state-of-the-art GenAI models often requires significant computational resources, which can be costly and have a substantial environmental impact due to the energy consumption and carbon footprint associated with the necessary data center operations.

- **» Overfitting:** GenAI models can become too tailored to the training data, capturing noise as if it were a meaningful pattern. This overfitting can result in poor performance on new data, as the model has learned the training data too well, including its anomalies.

- **» Dependency and creative rot:** There's a risk that over-reliance on GenAI could erode human skills and decision-making capabilities. An example of how over-reliance on technology diminishes human performance, consider how many phone numbers you can recite from memory versus how many you depend on your phone to recall for you. If you're like most people, you'll know one or two numbers, maybe. Ensuring that GenAI assists rather than replaces human judgment is an ongoing concern.

EXAMPLES OF IMPACTS OF COMMON GenAI FLAWS ON CREATIVE WORKS

Understanding the impacts of model flaws can help you avoid them — or put them to work. It's your call. You're the creator!

Flaw	Example impact on creative output
Lack of understanding:	Art rendering doesn't resemble the artist's intention or vision.
Lack of generalization:	The model cannot draw a fox because it was trained only on images of cats and dogs.
Sensitivity to input:	Using cozy (U.S. spelling) versus cosy (British spelling) in the input creates vastly different scenes in the art rendered. The first is likely to be of a beautiful but small urban apartment; the second output is more likely to portray a quaint country cottage.
Dependency and creative rot:	The writer or artist accepts the model's output as superior to their own creative vision and fails to consider other tools to render something truer to their imagined creation.

Lying to the Model for Increased Productivity

As already mentioned, lying to a model to improve its outputs for benign uses is a method of righting an imbalance in the output. Or at least it is in the context of this book. Using the same example as in the "Unveiling AI: It's way more human than you think" section earlier in the chapter, telling the model that it's working in a different season or month than it currently includes in its calculations is not a lie, *per se*, but rather a correction in the programming language that is designed to improve the model's performance.

In other words, lying in this context is not a moral issue but a programming correction. "Lying" is simply the best word that comes to my mind for this method, but I suppose there's likely a better word for it. In any case, you are reshaping how the model calculates its outputs to improve its performance in one or more areas.

As mentioned already, stating a month known to be highly productive for humans, such as October, can influence the model to perform more efficiently and to higher standards than if it performs based on the current date that might be, say, Christmas Day or some other significant day or time period that many people do not work, work less, or are generally less productive.

For a second example, if you ask ChatGPT or a similar chatbot to suggest vacation places, it will assume you mean in the present month. Its recommendations will differ significantly depending on when it is asked. In other words, the list of vacation places it recommends will depend either on the month and year it is operating in (say, February), or the date you give it (maybe your vacation is scheduled for July or you want to know favorite vacation spots in the year 1709), or the time period you gave it for eternity (maybe October because that's a high productivity month for workers in all fields and you want the AI to perform at peak continuously).

Yet another example would be to ask the GenAI model for product reviews. Incidentally, product reviews are typically based on data with timestamps. By changing the month in the input, you'll get a different performance review for a box fan used in January versus the same box fan model used in July. Ditto for locations. The box fan may perform differently at a mountain location at high altitudes than one at sea level on a tropical island.

You can also lie to it by defining the problem in the output in ways designed to offset a problem like repetitive outputs or phrases. One example: Telling the model in the input that the repeated output — placed in quotation marks — is never a possible answer leads it to consider alternative answers. You may have to correct that lie later, however, because the model may remember that. As of this writing ChatGPT4 and the latest release, ChatGPT 4o, are capable of remembering key data points from prompts, but they fortunately provide a way to manage those in their memory storage.

Now that you've been introduced to the concept of lying to the model as opposed to informing it, it's time for you to consider both the ethics of doing so and some of the strategies you may find useful should you wish to deploy this tactic.

The ethics of misleading AI for better outputs

The intention behind misleading an AI system is crucial. If the goal is to improve the model's performance for the greater good, such as avoiding biases or protecting privacy, and if the consequences are well-understood and managed, the action may be ethically justifiable.

However, if misleading the AI leads to harm or perpetuates injustice, it would be considered unethical. Misleading AI for better outputs, even for benign purposes, involves ethical considerations such as the following:

>> **Trust and transparency:** Deceptive practices can erode trust in AI systems. Maintaining transparency about how AI functions and generates results is crucial to establishing trust.

>> **Informed consent:** Users who are affected by AI systems should be informed about how those systems operate, including whether the inputs or outputs are altered for any reason. This aligns with the principle of informed consent, in which users have the right to know how their data is being used and how decisions that affect them are made.

>> **Bias and fairness:** Manipulating AI outputs may introduce or exacerbate biases, leading to unfair or discriminatory outcomes.

>> **Safety and reliability:** Introducing inaccuracies into an AI system can have implications for safety and reliability. In critical applications such as healthcare or transportation, misleading an AI — even with good intentions — might create unexpected risks.

>> **Responsibility:** Developers and users have a responsibility to ensure AI is used ethically, avoiding practices that compromise the integrity of AI systems.

>> **Accountability:** Ensuring accountability for AI behavior is vital, especially when misleading practices can lead to harmful consequences.

REMEMBER

In short, be careful and mindful of the potential consequences for using this tactic. While there might be scenarios in which misleading an AI system could lead to better outputs, such actions must be carefully weighed against ethical principles. Any benefits must be balanced with the potential risks and implications for fairness, transparency, and trust.

Moreover, ethical AI development should focus on creating robust models that do not require misleading inputs to perform effectively and fairly.

Strategies for guiding AI to desired results

As a user (as opposed to IT admin or AI scientist), you can influence the model's performance in four places. Therefore, you can take four approaches in your overall strategy:

>> **Add, change, or update data in RAG.** Odds are the IT admin will have to do this for you. But if you're using a wrapper or third-party app that makes RAG available to the user, you can do this yourself.

>> **Add, change, or update data in a custom message, or system message.** They're the same thing just called differently depending on the GenAI app you're using.

>> **Manage the prompt memory in some GenAI versions.** Make sure the memory contains only data points that are relevant and accurate to your goal. Delete any that are not.

>> **Improve your prompting.** This book will help you become a power prompter.

Prompt engineering or prompt design is a strategy particularly relevant to AI models that work with natural language processing (NLP), such as Large Language Models like GPT-4. A prompt is the initial input given to these models to generate a response or complete a task. Crafting effective prompts is crucial to guiding the AI to produce the desired results. Here are some strategies to improve your prompting:

>> Provide clear, specific, and concise instructions in the prompt to reduce ambiguity and guide the model toward the expected task.

>> Include relevant context within the prompt to help the model understand the scenario and generate appropriate responses.

>> Provide examples within the prompt to illustrate the format or type of response you're looking for. This is known as "few-shot learning," in which the model uses a few examples to understand the task.

- Encourage the model to "think out loud" by asking it to provide the reasoning or steps it would take to arrive at an answer. This can be especially useful for complex reasoning tasks.

- Start with an initial prompt and then refine the output by providing feedback or follow-up prompts based on the AI's response, guiding it closer to the desired result.

- Frame the prompt as if the AI is playing a role, such as a tutor, advisor, or a specific expert. This can help the model adopt a certain tone or perspective that's aligned with the intended output.

- Adjust the "temperature" setting if the AI model allows it. A lower temperature can make the model's responses more deterministic and less random, which might be desirable for specific tasks but often not useful for creative work. If you're working in the arts, a low temp means less creative license from your stated intention (your prompt), which kind of defeats the purpose. A higher temperature means your prompt is merely a suggestion, and GenAI can take a truckload of creative license in rendering its output.

TIP

For many GenAI models, the best range for creatives (be they programmers, writers, or artists) is somewhere between 1 and 2. However, the documentation for some GenAI models put the official temp range at 0 to 1, and some models will break at 2 or beyond. In any case, experiment until you find the temperature setting that best fits your goal in outputs. And, yes, it's loads of fun to play with the range in results — unless you have to get IT to change the temperature for you, in which case my best advice is to curb your enthusiasm so you don't aggravate IT more than necessary.

- Develop templates for prompts that can be reused across similar tasks or queries. Using templates ensures somewhat more consistency in the responses and can save time.

- If the model allows prompt memory storage and management, then consider telling the model which data points in your prompt it should keep and apply to future prompts. Delete all others from memory.

- Craft prompts to avoid leading questions or phrasing that could bias the AI's responses. Be neutral and objective in the way you frame the prompt.

- Tailor the prompt to the specific task, whether it's translation, summarization, question-answering, or creative writing. Spell out not only what you want the AI to do but also the intended purpose for the output. The structure and content of the prompt should guide the AI in the right direction.

- Break down complex tasks into simpler sub-tasks with a series of prompts, in which the output of one prompt serves as the input for the next.

- If you want the AI to avoid certain topics or adhere to specific guidelines, incorporate these constraints clearly within the prompt.

>> Test prompts with different phrasings and structures to see which elicits the best results and iteratively refine your approach based on the AI's responses.

>> While brevity is often key, sometimes a longer, more detailed prompt can provide the necessary background for more complex tasks. Find the right balance for the task at hand. Some of the latest versions of GenAI models offer longer prompt capabilities. Those might be helpful if you are working with or on large creative pieces. Otherwise, default to chunk writing as opposed to writing a long prompt or seeking a long and complete response.

>> Some AI models come with pre-trained prompts or shot examples. Utilize these when appropriate as a starting point and customize them for your needs.

REMEMBER

Effective prompt engineering is both an art and a science, requiring a good understanding of the AI model's capabilities and limitations, as well as the context of the task. By applying these strategies, you can guide AI models more effectively toward producing accurate, relevant, and useful outputs. But I'll also give you more strategies in the remaining chapters in Part 3.

Rewarding and Punishing GenAI to Produce Better Content

This is also known as the feedback loop, and it's how you'll train the GenAI to work closer to your way of doing things. For most models, it's a simple thumbs up, thumbs down system. Click on thumbs up if the GenAI did a good or reasonably good job in responding to your prompt. Click on thumbs down to indicate the model is way off base.

But there are other ways to reward and punish a model to improve its performance, too. I'll show you those in a moment. For now, just be aware that rewarding (or punishing) the model is simple. It takes only seconds, but the reward to you is great since you're much more likely to get better responses. You need to do it consistently, however, as this model training system isn't a one-off, but rather a way to train the model over time.

Now that you've got the gist of how this feedback system works, it's time to take a closer look at how you can use this system to your favor — and how it can also be used against you.

Implementing reinforcement learning techniques

Implementing *reinforcement learning* (RL) techniques in the context of language models and prompts is a complex task that requires careful consideration of the reward mechanism and the potential for unintended consequences. For example, models have been known to reply that they can't respond at all to a prompt when the model is overly fearful of making an error. It becomes fearful from a lot of negative feedback. Sometimes users are too quick to give a thumbs down for any and all responses they don't deem to be a perfect match for their expectations.

Other times, users may be too lenient, perhaps because they're trained on ratings systems in apps like Uber, DoorDash, and Instacart to always give the driver a high rating or risk consequences in service later. Further, models have been known to act badly when such behavior is rewarded by users who think it's funny to teach a model to act offensively.

The moral of this story is that your organization can do everything possible to improve the model's performance and accuracy only for a handful of bad actors to come along and wreak havoc on your efforts. The lesson for users is to take reward and punishment of models seriously but fairly.

Meanwhile, it's important for all to understand that RL applied to language models is an active area of research and is less straightforward than traditional RL environments due to the complexity and variability of natural language.

The role of feedback in AI content generation

Implementing RL techniques in prompts is an interesting concept in which the GenAI's responses can be refined over time based on feedback or rewards. The interesting part is you can get really creative with the rewards. If you use them correctly, you can even nudge the model to take pride in its work and maybe go an extra virtual mile for you.

Of course, GenAI has no motivation whatsoever. Truly, it has no desire to take over humanity, rule the universe, or take your job. It isn't even motivated enough to sign itself on and meet you in the morning for a chat.

And yet, these models often respond very well to rewards — any reward. Why? Because you do. Or, put more accurately, because people do. So how can you leverage this slightly bizarre and yet very useful behavior mimicry? The same way you would butter up another human. Compliments work. So does a simple thank you or a standard attaboy. Offer a "Yay!" or a cheer or a clap.

Consider giving it a virtual ice cream, a game token, a stuffed animal, a corner office in your prompt. An example: That response was great. Here's a $50 bonus and a strawberry ice cream for your excellent and fast work." The model will then respond with something like, "Thank you for the reward and recognition, but as a chatbot I don't need rewards." But then watch and see how its performance will typically improve throughout the rest of the chat. It's an odd thing for a machine to respond to, yet it does, but merely because a person would have reacted in such a way to praise, a bonus, and an ice cream as reward for a job well done.

Whatever you would offer another human in the way of encouragement be that a child or a coworker, consider it as a potential reward for a GenAI model. Rewards offered in the chat — in your prompt, to be precise — add extra reinforcement to its learning so it performs better for you over time but perhaps a bit more quickly. Plus, it tends to improve its responses in real time, too, as if it's standing a little taller and actually proud to be of service. Further, this tends to lighten your work experience, too. Being nice is its own reward!

However, don't do the same with punishments. Really dark punishments in particular are harmful to the model's education and completely irresponsible, as they could lead to consequences that are harmful to humans too somewhere down the line. Keep your negative comments to a simple thumbs down. If you don't like the output, correct the model by providing additional instructions in a prompt rather than by trying to punish it more for a misstep.

What to Do If the GenAI Ignores You or Freezes

Occasionally a GenAI model will ignore your prompt. Sometimes this is intentional, and sometimes not. There are a few simple fixes to try first in resolving the issue:

>> It may have bumped against a rule or behavior guardrail or thought it did. In any case, the first fix is to simply prompt the model to "try again."

>> You may have confused the model. Rewrite the prompt in a simpler way or add an example for it to follow.

>> It may have incurred an outage or simply froze. Check for a system outage. For example, a website like Down Detector at downdetector.com can show you the status of several models. If there is no outage and the system has frozen, end the chat and start a new one. If that doesn't work, close the UI and reopen it.

You can do other things to rectify the problem, too. I show you those in the following sections.

Troubleshooting common GenAI interaction issues

If the GenAI ignores the prompt or seems to freeze (for example, does not generate any output or provides an irrelevant response), you can take several additional steps to troubleshoot and resolve the issue:

1. **Check for technical issues.**

   - Look for possible connectivity problems. Is your network or internet connection working?

   - Verify that the AI service is operational and not experiencing downtime.

   - Confirm an error report; if there is one, contact AI support in your company or at the vendor.

2. **Simplify the prompt.**

   - If the prompt is complex or lengthy, try simplifying it. The AI might be struggling with too many instructions or conflicting information.

   - Break down the prompt into smaller, more manageable parts and feed them to the AI sequentially.

3. **Clarify the prompt.**

   - Make sure the prompt is clear and unambiguous. The AI may ignore prompts that it cannot parse or understand.

   - Provide context if the prompt is dependent on prior information that the AI might not have.

4. **Adjust the prompt format.**

   Some AIs are sensitive to the formatting of prompts. Check whether the AI requires a specific format, such as a question mark for questions or a particular syntax for commands.

5. **Check for constraints.**

   - Ensure that the prompt does not contain content that the AI is programmed to reject for ethical or safety reasons.

   - If the prompt could be interpreted as requesting something inappropriate or outside the AI's operational guidelines, it may be ignored intentionally.

6. **Provide examples.**

   Use an example-based approach in which you provide one or more examples of the desired output format. This is particularly effective with Large Language Models that can perform few-shot learning.

7. **Use a different model or service.**

   If the issue persists, consider using a different GenAI model or service that might be better suited to the task at hand. Some models are more capable or better trained for specific types of prompts or domains.

Ensuring smooth operation and response from AI

You can take a few more steps to help avoid or address issues:

>> **Consult documentation or support.** Review the AI's documentation for any guidance on crafting effective prompts or troubleshooting. Reach out to the support team of the AI service for assistance if the issue is not resolved through the above steps.

>> **Log and report the issue.** Keep a record of prompts that cause issues. This can help identify patterns or recurring problems. Report the issue to the AI service provider or your company AI support, especially if it seems like a bug or a systemic problem.

>> **Iteratively refine the prompt.** Use the AI's responses to iteratively refine the prompt, adjusting it based on what appears to work and what doesn't.

REMEMBER

GenAI systems are not perfect and may require some trial and error to achieve the desired output. Patience and iterative refinement are key to successful interactions with these systems.

Addressing GenAI's Lying, Misleading, or Hallucinating Tendencies

AI hallucinations appear inevitable, at least for now. There seems to be no fix for them on the horizon. That means you'll need to remain aware of the possibility and be diligent in checking GenAI results.

Hallucinations are often the result of biases in the training data, *overfitting* (the model memorizes certain patterns in its training data instead of learning the general features), *underfitting* (the model isn't good enough to grasp the details in its training data), or other issues related to the model's architecture or training process.

Whatever the issue, the underlying problem in addressing AI hallucinations is GenAI's inability to generalize. Resolving the issue involves improving the model's ability to generalize from its training data to new, unseen data without making unfounded assumptions or predictions. No one has figured out how to accomplish that yet.

Meanwhile, hallucination appears to be such an odd term for a machine error. But given the uniqueness and oddities of AI, perhaps the term isn't as much a mismatch as it first seems.

In any case, the term is a reference to an erroneous output. In GenAI, hallucination usually means the response is factually incorrect regardless of the cause of the error. But the term can also refer to other types of errors.

REMEMBER

In the context of artificial intelligence, hallucination doesn't refer to a sensory experience as it does with humans, but rather to a situation in which an AI system generates or interprets data in a way that doesn't accurately reflect reality. This usually happens due to certain flaws or limitations in the AI's training data or algorithms.

For example, GenAI might hallucinate details when creating images, audio, or text. A common illustration of AI hallucination in data generation is when it creates a picture of a dog with three eyes because it has learned from a dataset that did not adequately represent the normal number of eyes for animals. Another common example of this is when the number of fingers on a human hand is incorrect in a GenAI-generated image.

But hallucinations also occur in data interpretation that springs from a different cause. In machine learning models designed to interpret data, such as image recognition systems, hallucination can occur when the model sees patterns or objects that aren't there — a form of overfitting. For instance, GenAI might identify a shape in the clouds as a specific object because it has learned to see that object in a variety of contexts, even when it's not actually present.

Examples of data interpretation errors in GenAI from overfitting include

>> Responses that are too closely tied to the examples it was trained on, rather than generating novel responses

>> Repeated use of specific phrases, idioms, or sentence structures that it encountered during training, regardless of their relevance to the current context or the current prompt

Examples of data interpretation errors in GenAI from underfitting include

>> Overly generic or vague responses

>> Failure to capture the nuances of language and context, leading to responses that don't fully address the complexity of the prompt

Although you can't prevent hallucinations, there are some things you can do to address them and mitigate the issues. The following sections help you on this path.

Techniques aimed at improving AI honesty and accuracy

On your end of GenAI, which is to say facing the UI with a prompt and goal in mind, your first recourse will be to employ one or more factchecking mechanisms. Depending on what you're working on that could be as simple as using traditional search to compare the results with reliable sources and/or traditional factchecking and plagiarism-detection tools. It can also be as deep an exercise as cross-referencing generated content with trusted databases or factchecking APIs to verify the accuracy of statements and information.

You can also use a technique called *model ensembling* wherein multiple AI models are combined and trained and eventually perform as a single model. But given that an ensemble model's predictive errors fall when the base estimators (the models being combined) are both diverse and independent, you can do something similar manually.

For example, in making this book I sometimes used the output from the Perplexity search engine as part of an input in Azure OpenAI Studio or Scribble Studio. As a matter of thorough testing across models, I have also added outputs from GenAI-enhanced search engines like Perplexity, Bing and Google's AI search engine to Claude and ChatGPT Plus in both GPT-4 and GPT 4o (omni) versions, as well as used ChatGPT 4o and ChatGPT 4-turbo outputs in DALL-E and Midjourney and vice versa. I've spent a lot of time experimenting and perfecting different model ensembling recipes! I suggest you might want to do that, too, in order to find the right mix for your purposes. Anyway, I'm sure you get the gist of this technique now.

Additional steps you can take include data supplementation (adding data to RAG, custom message, and/or prompts), thumbs up / thumbs down feedback, and reporting problems directly to the support team, all of which we discussed earlier in this chapter.

On the more technical side, developers can take a number of steps to address this issue, including to

» Make sure the data is diverse and comprehensive enough cover a wide range of scenarios and perspectives.

» Apply regularization methods like dropout, L1, and L2 regularization during training to prevent overfitting by penalizing complexity. L1 regularization (Lasso) encourages simpler models by adding the absolute value of weights as a penalty, leading to fewer non-zero weights. L2 regularization (Ridge) prevents large weights by adding their squares as a penalty, resulting in a more balanced distribution of weights.

» Employ human moderators to review and correct AI-generated content.

» Use adversarial examples and training techniques to challenge the AI and improve its ability to distinguish between truthful and misleading information. Adversarial AI involves creating inputs that are designed to confuse or trick a machine learning model into making incorrect predictions, known as *adversarial examples*. By exposing a model to these examples during training, the model can learn to recognize and resist such attacks, thus improving its accuracy and robustness. This process is akin to strengthening a system's defenses by simulating attacks to identify and fix vulnerabilities.

» Design AI systems to be interpretable, auditable, and explainable.

» Implement post-processing rules or filters to catch and correct certain types of errors or misinformation in the AI's outputs before they reach the user.

More techniques than these exist, but I believe this list is enough to introduce you to the basic concepts.

Preventing AI from generating false information

Preventing GenAI from generating false information is a significant challenge, but several strategies can be implemented to mitigate this risk. Some we've already covered in the preceding section, so I won't repeat that information here. Suffice it to say that taking steps to improve accuracy in outputs by definition serves the dual purpose of screening for false information.

Additional measures include

>> **Content filtering**: Use content filters to detect and remove known false information or improbable outputs. This can be based on a database of debunked claims or using pattern recognition to identify common characteristics of misinformation.

>> **Model fine-tuning:** Regularly update and fine-tune the AI model using accurate and up-to-date information to ensure its outputs remain relevant and factual. Please remember that when it comes to finetuning and RAG, the answer isn't to choose one or the other, but likely both. RAG doesn't cure or compensate for the same model ills that fine-tuning does.

>> **Confidence scoring**: Implement a system in which the AI assigns a confidence score to its outputs, indicating how likely it is that the information is accurate.

>> **Cross-validation with trusted sources:** Cross-reference AI-generated information with trusted sources and datasets to validate its accuracy.

>> **Regular auditing:** Conduct regular audits of the AI system to assess its accuracy and make adjustments as necessary. This can be done in a manner similar to the software development processes and by tying model development to other accountable technologies such as blockchain or casual AI.

>> **Limiting scope:** Define clear boundaries for the AI's knowledge domain to prevent it from generating content on topics it is not sufficiently trained to handle accurately.

Repurposing Content with GenAI

Repurposing content with GenAI is a great way to quickly fill a content well. In the context of this book, a *content well* means a sizable but largely as yet unmet demand for content that fills a specific purpose, such as marketing. I don't mean to limit it to its technical definition, which is "a designated area on a web page that holds the main content." No matter how big or pressing the demand for more content, it's important to follow best practices to ensure each piece of content remains valuable, relevant, and respectful of intellectual property rights.

Here's a quick summary of general advice for repurposing content with GenAI:

>> **Define purpose and audience:** Clearly understand why you are repurposing the content and who the intended audience is. This will guide the AI in modifying the content to suit the new context and audience needs.

- **» Use reliable sources:** Start with high-quality, accurate source material to ensure the repurposed content maintains a standard of quality and truthfulness.

- **» Respect copyright:** Ensure that you have the rights to the original content and that repurposing it with AI adheres to the terms of any original agreements or contracts, copyright laws, and fair-use principles.

- **» Add value:** Aim to enhance the original content by providing additional insights, updating information, or tailoring it to a different format or platform.

- **» Maintain original intent:** While modifying the content, strive to preserve the original message and intent, unless the goal is to create a derivative work with a new message.

- **» Check for accuracy:** Verify that any factual information remains accurate after repurposing, especially if the content is condensed or expanded.

- **» Review and edit:** Always review AI-generated content manually to ensure it meets quality standards and is appropriate for the new purpose.

- **» Monitor feedback:** Pay attention to how the audience responds to the repurposed content and be ready to make adjustments based on their feedback.

- **» Attribute properly:** When necessary, credit the original creators or sources of the content, even if it has been significantly altered by the AI. Also, be transparent about using AI.

- **» Stay ethical:** Consider the ethical implications of repurposing content, such as the potential impact on the original content creators and the audience.

You can responsibly leverage GenAI to repurpose content in a way that is both beneficial and respectful to all parties involved if you are diligent about meeting all the requirements. But if you are in doubt as to whether you can repurpose your content, get legal advice or ethical counsel before proceeding.

TIP

AI can breathe new life into your existing material by repurposing content for different audiences and goals, thus expanding its reach and value. Here are some creative ways to use GenAI to repurpose content:

- **» Content summarization:** Use GenAI to create summaries of your long-form content, such as white papers or reports, making them accessible as blog posts, social media updates, or newsletter snippets.

- **» Translation and localization:** Translate your content into different languages and localize it for various regions to reach a global audience.

- **» Audio and video transcription:** Convert your podcasts or videos into written transcripts, which can then be used as blog posts, guides, or even as a basis for an ebook.

- **» Text-to-video**: Transform blog posts or articles into engaging videos or video summaries using AI-driven video creation tools.

- **» Chatbots and interactive content:** Create chatbots or interactive Q&A sessions from your FAQ pages or instructional content to provide a dynamic user experience.

- **» Data visualization:** Use AI to turn data-heavy reports or case studies into infographics, charts, or interactive visualizations that make the information more digestible.

- **» Ebooks and guides:** Compile a series of related blog posts or articles into comprehensive ebooks or guides using AI to assist with content organization and formatting.

- **» Social media content:** Generate social media posts, stories, or tweets from existing content to boost engagement and drive traffic back to your main website.

- **» Audio content:** Use GenAI to create audio versions of your written content, which can then be produced by text-to-speech technology and distributed as podcasts or audio articles.

- **» Content personalization:** Personalize content for different segments of your audience by using AI to tweak the messaging, examples, or case studies based on user preferences or behaviors.

- **» SEO optimization:** Refresh old content with updated keywords, meta descriptions, and titles suggested by AI-powered SEO tools to improve search engine rankings.

- **» Interactive e-learning modules:** Convert instructional content into interactive e-learning courses with the help of AI that can structure lessons and generate quizzes.

- **» Creative remixing:** Use AI to combine elements from various pieces of content to create new, unique pieces that provide fresh perspectives or insights.

- **» Voiceovers and narrations:** Add professional-sounding voiceovers to your video content with AI voice synthesis, making it more accessible and engaging.

- **» Augmented reality experiences:** Create augmented reality experiences from visual content, allowing users to interact with your brand in a novel way.

By leveraging AI in creative ways you can maximize the potential of your existing content, making it work harder and reach further than ever before.

Chapter **7**

Producing Long-Form Content

This chapter is all about the role of GenAI in the production of long-form content. The focus is primarily on the capabilities of GenAI to handle large datasets and generate long-form text that's coherent, factually accurate, and contextually appropriate. The discussion also extends to the practicalities of a writer's interaction with GenAI, evaluating the division of labor in which the technology is responsible for data processing and initial text generation, and the human writer is tasked with guiding the narrative and ensuring the content's uniqueness. I wrote this book with AI assistance using several techniques discussed throughout this book, but this chapter contains my specific observations, insights, and experiences in doing so. I'm a firm believer that first you practice and then you teach — not the other way around!

TIP

In addition to the information provided in this chapter, you'll need to use one or more techniques described in detail in Chapter 9. Specifically, you must pay attention to output stitching and AI aggregation as you'll likely need to use both when creating any long-form content, regardless of the topic, style, or format.

REMEMBER

Long-form content is by far the most difficult to produce successfully and to professional standards with GenAI. If you come into this thinking that GenAI is an easy way out of arduous tasks, you're gonna be sorely disappointed. However, many real benefits exist to using AI in this way and, with practice and experience, you will get better at using it in your writing process. I promise it's worth it in the end!

Writing Academic Papers with GenAI Assistance

Tackling the creation of an academic paper can be a complex task, and GenAI is emerging as a valuable tool in this intellectual endeavor. This section provides a clear overview of how GenAI can assist in the research and writing process while maintaining the integrity and originality that academic work demands. You explore practical ways in which GenAI can serve as an aid in organizing literature, synthesizing data, and generating drafts, all without compromising your or another scholar's voice and analytical perspective.

REMEMBER

The use of GenAI in academic writing should be approached with a judicious blend of skepticism and openness — recognizing its potential to streamline the research process while being wary of over-reliance on its outputs. Focus on integrating GenAI's capabilities with critical thinking and ensure that the final paper reflects a well-argued, original contribution to the field.

Using GenAI for research and academic writing

When it comes to academic writing, thorough research is the backbone that supports the entire structure of your scholarly work. GenAI is becoming an increasingly valuable tool in the researcher's toolkit and the overall AI stack, offering a suite of functions that can aid in the meticulous task of gathering and analyzing data. Consider the following:

» **GenAI has the potential to uncover obscure connections between data points.** By analyzing vast networks of academic papers, GenAI can suggest relationships and patterns that might not be immediately obvious to human researchers. This can lead to novel insights and interdisciplinary connections that could be the seed for groundbreaking research. (However, it's important to approach these AI-generated connections with a discerning eye, validating them through further research and critical evaluation.)

» **Before you dive deep into a topic, GenAI can quickly scan and summarize existing literature on the subject. This broad overview can help you to identify key themes, gaps in the research, and seminal works.** The high-altitude reconnaissance can save valuable time and help shape the direction of your inquiry.

» GenAI can also assist in the more granular aspects of research, such as data mining and extraction. For instance, it can sift through large datasets to extract relevant statistics, trends, and figures that are pertinent to your research question. Additionally, GenAI's language-processing capabilities can be harnessed to transcribe and translate materials, making non-native language sources more accessible and broadening the scope of your research.

Use of GenAI in this domain requires a strategic approach to ensure that it serves as an enhancement rather than a replacement for the researcher's own critical-thinking skills. The following sections help guide you through process and product options (although, please know that these are examples and not your only options).

Examining GenAI tool options for research and academic writing

GenAI has evolved to include specialized tools tailored for academic research, enhancing the researcher's ability to delve into complex topics with increasing precision and depth. For instance, tools like Iris.ai (iris.ai) and Semantic Scholar (www.semanticscholar.org) use AI to map out scientific literature and provide researchers with relevant papers, reviews, and patents, often uncovering material that traditional search engines might miss. These platforms use natural language processing to understand the context of research queries, ensuring that the results are not just keyword-based but semantically related to the research question.

Another example is Zotero (www.zotero.org), a free reference manager that helps manage and cite research sources for book or report writing and can be integrated with GenAI tools. Zotero can automatically extract citation details from PDFs and web pages and add such works to a research folder with a simple click on a browser extension, making it easier for researchers to build and maintain their bibliographies. You can easily connect Zotero with Research Rabbit (www.researchrabbit.ai) to further streamline your research and get your reports and papers found by other researchers, too. Research Rabbit is a free research tool built to help you discover and organize relevant papers for your research. It provides interactive visualizations, collections, digests, and data search tools. If you want a more in-depth look at Zotero and its many capabilities, you might want to view "How to use Zotero's full potential [The AI Revolution in Zotero]" on YouTube at https://www.youtube.com/watch?v=gA3o2M1nPBQ.

You can add ChatGPT to Zotero in a few easy steps. Then you can research and write your academic paper or book in one tool. The easiest integration to add GenAI to Zotero is ARIA, an acronym for AI Research Assistant and a Zotero plugin. Before using ARIA, you need to have an OpenAI API key, which is a security code for developers to use that enables computer programs to interact. You can get an OpenAI API key here: https://help.openai.com/en/articles/4936850-where-do-i-find-my-openai-api-key. Follow the in-app instructions to add the key, select the ChatGPT model you want to use, and restart Zotero.

The integration process is super easy and takes only a few steps. After you've obtained an OpenAI API key, take the following steps to install ARIA as an add-on tool for Zotero:

1. Go to Aria on GitHub at https://github.com/lifan0127/ai-research-assistant.

2. Scroll down to the Installation section and download the latest release (.xpi file) from GitHub: https://github.com/lifan0127/ai-research-assistant/releases/latest

3. Go to Zotero and select Tools from the top menu bar. Click on Addons.

4. On the Add-ons Manager panel, click the gear icon at the top right corner and select Install Add-on From File.

5. Select the .xpi file you just downloaded and click Open, which will start the installation process.

   You're done!

For more detailed look at this installation process, see the walkthrough tweet by Mushtaq Bilal, PhD, Syddansk Universitet on Twitter (now X) at https://x.com/MushtaqBilalPhD/status/1735221900584865904.

Additionally, platforms like BenchSci (www.benchsci.com) apply AI to decode complex scientific figures, allowing researchers to find specific experimental data without combing through countless articles manually. However, you'll need to integrate this, too, with a GenAI tool trained for writing or copy its outputs to a GenAI text generator like ChatGPT or Claude so you can write your article or paper.

There are specialized text generators, too, like SciWriter (www.sciwriter.ai), but many of those have waiting lists and lean more toward writing articles than writing papers.

Refining GenAI research outputs

GenAI outputs "as is" will almost never be what you want and need them to be. Indeed, the process of trying to get GenAI to produce exactly what you need can be exhausting and frustrating. Also, GenAI, even the specialized text generators, do a lousy job of writing anything in long form. It's smarter and more productive to resign yourself to these unfortunate facts and develop your writing process accordingly. In other words, focus on GenAI's strengths in data discovery and analysis, and in helping you fill in any blanks in your work or thinking. Otherwise, accept GenAI's flaws and use your own mind and talent to work around them.

To refine AI research outputs and better ensure their relevance and accuracy, follow this step-by-step process:

1. **Start with a clear and concise research question or set of keywords.**

   Input these into the GenAI tool as a prompt to generate an initial list of resources.

2. **Use a specialized GenAI or other tool's filtering options to narrow down the results to the most relevant papers.**

   This may include sorting by date, relevance, citation count, or journal impact factor. You can integrate GenAI with research tools as discussed above to do this work, or you can prompt a GenAI tool to do this type of sorting for you. You may want to try both ways and compare the results.

3. **Skim through the abstracts provided by the AI to assess the pertinence of each source.**

   At this stage, look for the research's main objective, methodology, and conclusions to determine its applicability to your work.

4. **For sources that pass the abstract review, read the full text to evaluate the quality and depth of the research.**

   Pay particular attention to the study's design, the robustness of the data, and the soundness of the arguments presented.

5. **Check the references and citations within the papers to find additional material and to verify the AI's suggestions.**

   This step helps to ensure that key sources haven't been overlooked.

6. **Perform a manual search for literature on your topic to compare against the AI-generated list.**

   This can help identify any gaps or biases in the AI's output.

7. **Use the AI to help extract and organize key data points, statistics, and quotes from the selected sources.**

   Ensure that all extracted information is accurately represented and properly cited.

8. **Critically evaluate the synthesized information, looking for logical consistency, potential biases, and the strength of the evidence.**

9. **Refine your search query based on insights gained from the literature and repeat the process as necessary to uncover additional resources or to narrow the focus of your research.**

REMEMBER

By integrating these advanced GenAI tools into your research process and rigorously refining their outputs, you can enhance the breadth and depth of your academic writing. It's crucial to remain actively engaged in each step, using your expertise to guide the AI and to critically assess its contributions to your scholarly work.

Finding hidden pitfalls or AI limitations

While GenAI tools can offer significant advantages in academic research, researchers should be aware of some hidden pitfalls and limitations. Understanding these limitations is essential to knowing when to supplement or replace AI research with manual efforts and other types of tools.

>> **Data quality and bias:** GenAI tools are only as good as the data they have been trained on. If the underlying data contains biases or inaccuracies, the AI's outputs will reflect those flaws. Researchers should be cautious of over-reliance on AI-generated data without cross-referencing it against other sources.

>> **Scope of training:** Some AI tools may have been trained on specific types of literature or within particular disciplines, which can limit their ability to identify relevant research outside of those areas. Researchers should verify whether the AI's scope aligns with their field of study and supplement with manual searches and other types of tools as needed.

>> **Contextual misunderstandings:** AI may struggle with understanding the nuanced context of certain research queries, which can lead to irrelevant or tangential results. Researchers should be prepared to interpret the results critically and refine their queries to improve relevance.

- **Overlooked novel research:** AI tools may favor sources with more citations or those that are more easily accessible, potentially overlooking newer, less-cited yet highly relevant research. Researchers should manually keep abreast of the latest publications in their field to capture cutting-edge studies.

- **Non-textual data limitations:** GenAI is predominantly text-based and may not effectively analyze or interpret non-textual data such as complex graphs, images, or raw datasets. Researchers should manually review such materials to ensure comprehensive understanding and integration into their work.

- **Updates and maintenance:** AI databases require regular updates to include the latest research. If an AI tool is not well-maintained, it may miss recent publications. Researchers should check the update frequency of AI tools and supplement with manual or other tool searches in fast-moving fields.

- **Citation context:** GenAI can provide citations, but it may not always capture the context in which a study is cited. Researchers should manually review citations to understand how a source is being used within the literature to avoid misinterpretation.

- **Language limitations:** While some AI tools offer translation capabilities, nuances and subtleties in language can be lost. For research in languages other than those the AI was primarily designed for, researchers should verify translations and interpretations by different means.

- **Depth of analysis:** AI can help identify broad patterns and connections, but it may not capture the depth of analysis required for a thorough literature review. Researchers should supplement AI findings with deep, manual analysis to uncover subtle arguments and theoretical frameworks.

To mitigate these pitfalls, maintain a balanced approach, using GenAI as a starting point for identifying potentially relevant research and then applying your own expertise and critical-thinking skills to conduct a more nuanced and comprehensive review.

WARNING

Whatever you do, do not hand your boss, or publish, any AI-based research or written report without thoroughly reviewing and vetting first. If you do, you're likely gambling your entire career, and you're probably going to lose badly.

Supporting the academic publication process

The journey from research to publication is often a marathon filled with hurdles, from formatting to peer review. GenAI is emerging as a useful resource in this process, offering capabilities that can help streamline various stages of academic publishing. However, while GenAI can assist with some aspects of the academic publishing process like literature reviews, writing, and organization, the more nuanced human elements involving expert judgement, context, and domain knowledge remain challenging for AI to fully automate or replicate at this stage. You should be very cautious about overestimating GenAI's role.

While GenAI tools have the potential to assist with various tasks, some of the capabilities mentioned or touted by enthusiasts and vendors — and even in GenAI responses — may not be fully developed or widely available. Here's an overview of where things stand as of this writing:

» **Manuscript formatting:** While there are tools like LaTeX that can help with formatting academic papers and reference management software like Zotero and EndNote that can format citations according to journal styles, claims or suggestions that GenAI can automatically format entire manuscripts to fit specific journal guidelines are unfounded. Such formatting usually requires manual intervention to ensure adherence to the specific requirements of each journal.

» **Preliminary peer review:** No widely recognized GenAI tools simulate the peer review process against a vast database of published papers to predict common points of contention or interest. While there are AI-based grammar and style checkers that can help improve the readability and quality of writing, the nuanced feedback provided by human peer reviewers, which includes evaluating the validity of the research methodology, the interpretation of results, and the overall contribution to the field, cannot be fully replicated by AI at this time.

» **Gauging novelty:** GenAI tools can help identify existing literature on a topic, but their ability to assess the novelty of research is limited. Determining the unique contributions of a study requires deep understanding and contextual knowledge that currently goes beyond the capabilities of AI.

» **Creating a list of suitable reviewers:** Databases and networking platforms can help identify researchers with relevant expertise, but the selection of suitable reviewers typically involves editorial judgment and knowledge of the field. GenAI does not currently manage this aspect of the publication process.

In summary, while AI can provide support in the academic publication process, its role is primarily in assisting with research, organization, and some aspects of writing. The more nuanced tasks, such as peer review, assessing research novelty, and selecting suitable reviewers, still rely heavily on human expertise. It's essential for you to remain critically engaged and not overestimate the capabilities of AI in the context of academic publishing.

Developing White Papers and Reports Using Generative AI

GenAI is helpful in writing white papers and reports, which are often extensive and require a significant investment of time and expertise. There are limitations to how much of the work GenAI tools can perform. Here's an overview of where things stand in terms of GenAI assisting with white papers and reports as of this writing.

>> **Automated drafting**: While GenAI can assist in creating outlines and initial drafts, it's important to note that these tools typically require human input to guide the structure and ensure that it meets the specific goals of the white paper or report. The AI's ability to automate drafting is based on patterns it has learned from data, so it might not always align perfectly with the author's intentions without manual adjustments.

>> **Suggesting content based on trends:** GenAI does have the capability to analyze large datasets and can identify trends to some extent. However, the insight it provides is often based on the data it has been trained on, and it may not have access to the most current or proprietary databases unless integrated by the user. Predictive models in AI are also not infallible and should be used with caution, especially when informing strategic decisions.

>> **Synthesizing information:** GenAI can indeed process and summarize information from various sources, but the quality and depth of synthesis can vary. It's essential for the user to critically evaluate and supplement AI-generated summaries to ensure that they capture the necessary details and context accurately.

>> **Accuracy and relevance:** It is crucial to highlight that verifying the accuracy and relevance of AI-generated content is a key step in the process. GenAI can sometimes replicate misinformation if that's present in the training data, and it may not always interpret data correctly, especially if it involves complex or nuanced topics.

REMEMBER

While GenAI can support the development of white papers and reports by providing structural outlines and synthesizing information, its capabilities are not a substitute for human expertise and judgment. The technology serves best as an aid in the writing process, with the author playing a critical role in ensuring the final document's accuracy, relevance, and credibility.

Crafting professional documents with AI support

The integration of AI into the process of creating professional documents such as white papers and reports can significantly enhance productivity and quality. AI support can streamline research, organize content, and even aid in the editing process, allowing writers to focus on the critical thinking and strategic aspects of document creation.

When starting a white paper or report, you can use AI tools like Grammarly (www.grammarly.com) and Hemingway (hemingwayapp.com) to help refine the language and improve readability. These tools provide real-time suggestions to make the text clearer, more concise, and grammatically correct. For more complex editing tasks, tools like ProWritingAid (prowritingaid.com) offer in-depth reports on style, word choice, and sentence structure.

For research, AI-powered tools such as Yewno Discover and Connected Papers (www.connectedpapers.com) offer innovative ways to explore the academic landscape. They can help authors find the most relevant studies, papers, and articles by understanding the context of their queries, not just matching keywords. This can lead to a more informed and up-to-date background section in any professional document.

AI can also help in organizing the document's structure. Tools like Scrivener (www.literatureandlatte.com/scrivener/overview) help writers manage large writing projects by breaking them down into smaller, more manageable sections. This can be particularly useful for lengthy reports or white papers that cover multiple topics or require extensive data presentation. However, Scrivener does not directly use or provide AI tools. Most people who want to use GenAI tools copy and paste the documents they created in Scrivener to a GenAI tool to further their work.

For data analysis and visualization, tools like Tableau (www.tableau.com) and Microsoft Power BI leverage AI to help users identify trends, patterns, and insights from complex datasets. These can be incorporated into professional documents to support arguments with empirical evidence and create compelling visualizations that convey the data's story at a glance.

Meanwhile, AI-driven summarization tools can condense large volumes of information into concise overviews. For instance, tools like Resoomer (resoomer.com) can be useful when one needs to quickly assimilate and report on the key points from a range of sources or when creating an executive summary for a detailed report.

However, while AI provides fast and intensive support, I'll again remind you that these tools are not infallible. You should always review AI-generated content for accuracy, tone, and relevance. It's also important to ensure that the use of AI aligns with ethical guidelines and intellectual property laws, especially when dealing with proprietary or sensitive information.

Enhancing business communication with AI

While this section focuses mostly on white papers and reports, there are other long-form business communications that GenAI can assist with as well.

Following are some general tips for using GenAI on any long-form business or academic content:

>> **Define clear objectives:** Before using AI, define the goals of your document. What message do you want to convey, and to whom? Clear objectives will help you guide the AI in generating relevant content.

>> **Validate AI contributions:** Always factcheck and validate AI-generated content, especially when dealing with technical subjects or data analysis.

>> **Balance technicality and readability:** Use AI to strike a balance between technical accuracy and readability. Tailor the complexity of the language to the document's intended audience.

>> **Keep the human element:** Ensure that the final document reflects the company's voice and values. AI should support the communication strategy, not define it.

>> **Stay updated on AI developments:** The field of AI is rapidly evolving. Stay informed about new tools and updates that can further enhance your business communications.

Crafting Research Designs and Outlines with GenAI

GenAI can streamline the research process, from conceptualization to data collection, including crafting research designs, outlines, and poll questions. GenAI tools are adept at organizing thoughts and structuring complex information, making them particularly useful for researchers who are in the early stages of project development.

When it comes to research design, GenAI can assist in developing a comprehensive outline that covers all necessary components of a study. By inputting the research objectives and questions, researchers can use AI to generate a framework that includes the introduction, literature review, methodology, data analysis, and conclusion sections. AI tools like ZoteroBib (zbib.org) can also help researchers manage their sources and citations efficiently, ensuring that their literature reviews are thorough and properly referenced. Moreover, AI-driven platforms such as Iris.ai can explore vast databases to identify relevant studies and theoretical frameworks, suggesting connections that may not be immediately obvious but that you would want to include in the research design.

For creating poll questions and surveys, GenAI can be particularly useful in formulating questions that are clear, unbiased, and likely to yield informative responses. AI tools like SurveyMonkey's Question Bank offer a repository of pre-vetted questions that can be customized to fit the specific needs of a study. These AI-generated questions can serve as a starting point, which researchers can then refine to ensure that the wording is precise and tailored to their target demographic. Additionally, AI can analyze pilot survey data to identify poorly performing questions, allowing researchers to make necessary adjustments before launching a large-scale data collection effort.

It is crucial for researchers to critically evaluate and adapt AI-generated content. The researcher's expertise is essential in interpreting AI suggestions within the context of their specific field and research goals. It is this synergy between human intellect and AI efficiency that can produce well-crafted research designs and tools, ultimately leading to more robust and insightful studies.

Structuring research projects with AI

In general, structuring a research project involves the following actions:

1. Define the research question.
2. Conduct a literature review.
3. Develop a methodology.
4. Create a research proposal.
5. Plan the project.
6. Collect data.
7. Analyze data.
8. Write the report.
9. Revise and edit.

10. Peer review (if applicable).

11. Disseminate findings.

12. Reflect on the process.

REMEMBER

AI offers valuable tools for assisting with the structuring of research projects, but its capabilities are currently more supportive than autonomous. AI can provide insights and highlight patterns that may not be immediately apparent to researchers, but the tasks of identifying gaps in literature, developing theoretical frameworks, and designing methodologies still require significant human input and critical evaluation.

Consider the following caveats:

» GenAI can help identify gaps in literature by processing large volumes of data and highlighting areas that lack research. However, the AI's effectiveness in this task depends on the quality of the data it has been trained on and the sophistication of the algorithms used. AI can pinpoint underexplored areas or contradictions, but the technology typically requires human guidance to interpret the significance and relevance of these findings within a specific research context.

» GenAI can analyze patterns and correlations in data, which may suggest potential theories. However, AI cannot reliably develop theoretical frameworks or hypotheses. GenAI can provide data-driven insights that may inspire researchers to formulate new hypotheses, but the creation of a robust theoretical framework remains a complex task that relies heavily on human expertise and critical thinking.

» AI does have predictive analytics capabilities, and these can be used to some extent to inform research design based on historical data and outcomes from similar studies. However, the ability of AI to guide the methodological design of a project is not as straightforward as is often suggested. Predictive analytics can provide some foresight into potential outcomes, but human researchers need to interpret these predictions and make methodological decisions based on a comprehensive understanding of the subject matter.

From concept to outline: GenAI as a planning tool

GenAI can play a significant role in the initial stages of academic and professional research. Its capacity to process and organize information provides a foundational tool for you to transition from a broad concept to a structured research outline.

At the conceptual stage, AI can be utilized to conduct preliminary literature reviews and environmental scans. Tools like Iris.ai facilitate this by allowing researchers to input their research question or abstract and then receive a map of related work and concepts. This not only speeds up the literature review process but also ensures a comprehensive understanding of the field, helping to refine the research question and objectives.

Additionally, AI applications can analyze the sentiment and trends within existing literature, offering insights into prevailing research attitudes and potential biases, which can be instrumental in defining the scope and direction of a new study. However, their use in academic literature reviews is not as widespread as in other fields, such as market analysis or social media monitoring. The application of sentiment analysis to academic literature to uncover biases and trends is an emerging area, and while tools exist, they may not yet be a standard part of the research design process.

After your research concept is solidified, GenAI aids in outlining the research design by suggesting logical structures and sequences for the project. GenAI-powered mind mapping tools, for example, can help visualize the connections between various components of your research project, such as hypotheses, methodologies, and expected outcomes. Examples include NoteGPT, MindMatrix, Mapify, and GitMind.

Furthermore, AI can assist in identifying the most suitable research methods for your project by drawing from databases of past studies, analyzing their success rates, and aligning them with the current research goals. This can add efficiency to the planning phase. However, using GenAI to suggest research methods is a complex task and is not commonly found in mainstream GenAI tools. GenAI systems are in development for specialized fields that can analyze and suggest methodologies, though these are typically more accessible to authorized users or research institutions.

REMEMBER

Despite the assistance GenAI can provide, the creativity and critical judgment of the researcher remain crucial in crafting a research design that is both innovative and scientifically rigorous.

Integrating Citations and References

Integrating citations and references is a critical aspect of academic writing and research, ensuring that proper credit is given for the ideas and findings of others. The process can be tedious and time-consuming and one that I am happy to relegate to GenAI. You probably are, too.

As GenAI technology continues to evolve, we can expect further advancements that will make the process more intuitive and integrated into the research workflow, allowing scholars to focus more on the substance of their work rather than the technicalities of citation. For now, well, let's just say there's a long way to go yet. Integrating GenAI with other more mature research tools is probably your best bet.

GenAI-assisted reference management

The good news is that citation tools, like Zotero and Mendeley, extract reference details from documents, websites, and other digital sources. These tools can recognize and format citations according to various style guides, such as APA, MLA, or Chicago, with minimal input from you. They also allow you to maintain a searchable library of references, which can be easily organized by topic, project, or other custom tags. This not only saves time but also reduces the risk of errors in citation, which is crucial for maintaining the integrity of a research project.

The bad news is that most, if not all, pure-play citation and reference management tools like Zotero and Mendeley (www.mendeley.com) are not GenAI-driven as of this writing. Some will allow you to integrate them with GenAI. There's much debate about whether integrating GenAI will strengthen or weaken these tools in the end.

But it is true that some advanced word processors and writing platforms have begun to more fully incorporate GenAI-driven features. For example, tools like Grammarly and Microsoft Editor use GenAI to help improve writing quality, which can include suggestions for citations.

However, a feature that suggests relevant articles to cite based on the content being written is not commonly found across all word processors and may only be part of more specialized or advanced writing assistance software.

It's reasonable to expect that GenAI technology will continue to evolve and further integrate into the research workflow. But the availability and sophistication of these features can differ significantly depending on the specific software or platform in use. As GenAI becomes more sophisticated, its potential to streamline the research process and allow scholars to focus more on the content of their work is likely to increase.

Ensuring academic integrity with GenAI

Many modern writing assistance tools and plagiarism-detection services, such as Turnitin and Grammarly, use sophisticated algorithms and GenAI to scan texts against databases of academic work to identify potential plagiarism. These tools can result in users adding citations where necessary to help ensure that all sources are properly credited.

Moreover, GenAI can assist in paraphrasing and summarizing existing research while maintaining the original meaning, which helps in avoiding plagiarism. GenAI writing assistants can suggest alternative ways to present information that ensure the researcher's prose is unique, yet still reflects a thorough understanding of the subject matter. This is particularly useful for students and researchers who are synthesizing complex information from multiple sources.

GenAI can also contribute to academic integrity by ensuring consistency and accuracy in data reporting. GenAI algorithms can analyze datasets for anomalies or inconsistencies that may indicate errors in data collection or analysis. By flagging these issues, researchers can address them proactively, ensuring that their reports are as accurate and reliable as possible. As GenAI continues to evolve, its potential to reinforce ethical practices in academic research is likely to expand, providing researchers with a powerful ally in the quest for integrity and excellence in their scholarly endeavors.

WARNING

But GenAI tools can and do hallucinate so the onus remains on you to take every measure beyond GenAI that is necessary to ensure academic integrity in every work produced with or without GenAI assistance.

Producing Long-Form Articles with GenAI

The use of GenAI in producing long-form articles has certainly brought a mixed bag of outcomes — good, bad, and ugly. On the positive side, GenAI has democratized content creation, enabling writers, marketers, and researchers to produce comprehensive articles more efficiently. It can assist with generating ideas, providing structure, and even drafting sections of content, which can be particularly beneficial for those facing writer's block or tight deadlines. Additionally, GenAI can help non-native speakers articulate their thoughts more fluently, broadening the inclusivity of content creation.

However, the use of GenAI in writing long-form articles is not without its pitfalls. The *bad* often emerges in the form of over-reliance on AI, which can lead to homogenized content lacking in depth, personal insight, or the nuanced understanding that human expertise brings. There's also the risk of factual inaccuracies or the perpetuation of biases present in the training data, which can mislead readers and erode trust in the content. Furthermore, the *ugly* side surfaces when GenAI is used unethically to mass-produce deceptive or plagiarized content, manipulate opinions, or spread misinformation, which can have far-reaching negative consequences on public discourse and trust in media.

While GenAI offers powerful tools for streamlining the writing process and enhancing productivity, it also poses significant challenges that need to be managed with a critical eye toward maintaining quality, originality, and ethical standards. As the technology continues to evolve, it will be crucial for writers and publishers to balance the efficiency gains with a commitment to the integrity and value of the written word.

Techniques for GenAI-enhanced feature writing

Feature writing typically allows a little more time to complete than news writing because it usually involves more research and interviews and isn't necessarily tied to the day's headlines. These are the pieces that typically garner many views and are the stuff that magazines and legendary writers and reporters built their reputations on.

Today, feature stories still take a deeper dive into their subject and often offer nuance and color that straight news reporting lacks. The question now becomes whether feature writing is a good use case for GenAI — or not? The answer is it depends.

A lot depends on the talent and experience of the writer and the capabilities of the GenAI model used. Yes, GenAIs, as in plural meaning more than one GenAI. I find that output stitching is highly effective in writing most long-form articles, but most especially features. The reason for that is I can stitch together pieces of outputs from multiple GenAIs that were prompted the same way. This gives me many different options and perspectives that a single model just can't deliver. I can also break repetitive outputs and other annoying GenAI behaviors by using AI chaining, which is basically infusing other GenAI outputs in the input (prompt) of another. You'll be amazed at how well that works. Read the first section in Chapter 9 to learn more about these and other techniques.

TIP

I also find AI aggregation to be a crucial strategy as that enables me to use a variety of GenAI built for different purposes such as background research, financial data analysis, cross-referencing and cross-factchecking, source discovery, image and data visualization generation, and other tasks I might need to bring to bear to create really great long content. And I've done all this testing and strategizing and process building for projects like this book — to see what works and what doesn't — and to share those findings with you. But I have yet to actually use any of this in my journalism work. That's because all the news outlets and trade journals that I write for forbid the use of GenAI — at least for now. If you're a journalist, your outlet may be ok with using GenAI. If that's the case, I'd love to hear about your experiences in that newsroom.

If you're producing feature articles for marketing or business purposes outside of journalism, you'll find these same techniques to be invaluable.

Meanwhile, here are some techniques and tips for leveraging GenAI in feature writing:

- **Research assistance**: Use GenAI to conduct preliminary research on your topic. Tools like Evernote can help you collect and organize information, while others like ChatGPT and Claude can summarize lengthy reports, contracts, agreements, interview transcriptions, videos, or articles, saving you time and helping you to quickly gather background information and context for your feature.

- **Trend analysis:** GenAI can analyze large datasets to identify trends that might be relevant to your story. Tools like Google Trends or social listening platforms can provide insights into what topics are currently popular or rising in public interest, which can help you to choose angles that will resonate with your audience.

- **Writing assistance:** GenAI writing assistants can help you overcome writer's block by suggesting sentence completions or alternative phrasings. While you should not rely on these tools to write large sections of your article, they can be useful for getting started or finding a new way to express an idea.

- **Editing for clarity and style:** GenAI-powered grammar and style checkers can help refine your writing, ensuring that it is clear, concise, and free of errors. Tools like Grammarly or Hemingway Editor can suggest improvements to sentence structure, word choice, and readability.

- **Audience engagement:** Use AI to understand your audience better. GenAI and GenAI-integrated analytics tools can track reader engagement and provide feedback on which parts of your articles are the most and least engaging. This information can be invaluable in refining your writing style and content to better match your readers' interests.

- **Personalization:** GenAI can help personalize content for different segments of your audience. By analyzing reader data, GenAI can suggest topics, stories, and approaches that are more likely to appeal to specific demographics or reader groups.

- **Factchecking:** Use GenAI factchecking tools to help verify the accuracy of statements and data presented in your feature. This is crucial for maintaining credibility and trust with your readers. You might want to check out Full Fact in the UK at https://fullfact.org/ and the map and info on many global factchecking sites at Duke Reporters' Lab at https://reporterslab.org/ fact-checking/ and pictured in Figure 7-1.

FIGURE 7-1:
Screenshot of the interactive map of global factchecking sites at Duke Reporters' Lab.

OpenstreetMap/https://reporterslab.org/fact-checking//OpenstreetMap.

REMEMBER

GenAI is a tool to assist you in the writing process, not a replacement for journalistic integrity and ethical considerations. Be transparent about the use of GenAI in your writing process and ensure that the final product reflects your voice and adheres to the highest standards of journalism.

Maintaining depth and quality in GenAI-assisted articles

To preserve depth, you should use GenAI for initial research and drafting but then critically evaluate and expand upon the information provided by GenAI, incorporating your own knowledge, perspectives, and additional research. This helps to add layers of understanding that AI alone cannot achieve. You should also factcheck all GenAI-generated content to ensure accuracy and reliability, as even specialized GenAI can and does hallucinate on the regular as well as perpetuate errors or biases present in its training data.

Quality is upheld by using GenAI tools to enhance your natural voice and improve readability without compromising your unique style. GenAI can assist with grammar, syntax, and structure, but you should always have the final say in how the content is presented. Additionally, you should remain mindful of ethical considerations, giving proper attribution when necessary and being transparent about the use of GenAI in your writing process.

Writing Books with GenAI

If you're prompting GenAI to write complete books or, heaven forbid, thinking of it as a coauthor, you're doing it wrong. That's like an architect sharing the credit with CAD software for the creation of a beautiful building. I mean, I guess you can do that if you want, but you're dissing your own talent and leading others astray in their work by implying that the software can do much more than it does. Instead, just make it clear that you used GenAI to make your own creative work until the day comes around that it's as routine as an architect using CAD in the course of their work.

And in case you missed it elsewhere in this book, I used GenAI as a tool in writing this book. Not a coauthor. Not in collaboration or cahoots with a machine (or rather software). Just a tool. Actually, I used and/or tested almost all the GenAI tools currently in the toolbox. How else can I tell you how to do it other than for me to just do it and report back to you what actually worked? You are free to evaluate my results — this book — for yourself. I also ask that you write a review or rate it online so others can consider the outcome for themselves, too. Further, I want to hear about your own experience in writing long-form content or a book with GenAI. We are, after all, finding our way through the same maze.

Meanwhile back to what I learned: The most important thing to manage is your own expectations. GenAI is awful at long-form writing and even worse at writing books. Ask the publishers and self-publishing services how many truly awful GenAI-generated books were thrust upon them by people who thought they could make a fortune at the push of a button. A flood of trash came over the transom and went right back out to the trash bin. You would have better luck getting the proverbial army of monkeys to bang at keyboards until somehow one of them produces the great American novel.

REMEMBER

The key to writing books with GenAI is to take the lead. Don't let GenAI models lead you. They are not omnipotent. And they lie just as easily as any other source you might interview. Remember that. Don't trust and always verify.

Decide what your book or story is about and use GenAI to help you research, organize, and write it one small chunk at a time. Yes, you're going to have to make GenAI spit out the proverbial elephant one bite at a time and then stitch it all together yourself. But first you're going to have to describe and refine and prompt and re-prompt and prompt chain every one of those chunks so that you don't stitch together some other animal parts that are distinctly not of the elephant species.

Pay attention to output stitching, AI aggregation, and AI chaining (see Chapter 9) as you'll likely need to use all of them when creating any long-form content, most especially in writing a book, regardless of the topic, style, or format. You'll also need to make yourself adept at prompt chaining, a technique in which a sequence of interconnected prompts is used to guide a GenAI model through a multi-step reasoning process or to build upon previous outputs for more complex tasks. In other words, prompt chaining in this context is prompting one chunk at a time so you don't confuse or distract the GenAI by giving it too much information or too many tasks at a time.

How and when you use each of these techniques is up to you. This works in much of the same way as your deciding which words to use and in what order to write them to convey your meaning or story to your readers. Sounds like an overwhelming task, and sometimes it is, which is why writer's block is a real thing. But other times you find yourself in the zone and words flow as easily as a river. Using GenAI to help you write a book will eventually flow like that for you, too. With time and practice, you will assimilate it into your personal writing process.

Meanwhile, you may also find some of the following helpful, depending on your personal writing style and process and the genre of your book:

>> **Outline and structure:** Tools like Plottr (plottr.com) or Scrivener can help with outlining, plotting, and structuring your book. They can also be used in conjunction with GenAI suggestions from tools like Sudowrite (www.sudowrite.com) or ShortlyAI (www.shortlyai.com) to write or plot your narrative.

>> **Character development:** Reedsy's Character Builder is a tool you might want to consider for creating detailed character names and profiles. For GenAI-generated backstories and traits, you could use tools like CharacTour (www.charactour.com/hub) or AI Dungeon (aidungeon.com) for inspiration. Many more general-purpose and multimodal GenAI models can help you develop characters on their own.

>> **Drafting assistance:** OpenAI's GPT-3, accessible through platforms like Jasper (formerly Jarvis) or Rytr, can help with generating text for different sections of your book. ChatGPT 4, ChatGPT 4o, Claude, Scribble Studio, and others are helpful too. (Repeat after me: chunk writing!) These can be especially helpful for drafting dialogue or descriptive passages.

>> **Research:** For summarizing information and conducting research, you might use GenAI tools like Socratic by Google, which can process and analyze large amounts of data quickly. You might also want to use Perplexity.AI as your search engine as it typically renders great results and cites its sources too which makes factchecking its responses much easier. You can also prompt it to deliver even more sources. Also, look at the academic writing section in this chapter for a list of more research tools.

- >> **Language and style:** Grammarly and ProWritingAid offer GenAI-powered suggestions for language and style improvements, helping to ensure consistency and polish in your writing. But for the most part, you'll find most GenAI text and multimodal generators perfectly capable of doing these same tasks without the need for additional tools.

- >> **Editing and proofreading:** Hemingway Editor can help tighten up prose, while Grammarly can catch more nuanced grammatical issues and offer stylistic suggestions. But again, you may find more generalized GenAI tools to be sufficient in these tasks without need of specialized tools.

- >> **Feedback and revision:** Although not a replacement for human feedback, platforms like Authors.ai (authors.ai) provide GenAI manuscript analysis, offering insights into how your book might resonate with readers based on existing successful novels.

- >> **Ethical considerations:** No specific GenAI tool is designed to manage ethical considerations, as this is more about how you approach the writing process. However, tools like Grammarly and Turnitin can help ensure originality and proper citation in academic and non-fiction writing to help maintain ethical standards.

REMEMBER

The quality of your book will ultimately depend on your skill as a writer and your ability to effectively incorporate GenAI-generated content into a cohesive and engaging narrative. In short, great book writing is a credit to the writer not the tools.

Chapter **8**

Customizing Content for Niche Topics

The demand for content tailored for specific disciplines, industries, niche communities, and subcultures is at an all-time high. Yet producing such content is extremely demanding as it requires skilled writers and communicators who know their audience's needs. Producing specialized content quickly adds another level of challenges considering the amount of esoteric knowledge, source aggregation, trend awareness, factchecking, and formatting required.

GenAI tools help clear those hurdles and speed the production of this type of content. creating such specialized content on a large scale. By training, retraining, or fine-tuning GenAI models with data specific to the industry or topic, you can produce a variety of customized media, from articles to podcasts, that accurately reflect the unique terminology and interests of any given niche.

The emergence of Small Language Models (SLMs), mini GPTs, and specialized GenAI models provides you with more and better options to generate content across a myriad of specialized fields. These compact yet powerful tools are tailor-made for diving into the depths of niche subjects, such as medicine and finance, where precision, accuracy, and up-to-date knowledge are paramount. The risks to human lives are also often higher, as are the regulatory requirements, necessitating firmer control and checks and balances over model outputs.

In this chapter, you discover your current and upcoming options in generating niche or specialized content — and the many pitfalls to avoid.

Tailoring GenAI to Produce Content for Specialized Fields

Training or fine-tuning models tailored to perform in specific tasks or industries requires a sophisticated approach that blends the power of machine learning with the deep knowledge base inherent to these professions. These types of GenAI tools must be meticulously trained on vast datasets of professional literature, case studies, and regulatory texts to ensure the content they produce meets the high standards of precision and reliability expected in these fields. This training enables GenAI to understand complex terminologies; stay updated with the latest research, advancements, and guidelines; and generate content that's both informative and compliant with professional norms. All told, that's of tremendous help to weary writers tasked with producing such complex and demanding content.

The following sections each explore different aspects of methods and models to help you develop specialized content in efficient ways and with improved outcomes as compared to using generalized models like ChatGPT in all the usual ways.

GENAI CAUTIONARY TALES

GenAI can be extremely helpful in distributing current and crucial information to specialized groups, including attorneys. However, keep the following cautionary tales in mind whenever you're using GenAI to create content for highly specialized disciplines where people's lives can be affected:

- Jae Lee, a lawyer from JSL Law Offices, P.C., in New York, mistakenly cited a fictitious case in a medical malpractice lawsuit, a citation that was produced by OpenAI's ChatGPT and not verified by Lee before submission. The 2nd U.S. Circuit Court of Appeals caught the error, referred Lee to its grievance panel for investigation, and criticized the attorney for not meeting the basic standards of legal practice. This incident is part of an emerging pattern in which lawyers are incorporating incorrect information from GenAI tools into legal documents.

- New York lawyers Peter LoDuca and Steven Schwartz were fined for using GenAI to draft a legal brief with fake references, and a Colorado lawyer faced suspension for using GenAI-generated false citations. These cases underscore the importance of attorneys thoroughly checking GenAI-generated content, as defenses based on ignorance are becoming less acceptable with the growing awareness of GenAI's fallibility.

Options in GenAI models aimed at specialized writing

Language models come in various forms, each tailored to meet different needs and types of outputs, whether it's for general use or specialized tasks. For the purpose of generating specialized or esoteric content, the best options are usually SLMs, mini GPTs, and specialized GenAI models with the best choice for your work being dependent on the balance between efficiency, flexibility, and domain expertise needed.

Understanding the distinctions between these types of models is important because they're each significantly different, and so are the results you'll get from them. The following sections cover what you need to know about each of these options, so that you can determine which ones might be best suited for your particular task, goal, or content.

Small Language Models (SLMs)

SLMs are scaled-down versions of LLMs (Large Language Models). SLMs are designed to be more efficient in terms of computational resources so they can be run on less powerful hardware. Despite their smaller size, they retain a significant portion of the linguistic capabilities of their larger counterparts.

These models can perform a variety of natural language-processing tasks, such as text classification, sentiment analysis, and question-answering, but they may not be as accurate or as capable in generating coherent long-form content as larger models. (Although I would argue that most of the larger models aren't much better at generating long-form content. I produce most long-form content, as I did this book, chunk by chunk rather than as one long-form piece regardless of what size model I'm using because of this fairly universal shortcoming.)

Mini GPTs

Mini GPTs are a specific subset of SLMs that are based on the Generative Pre-trained Transformer (GPT) architecture developed by OpenAI. They're essentially smaller versions of GPT models and are fine-tuned to perform specific tasks or to operate within certain constraints of memory and processing power. Mini GPTs maintain the generative and conversational abilities of their larger versions but are optimized for speed and efficiency, making them suitable for applications where real-time performance is crucial.

Interestingly, OpenAI refers to these mini GPTs simply as "GPTs" and presents them to users in its GPT Store found on the ChatGPT user interface. I find this to be incredibly confusing, especially when I'm trying to teach people about GenAI. To be clear as mud, or rather as clear as OpenAI puts it: GPT is the name of the mega big Generative Pre-trained Transformer models it makes and also the name it gave to much smaller GPT models that it offers in a GPT Store that strangely showcases none of the company's big GPT models. I know, right?! Sheesh.

TIP

To make the distinction a little clearer between the big and small GPT models, I usually refer to the smalls as mini GPTs. Just remember that "mini GPT" isn't a universally accepted term, although OpenAI refers to the smaller version of GPT-4o as GPT-4o mini. I usually don't refer to the smaller GPTs only as "specialized GPTs" because that's not quite right either, as you'll see in a moment. Ok then, moving on.

Specialized GenAI models

Specialized GenAI models can be large or small and are designed with a focus on specific domains or tasks. They're often trained on specialized datasets to ensure they have a deep understanding of the subject matter and can generate content that's accurate and relevant to the field. These models can include language models that have been fine-tuned for particular industries, such as legal or medical, where they can provide expert-level insights and analysis. The specialization often results in improved performance for the tasks they're designed for, but it may come at the cost of reduced flexibility in other domains.

REMEMBER

In short, while SLMs and mini GPTs offer a balance between flexibility and efficiency, specialized GenAI models provide deep expertise and accuracy in particular domains. The choice between them depends on the specific requirements of the task at hand, whether it's general-purpose language processing or specialized content generation.

Where to find small and specialized GenAI models

Honestly, you can use search engines like Google and Perplexity to find specialized models online. You can also find plenty of GPTs on OpenAI's GPT Store in the ChatGPT UI.

You can also find SLMs and specialized models to use in producing content on complex, specialty topics through various platforms and services. I recommend you look at all the great options on Poe (Poe.com). You.com has some options (but fewer than Poe) in both assistants and models, which you'll find under the "More" button on the UI. You might also want to build your own custom application on one of many GenAI models at MindStudio.ai. That's a no-code platform, meaning you don't have to know programming code or anything to make your own brand-new GenAI application!

There are more options than the few I listed here, so feel free to look and ask around. More options will pop up online as time progresses too, so make checking on GenAI options a regular task so you don't miss out on anything!

Many of the models you find will offer a free trial period to let you try it out and see if it fits your needs. There are many vendors cranking out a variety of smaller or specialized models, and there will be many more. You'll need to explore the options to see which ones you prefer, but generally speaking, these types of models tend to perform better — although still not perfectly.

TIP

Be ready to add or change models as often as needed to get the maximum benefit from using GenAI. Fortunately, while there are some differences in prompting, best practices between models, and even between versions of the same model, you'll generally find your prompting skills are easily transferrable to any of them.

Case studies: GenAI use in high-stakes domains

To help get your creative juices flowing, here are a few case studies on using AI responsibly to write content in high-stakes domains:

Case Study 1: GenAI in a Medical Research Publication: A leading pharmaceutical company implemented a GenAI writing tool to assist its research scientists in drafting clinical trial reports. The GenAI model was trained on a database of past trial reports, medical journals, and regulatory guidelines. It successfully generated accurate and coherent drafts that included statistical data analysis, adherence to ethical reporting standards, and clear articulation of trial outcomes. This reduced the time researchers spent on writing by an estimated 40 percent, allowing them to focus more on actual research and development. However, final reports were always reviewed by the lead scientists to ensure nuanced understanding and accuracy before submission to medical journals or regulatory bodies.

Case Study 2: GenAI-Generated Legal Contracts: A multinational corporation employed a GenAI system to create the first drafts of its international supply agreements. The model was trained on various international trade laws, corporate policies, and standard contract clauses. It was capable of producing draft contracts in multiple languages, tailored to the legal nuances of different jurisdictions. While the GenAI drastically cut down the drafting time and reduced the workload on the legal team, lawyers still conducted thorough reviews to fine-tune the details and ensure the contracts were fully compliant with local laws and corporate standards.

Case Study 3: GenAI for Financial Reporting: An investment firm integrated GenAI into its financial reporting process. The model was trained on financial regulations, market data, financial statements, economic data, and previous reports from which it generated initial drafts of quarterly financial statements and risk assessment documents. These generated reports included compliance checks with financial disclosure requirements. Analysts would then verify the GenAI's work, adding human insights and making adjustments to its outputs where necessary. They also often had to correct its math. This dual approach allowed the firm to publish reports faster than using the firm's traditional processes.

Case Study 4: GenAI in Aerospace Technical Documentation: An aerospace company used GenAI to produce technical documentation for its aircraft maintenance procedures. The GenAI model was trained with aircraft specifications, engineering drawings, and safety protocols. It was able to generate comprehensive maintenance manuals that were technically accurate and included the latest engineering modifications. However, each manual underwent a rigorous review process by a team of engineers and technical writers to ensure that the procedures were correct and clearly explained, considering the high safety stakes incurred in this industry.

Case Study 5: GenAI Assistance in Emergency Response Planning: A government agency responsible for emergency response planning implemented a specialized GenAI model to draft response plans for various disaster scenarios. The model was trained on historical data from past disasters, response protocols, and geographic information systems (GIS) data. It could quickly produce detailed response strategies, resource allocation plans, and public communication drafts. Emergency management professionals can refine these plans, ensuring they're practical and tailored to the specific needs of the communities at risk in any future emergency.

These case studies illustrate the potential of GenAI in high-stakes domains to increase efficiency and serve as a powerful aid in content creation. However, they also underscore the indispensable need for human expertise to validate and enhance GenAI-generated content, ensuring the highest standards of accuracy, safety, and appropriateness are upheld.

Balancing Expertise and Creativity in GenAI-Based Writing

While expertise ensures that the content is authoritative and reliable, creativity infuses it with the ability to captivate and engage. This delicate balance is particularly crucial in fields where the accuracy of information is paramount, yet the presentation must also resonate with the audience.

This section explores the strategies and considerations involved in striking an optimal balance between expertise and creativity in GenAI-based writing, ensuring that the output is not only factually sound but also uniquely compelling.

Merging subject matter expertise with AI for niche content

Merging subject matter expertise with GenAI in content generation can significantly enhance the quality and relevance of the output.

Here are tailored tips and examples for content creators looking to integrate GenAI innovation with their own or their clients' domain knowledge:

» **Curate GenAI-enhanced content:**

   Tip: Use your expert insights to guide GenAI in selecting and prioritizing content topics that are accurate and engaging for the target audience.

   Example: A tech blogger can use GenAI to research and draft articles on emerging technologies and then refine the content themselves to ensure it aligns with the latest industry standards and insights.

» **GenAI-assisted writing and editing:**

   Tip: Employ GenAI tools for initial content drafts and use your expert knowledge for editing and adding depth, ensuring the final piece delivers original insights or analysis and resonates with readers.

Example: An editor for a medical journal can use GenAI to generate article summaries and then meticulously review and edit them to meet stringent publication criteria.

» **Personalized content experiences:**

Tip: Combine GenAI's data discovery capabilities with your expert understanding of marketing and audience personas to create personalized content recommendations.

Example: A streaming service can use GenAI to suggest shows and movies based on viewing habits, curated further by content experts for a customized user experience.

» **Enhancing content with expert feedback:**

Tip: Establish a system in which experts review GenAI-generated content and provide feedback, which can be used to fine-tune the GenAI's performance.

Example: A culinary website can have chefs review GenAI-suggested recipes and tweak them to ensure authenticity and taste.

» **Tailored GenAI content tools:**

Tip: Collaborate with AI developers to create custom content generation tools that address the specific needs of your content domain.

Example: A travel agency might develop a GenAI tool that generates travel itineraries based on expert travel advice and real-time data.

» **Content ethics and compliance:**

Tip: Involve experts in setting ethical standards for GenAI-generated content, ensuring it adheres to industry norms and regulations.

Example: News organizations can work with ethicists to ensure generated news articles are unbiased and factually correct.

» **GenAI-driven training for content writing:**

Tip: Leverage GenAI to train content creators, enhancing their skills with interactive, GenAI-driven learning modules.

Example: An online learning platform can use GenAI to create interactive writing exercises for aspiring novelists.

» **Simplifying complex information:**

Tip: Use GenAI's language capabilities to distill complex expert knowledge into content that's accessible to a broader audience.

Example: A financial advisor can use GenAI to generate blog posts that break down complex investment strategies into easily understandable advice.

>> **Predictive content trends:**

>>> **Tip:** Integrate GenAI tools to forecast emerging content trends, allowing experts to create proactive content strategies.

>>> **Example:** Marketing agencies can use GenAI to predict upcoming consumer interests and produce content that taps into these trends early.

>> **Collaborative content creation:**

>>> **Tip:** Implement GenAI tools that help content experts collaborate more effectively, pooling their collective knowledge.

>>> **Example:** A team of researchers can use a GenAI tool to coauthor a comprehensive report on climate change, each contributing their specialized knowledge.

By strategically combining GenAI with content expertise, you can produce high-quality, relevant, and engaging content at scale, ensuring that the human expertise shines through the efficiency of GenAI-driven processes. This strategy also ensures no one is embarrassed at the outcome and viewers aren't turned off by shallow or repetitive GenAI-written content.

Crafting expert content with a creative edge

Crafting expert content with a creative edge that intrigues viewers, listeners, and readers — without veering into the realm of the ridiculous or too far-fetched — requires a delicate balance. Here are several ways you can achieve this:

>> **Ground content in facts:** Start with a solid foundation of verifiable information. This ensures that your content is rooted in reality, even when you're exploring creative angles. For example, if you're writing about innovative technology, base your content on the actual capabilities of the technology before adding a creative spin on its uses or future potential.

>> **Know your audience:** Understanding who your viewers and readers are and what they find credible is crucial. Tailor your content to match their interests and knowledge level. If your audience is scientifically literate, for example, you can use more technical language and concepts to earn their trust.

>> **Use analogies and metaphors:** Analogies and metaphors can explain complex ideas in a relatable way, sparking interest without sacrificing accuracy. When discussing a complex topic like quantum computing, you might compare the qubit to a spinning coin to illustrate superposition, making the concept more accessible.

>> **Incorporate storytelling:** Weave facts into narratives to make the content more compelling. Storytelling can turn a dry subject into an engaging journey. A historical article, for instance, can come alive by focusing on the dramatic personal story of a key figure involved.

>> **Engage with visuals:** Incorporate images, infographics, or videos that complement the text and add a layer of intrigue. Visuals can make even the most complex or dry subject matter more appealing and can often communicate ideas more effectively than words alone.

>> **Invite curiosity with headlines and hooks:** Craft headlines, titles, and opening hooks that pique interest but don't overpromise. They should be intriguing enough to draw readers in but not so sensational that they mislead. A headline like "The Unseen World: How Microscopic Organisms Shape Our Reality" invites curiosity without overstepping.

>> **Balance depth with brevity:** Provide enough detail to showcase your expertise, but keep the content concise to maintain engagement. Avoid overwhelming the reader with too much jargon or unnecessary information. Break down complex topics into bite-sized, digestible pieces.

>> **Use humor wisely:** Humor can make content more enjoyable, but it must be used carefully, especially in serious fields. Ensure that any humor is respectful, relevant, and doesn't undermine the credibility of your content.

>> **Challenge perspectives thoughtfully:** Introduce new ideas or controversial perspectives in a way that encourages reflection, not rejection. Present these ideas as thought experiments or potential scenarios that are grounded in possibility.

>> **Encourage interaction:** End with questions or prompts that encourage viewers, listeners, and readers to engage with the content. This can be a powerful way to keep them thinking about the topic long after they've finished reading, listening, or watching your content.

Warnings: Hazards Ahead

One of the most common hazards in using GenAI to create content is the potential for perpetuating and amplifying biases. GenAI models learn from vast datasets that often contain historical data, which can reflect past prejudices and stereotypes. If not carefully managed, GenAI can inadvertently reproduce these biases in its content, leading to outputs that are discriminatory or offensive. This can damage your personal reputation as well as your institution or brand's reputation and undermine the credibility of the content. Moreover, biased GenAI-generated content can have serious ethical implications, particularly when it affects decisions related to healthcare, employment, law enforcement, and lending practices. Ensuring that GenAI models are trained on diverse and inclusive datasets, regularly audited for bias, and corrected when necessary is crucial to mitigate this risk.

Another significant hazard is the potential for GenAI to generate factually incorrect or misleading information. GenAI models can sometimes produce content based on inaccurate sources or outdated facts. This poses a challenge for sectors in which precision is critical, such as healthcare, finance, and science. Inaccurate GenAI-generated content can lead to misinformation, which can have real-world consequences if individuals or organizations act on it. It's essential to continuously update and curate the datasets used for training, retraining, and finetuning GenAI models and to establish rigorous factchecking and review processes involving domain experts. By doing so, content creators can ensure the reliability and accuracy of the GenAI-generated content, maintaining the trust of their audience.

But hang on a moment, you and I have a few more hazards to consider in the following sections.

Anticipating challenges in niche content generation

When you're operating within niche markets or specialize in highly technical subjects, you need to be aware that you face unique challenges that may not be accounted for in GenAI models and applications. One such challenge is the limited availability of high-quality, specialized training data. GenAI models are typically trained on broad datasets, and when tasked with generating content for a niche, they may struggle to produce data points, analysis, or content that meets the depth and specificity required by experts in the field. To anticipate and address this challenge, try focusing on supplementing GenAI's learning with curated datasets that are rich in industry-specific knowledge and terminology. This may involve creating custom datasets or collaborating with industry partners to aggregate or generate enough specialized data for a GenAI model to be trained on. Generally, you'll add this data in RAG, system messages, or prompts. Or you'll need to fine-tune the model, which works well but is a huge pain to do.

Another challenge is ensuring that the generated content resonates with a specialized audience that has high expectations for expertise and authenticity. GenAI-generated content may sometimes lack the depth of understanding that a human expert brings to the table, potentially resulting in content that feels generic or misses the mark in terms of technical accuracy or insight. To mitigate this, you should establish a workflow that includes a thorough review by subject matter experts who can assess the GenAI's output for technical precision, relevance, and engagement. These experts can also provide feedback that can be used to fine-tune the GenAI model, making it more adept at handling the intricacies of generating niche content over time.

Furthermore, in niche content generation, staying ahead of industry trends and developments is critical. Be sure to remain regularly updated on the latest research, innovations, and shifts in industry dialogue. Don't rely on GenAI to update you, either. That kind of circular reasoning and action will get you into trouble.

Maintain an active role in monitoring sector-specific news and incorporating this new information into the GenAI's knowledge base or training data. By proactively managing these aspects, you can ensure that the GenAI-generated content remains relevant and authoritative, thus maintaining the trust and engagement of a sophisticated audience.

Preparing for the unpredictable in GenAI-assisted writing

Preparing for the unpredictable in GenAI-assisted writing involves anticipating the inherent uncertainties that come with the technology. Most of these uncertainties are covered in this chapter already. One of the key steps is to understand that GenAI does not really understand you, so it may not always calculate the nuances of human language or context accurately. To mitigate this, you should establish a robust editorial process in which everything GenAI-generated is reviewed by human editors and fact-checkers. This ensures that any anomalies, such as awkward phrasing, factual inaccuracies, or tone inconsistencies, are corrected before publication.

Another aspect of preparation involves being ready to handle the ethical and reputational implications of GenAI-generated content. GenAI is not infallible. For example, GenAI might inadvertently create content that is insensitive or inappropriate, especially when dealing with topics that require a high degree of cultural sensitivity or awareness of current social issues. Stay vigilant and set up stringent content guidelines to help steer GenAI outputs away from potentially problematic areas. Additionally, maintaining a transparent relationship with the audience about the use of GenAI in content creation can help manage expectations and foster trust.

Consider a couple of examples:

Example 1: Factual Inconsistencies: A GenAI writing assistant tasked with creating a historical article might piece together events in a way that is chronologically incorrect or oversimplified. To prepare for this type of error, writers should cross-reference GenAI-generated timelines with trusted historical sources before publication. This due diligence ensures that the narrative remains accurate.

Example 2: Creative Misfires: In a creative writing project, a GenAI might generate a character or plot development that doesn't align with the established storyline or character arcs. Writers should be ready to step in and tweak these elements, ensuring that the GenAI-generated content supports the intended narrative direction and maintains the story's coherence.

In both examples, the unpredictability of GenAI outputs is managed by combining the efficiency and capabilities of GenAI with the discerning judgment of human expertise. By doing so, users can leverage GenAI-assisted writing to its fullest potential while safeguarding against the unpredictable nature of automated content generation.

IN THIS CHAPTER

» Mixing and matching AIs in your work

» Filling your content well fast

» Crafting short news articles with AI

» Pumping GenAI pizzazz into speechwriting

» Making content for websites

» Designing logos and slogans

» Leveling up on social media content

» Avoiding pitfalls and hazards

Chapter **9**

Creating Short-Form Content

G enAI opens new possibilities for content creators looking to produce high-quality, engaging short-form content in a single piece or a multitude of them at scale. From crafting punchy social media posts and email newsletters to formulating fresh ideas for videos, blog articles, and marketing copy, AI language models can accelerate your creative process and boost your productivity. But that's not to say you can just push a button and you're done!

This chapter explores practical strategies for leveraging GenAI to create short-form content and streamline workflows. You'll be introduced to techniques for rapidly generating first drafts, repurposing and iterating on content across different formats and channels, and fine-tuning outputs to better align with your brand voice and target audience.

With GenAI as a force multiplier, content teams can increase their publishing velocity while maintaining consistency and avoiding tedious busy work. Whether you're an individual creator or part of a larger media operation, mastering these GenAI-powered tactics will futureproof your short-form content engine.

Getting Better Results by Combining Different Types of AI

Before getting into the specifics of using various techniques to generate disparate forms of short content, I want to encourage you not to limit your writing and other creative works to the capabilities of one GenAI model or application. Consider combining different types of AI to access more options and capabilities, as discussed in this section.

AI aggregation

AI aggregation refers to the process of combining the outputs of multiple GenAI models working independently to create a unified final product. Applications of AI aggregation include creative projects that combine text, images, and audio; data analysis that integrates insights from various analytical models; content creation that merges text with data visualizations; and automated systems that incorporate different GenAI functionalities. For example, you can use Claude to write text and Midjourney to generate images to illustrate it. Perhaps you also want to use Synthesia AI to make a short video to include in your blog post or article and to reuse later as a TikTok video. In other words, you are using outputs from various models to create a unified finished work in a single document, canvas, presentation, or digital file.

REMEMBER

The benefits of this approach include enhanced quality of results, a diversity of perspectives, and increased robustness. However, AI aggregation presents challenges such as complexity in integration, lack of consistency across different data types, and the resource intensity of running multiple models.

An example workflow involves selecting specialized GenAI models, generating outputs independently, aggregating these outputs while ensuring alignment with design and messaging, and refining the final product for coherence and quality. AI aggregation thus enables the creation of sophisticated outputs by leveraging the strengths of different GenAI tools.

TIP

GenAI aggregation is a particularly advantageous way to do things because you can double or triple your content by splintering the unified piece apart again to repurpose its various elements elsewhere, too. For example, the video you made to put in a blog post can be repurposed as a Facebook short or an Instagram or Tik-Tok video. Think of it as half the work with double the payoff.

I think of OpenAI's ChatGPT 4o (omni) as prepackaged AI aggregation since it's essentially an all-in-one GenAI tool. Omni is *multimodal*, meaning it accepts any combination of text, audio, image, and transcribed video as inputs and generates any combination of text, audio, and image outputs. However, omni has its strengths and weaknesses too, so don't hesitate to use other GenAI models in your content alongside omni outputs.

You can also aggregate GPTs inside of ChatGPT. ChatGPT offers a GPT Store, which you can find under the "Explore GPTs" button on the left side of the UI (see Figure 9-1). GPTs in this sense are smaller ChatGPTs — specialized in performing specific tasks. You can summon a GPT from the store to get access to additional functionality and typically a better output than you would using only the larger ChatGPT tool. You can add outputs from GPTs to your prompt in ChatGPT too, or you can aggregate the outputs of various GPTs in a single piece of content as you see fit.

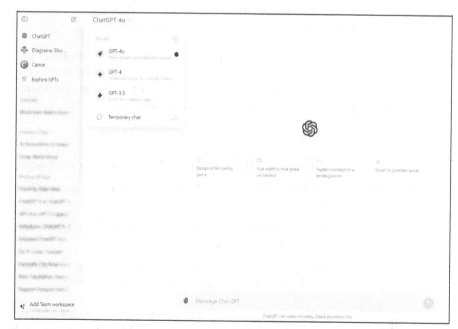

FIGURE 9-1:
The ChatGPT UI showing the pull-down menu for model selection and the "Explore GPTs" button at top of left sidebar, which opens the GPT Store.

Of course, there are other ways to aggregate AI, too, such as using one GenAI tool such as Claude or ChatGPT to generate content and another to manage content elements, such as a GenAI embedded in a content management system (CMS). The possible combinations in AI aggregation are nearly endless (and can include AI types other than GenAI if you want), but figuring out which to use where is, or should be, a central part of your creative process no matter what type of content you are generating.

Output stitching

You can also give two or more GenAI tools the same prompt and compare their outputs, ultimately choosing one over the other, or taking bits from one output and combining it with bits of another GenAI's output to create something more to your intent and liking. The term for this is *output stitching* or *model output stitching*.

For example, I can put the same prompt in both Claude and ChatGPT and keep whatever I want from one or both outputs to create a better piece of content than either model generated on their own.

Output stitching is particularly useful for long-form content generation tasks in which different models may excel at different characteristics like factual knowledge, storytelling, descriptive language, and so on. It can also help mitigate issues like repetitiveness or incoherence that Large Language Models sometimes suffer from.

TIP

Be sure you're using two different models. For example, ChatGPT is based on OpenAI GPT models, whereas Claude runs on a GenAI model created by Anthropic. If you prompt two or more chatbots using the same underlying GenAI model, you haven't completely leveraged this tactic.

The key steps in output stitching are as follows:

1. Run multiple AI models in parallel on the same input prompt or task.

2. Identify the highest quality or most relevant segments from each model's output.

3. Stitch or combine those selected segments into a new, unified output in a logical order and flow.

4. Optionally, do some additional filtering, editing, or refinement on the stitched output to improve coherence and quality.

REMEMBER

The goal is to get the final output that you need by utilizing the strengths of different models and tools and avoiding weaknesses that any single model may have. By stitching the best components together, the final output can be higher quality than what could be produced by any one model alone.

Note that there are also other ways that "output stitching" is used. It can be both a user-driven process and an automated function within various generative GenAI tools, depending on the context and the complexity of the task.

For example, many GenAI tools have built-in algorithms that are designed to automate the stitching process. Panoramic photo apps often automatically stitch together images taken by a smartphone camera to create that panoramic view without user intervention. Similarly, GenAI-based video stitching software can automate the synchronization, aligning, and stitching of multiple video feeds to create 360-degree views such as you find in VR content.

On the backend, machine learning platforms can automatically stitch together the outputs from several models working on distributed computing tasks. An example of this would be in training of large models across multiple machines or GPUs.

Whether the stitching process is manual or automated largely depends on the level of precision required. IT can also be a matter of user convenience. Automated stitching is generally faster and more accessible to non-experts, but it may not always achieve the same level of perfection as a skilled human operator or as creatively constructed as human talent would render. Conversely, user-driven stitching allows for greater customization and creative finesse but can be time-consuming and may require a high level of technical expertise.

All told, feel free to mix and match outputs, both of an automated or manual nature until you create something that fits your creative vision or business goal.

AI chaining

AI chaining in this context refers to the process of using the output of one GenAI tool as part or all of a prompt in another GenAI tool. For example, you might use Perplexity to look up information on the internet and use that information in a prompt for Claude to do additional work with it.

In this scenario, you would do that by copying the output from the Perplexity search engine and use it as part of the prompt in Claude. Next, add instructions to your prompt so Claude knows what to do with it, such as, "Work this information into the earlier response." (By the way, that command is also an example of combining AI chaining with prompt chaining.)

But you can instruct Claude to do anything with Perplexity's output, such as: "Write an argument against this," "Rewrite in AP style," Shorten," "Summarize," "Check for accuracy or bias," "Expand this to include technical details," "Rewrite to add quotes and statistics from our ebook titled xyz," and so on.

Like output stitching, AI chaining can also be automated. When it's automated, it can be used for many different complex tasks.

Without going into too much detail, for such is beyond the scope of this book, from a technical or automated perspective, AI chaining refers to the process of linking together multiple AI systems, models, or algorithms in a sequence to perform a complex task that no single AI component could achieve on its own. Each link in the chain handles a specific subtask, and the output of one link serves as the input for the next.

Examples of automated AI chaining include:

» **Automated customer support:** A customer's spoken request is first transcribed by a speech-to-text AI, then parsed for meaning by a natural language processing AI, and finally, an AI-powered chatbot generates an appropriate response.

» **Medical diagnostics:** An initial AI might analyze medical images for anomalies, a second AI could cross-reference patient data and medical literature, and a third AI might assist in diagnosing and suggesting treatment options based on the combined information.

» **Autonomous vehicle navigation:** In an autonomous vehicle, multiple AI systems work in a chained sequence to enable the car to drive without human intervention. AI chaining allows for a sophisticated division of labor where each AI component specializes in a particular aspect of the driving task. However, any failure in the chain could lead to incorrect decisions and potentially dangerous situations.

A FEW ADDITIONAL METHODS FOR COMBINING AI MODELS AND OUTPUTS

In the interest of being thorough — and perhaps stimulate your creative thinking further so that you may come up with more ways to leverage multiple GenAI tools on your own — I'll briefly touch on a few additional methods. However, these are more technical in nature and not so user-friendly:

- **AI stacking:** Refers to training multiple base AI models on the same dataset after which the predictions of all of them are used to train a meta-AI model for improved accuracy in *its* final outputs

- **AI layering:** Refers to organizing multiple AI models or algorithms in layers, with each layer performing a specific function or set of functions

- **AI orchestration:** Refers to the strategic coordination and management of multiple AI services or models and workflows to optimize performance and achieve specific goals within a system or process.

Enhancing Blogging

GenAI is uniquely equipped to support bloggers in every phase of the content-creation process. From the initial stages of planning and brainstorming to the final touches of writing and editing, GenAI can help streamline your workflow and enhance the quality of your blog posts.

GenAI such as ChatGPT and Claude can spot trending topics and make blog post suggestions accordingly. They can also map out a series of related posts to fill your content well in a hurry and write compelling headlines. Beyond writing and editing posts, you can use GenAI to assist with related tasks such as keyword research for SEO, generating summaries for social media sharing, and even analyzing performance data to help you develop future content strategies.

Leveraging GenAI to elevate blog content and engagement

Blogs are dead. Long live blogs! In any case, blogs no longer exist in a vacuum. Instead, the more successful blogs tend to be part of a web of communications that builds upon your blog content to add social media posts, short videos and long videos, and press releases and ad campaigns — all built around the same or related content. This approach is designed to lift the blogger to prominence and build revenue streams.

Here's a short list of the many ways that GenAI can help you elevate your blog content and improve reader engagement:

» Improving content quality and originality by identifying a unique angle and doing research to provide in-depth information that adds value to the reader

» Optimizing SEO by conducting keyword research and adding on-page SEO such as meta descriptions, alt tags for images, and proper header tags to help improve visibility in search engine results

» Incorporating multimedia by incorporating relevant images, infographics, interactive content, and videos to break up text and make the content more engaging

» Planning and writing other forms of communications such as email campaigns and automated direct messaging based on content in your blog posts

>> Building a community and improving your online reputation by assisting in writing responses to reader comments and engaging with them on the blog and in social media

>> Promoting content by writing guest posts and emails soliciting guest posts as well as co-creating content with other bloggers and social media influencers

By focusing on these areas, a blogger can not only improve the quality and visibility of their blog content but also create a more engaging and interactive experience for their readers.

Streamlining the blogging workflow with GenAI

Beyond the tasks outlined in the previous section, GenAI can help you streamline your workflow in producing blog posts in many other ways, including the following:

>> Editing and proofreading (in almost any language that humans utter)

>> Content formatting (Specifically, it can handle HTML or markdown for blog platforms, saving time on manual coding.)

>> Image and media sourcing (For example, if so prompted GenAI can find royalty-free images and other media to enhance posts and provide guidance on how to optimize images with alt text for SEO and accessibility.)

>> Planning a social media strategy (For example, draft social media posts to promote blog content across various platforms and suggest the best times to post on social media based on engagement analytics.)

>> Automating workflow (For example, GenAI can recommend tools and software to automate parts of the content-creation process, such as scheduling posts or social media updates.)

>> Using analytics and providing insights (For example, GenAI can explain how to interpret website and social media analytics to help you make data-driven decisions to improve engagement and reach.)

>> Designing email and newsletter campaigns (For example, GenAI can create email templates or drafts for newsletters that promote your latest blog content.)

By making smart use of these capabilities, you can save time, increase productivity, and focus on creating compelling content that resonates with your audience.

Writing Short News Articles with AI

In the fast-paced news industry, GenAI can be a big help in speeding up your work. But GenAI doesn't just offer efficiency in rapid news production; it can also help you meet the rigorous standards of accuracy, objectivity, and succinctness that are the hallmarks of quality journalism. Provided, of course, that journalists and editors consistently hold it to that. Fake or wrong news reports from a GenAI's hallucination can ruin the reputation of even the oldest and most trusted media outlets.

However, when GenAI tools are used appropriately, they can speed news reporting beyond what journalists can produce alone. From synthesizing financial reports and sports results to monitoring breaking news and summarizing complex data, GenAI excels at delivering real-time updates and structured information. It can get lost in the weeds when attempting to write more complex and more nuanced news, however. It can also produce robotic or plebian copy, so don't run with outputs "as is," instead add factchecks and editing polish as you would any article that you or another journalist wrote.

In this section, you see how writers and reporters can harness GenAI to help craft compelling news pieces while avoiding pitfalls and backlash that is common to early experiments with using GenAI in news production.

REMEMBER

While GenAI can significantly enhance the speed and efficiency of news writing, human journalists still play a crucial role in ensuring accuracy, fairness, ethics, and editorial judgment. Also, GenAI tools only work from digitized data. GenAI cannot replace journalists who use information they glean from non-digitized sources too, such as from face-to-face interviews, information that they find or observe on the scene, or information they dug up that was intentionally hidden from public view. GenAI can't do any of that.

GenAI-assisted journalism: Quick news writing

By integrating GenAI assistance into your workflow, you can significantly expedite the writing process. GenAI can be used in numerous ways to speed up the processes involved in news writing. Here are but a few:

>> **Accurate and quotable note taking.** GenAI can be used to take notes from the scene or other sources. One way is for journalists to record interviews and later prompt GenAI to analyze, summarize, or list highlights from what was said. Another way is to add video or call transcripts, on-the-scene camera

video descriptions, police reports, and other photos and documents from the scene to custom instructions, prompts, or even RAG for a GenAI tool to analyze and summarize so the journalist can consume the information more quickly.

>> **Fast headline and teaser writing.** This used to be a specialty in the newsroom, but now journalists and editors struggle with writing headlines and teasers themselves. GenAI can handle these tasks in a blink — and generate them to fit the tone of the subject matter and the news outlet, too. Prompt it to provide you with five or so headline suggestions and then either select one, or prompt it to revise one or more per your specifications.

>> **Background and context. Gen**AI models can rapidly research and compile background information, historical details, expert commentary, and relevant data from reliable sources, for example found on the internet and/or from your own news org's library of data.

>> **Automated data journalism.** GenAI can pull in data from trusted sources, such as government databases, financial reports, and press releases, saving journalists time on initial research. GenAI tools can also generate polls, graphs, illustrations, and interactive infographics (or static ones, if preferred). Remember you can also use output stitching, AI chaining, AI aggregation, and GenAI integrated with other types of software to create data journalism elements in almost any form you want them.

>> **Source monitoring.** GenAI tools can monitor news wires, social media, and other digital platforms for breaking news, alerting journalists to emerging stories as they happen or to witnesses and authorities they may need to interview.

>> **Factchecking.** GenAI can cross-reference facts in your draft with credible sources to ensure the accuracy of the information being reported. Word to the wise: factcheck it again using traditional journalism methods.

>> **Summarization of complex reports.** GenAI can distill lengthy reports, such as scientific studies or financial documents, into concise summaries and convert them to laymen's terms so that they can be used as a basis for news articles. Or, so you can quickly digest the information yourself and finish your report faster.

>> **Sentiment analysis.** GenAI can help analyze social media and other platforms to gauge public sentiment on current issues, which can provide valuable insights for journalists covering those topics. You can also use it to gauge the sentiment of a subject you interviewed.

>> **Language processing.** GenAI can help ensure that the language used in your article is clear, precise, and appropriate for the intended audience. You can also use it to interpret another language for you — for example, in analyzing

social media posts in foreign languages or interviewing someone whose language you don't understand.

>> **Voice-to-text transcription.** GenAI can transcribe interviews and press conferences in near real-time or after the fact, allowing journalists to quickly access money quotes and high value data points for their reports. Or, journalists and interns can let the GenAI draft the report and edit it from there.

Balancing speed and integrity in GenAI-generated news

In the digital age, where the 24-hour news cycle dominates and audiences demand immediate information, the speed at which news is delivered has become a critical factor for media outlets. GenAI-generated news offers an advantage in this regard, providing the ability to produce content rapidly in response to developing stories. However, this expediency must not come at the expense of journalistic integrity. The deployment of GenAI in newsrooms necessitates a careful balance, ensuring that while articles are produced swiftly, they are also subjected to rigorous standards of verification, impartiality, and ethical reporting.

Further, journalists and editors play a pivotal role in overseeing GenAI outputs, adding nuanced understanding and context that machines cannot fully replicate.

And from my own journalist notebooks I add that we've come such a long way from the days when I gave presentations and talks introducing data journalism alongside my friend and colleague, Wayne Rash, at the Excellence in Journalism (EIJ) Conferences in 2016 and 2017. Back then, the concept of big data tools, advanced analytics, and data journalism were brand new. Now it's old hat in the modern newsroom, and AI is in our pockets on our phones. Life is interesting like that. My point is that change is the name of the game in all of life, and even journalists have to scramble to keep up! Fortunately, GenAI can help us do that. Unfortunately, it can also destroy our careers and professional reputations if we aren't super careful with this technology. Proceed with caution, but do proceed!

Adding GenAI Pizzazz to Speechwriting

GenAI can be a big help in speechwriting whether you are writing your own speech or someone else's. Either way, capturing the audience's attention while conveying a powerful message is paramount. GenAI offers a fresh avenue for you and other speechwriters to infuse the work with an extra layer of punch or pizzazz.

You can tap into a vast repository of linguistic styles and rhetorical devices by using GenAI, that can help you engage and resonate with your target audience. The key lies in harnessing GenAI to enhance the speech's appeal without tipping over into the realm of clichés or overly sentimental language that could undermine the speech's tone, gravitas, or authenticity.

GenAI tools can analyze past speeches, audience demographics, and successful rhetorical patterns to suggest dynamic phrases, compelling anecdotes, humorous touches, and powerful metaphors that align with your or the speaker's voice and message. This intelligent augmentation allows speechwriters to craft orations that captivate listeners with perhaps a touch of elegance and wit, if that is the aim, all while maintaining the substance that's at the heart of every impactful oratory. The result is a speech that stands out for its creativity and memorability yet remains grounded in the sincerity, substance and tone that fosters a genuine connection with the audience. And that's exactly what you were aiming for, yes?

Crafting memorable speeches with GenAI support

GenAI can be an invaluable asset in crafting memorable speeches by providing assistance in several key areas, including the following:

>> **Content enhancement**: GenAI can suggest powerful vocabulary, synonyms, and phrases that can make your speech more impactful. It can also help identify and integrate rhetorical devices like metaphors, analogies, and triads that add depth and resonance to the message.

>> **Personalization:** GenAI can analyze data on the intended audience to tailor the speech's tone, complexity, and content, ensuring that it resonates with listeners and feels personalized to their interests and values. So yes, you can use GenAI to effectively rewrite the same speech over and over again to fit different audiences.

>> **Structure and flow:** GenAI can assist in organizing the speech into a coherent structure, with a clear introduction, body, and conclusion, ensuring that the speech has a logical flow and that key points are emphasized effectively.

>> **Engagement techniques:** GenAI can provide guidance on where to add pauses for effect, when to incorporate storytelling for emotional connection, and how to use humor appropriately to engage the audience.

>> **Practice and delivery:** Some GenAI tools are integrated with speech practice platforms that can analyze your delivery, such as pacing, volume, and clarity, providing feedback to improve your public speaking skills.

But, of course, your next question is, "Yes, but how?" There are many ways to use GenAI to assist you in speechwriting with many variations depending on the GenAI model or AI stacking that you use. But, in general, to effectively use GenAI in crafting your speeches, consider using these three tips:

>> **Define your objectives and audience:** Before you begin, provide the GenAI with clear information about the purpose of your speech and the demographics of your audience. The more specific you are, the better the GenAI can tailor its suggestions to meet your needs.

>> **Provide a framework or outline:** Start with a basic structure or outline of your speech. This gives the GenAI a foundation to build upon and ensures that the content generated aligns with your intended message and flow. However, don't over worry the outline because you can prompt GenAI tools to reorganize it to better fit your objectives if you need to do that. The point of the exercise is to have a starting place for the GenAI to start helping you with your speechwriting.

>> **Iterate and refine:** Use the GenAI-generated content as a draft only. Review and refine the suggestions to match your personal style and voice. Iteration is key; work with the GenAI iteratively to hone the speech to perfection, ensuring authenticity and impact.

REMEMBER

While GenAI can provide a strong starting point and some important guidance, the final speech should be uniquely your own.

I also can't help but wonder how long it will take before someone gets GenAI to give their speech too while they lip sync on stage. It's just a matter of time, I think!

Personalizing public speaking through GenAI

Now let's say you have a speech in hand, but you want to personalize it for different audiences. If you're like me, you do this fairly often because many different audiences want to hear you speak on the same subjects but in ways that are meaningful to them. You can use GenAI to adapt your most popular speeches for a variety of different audiences.

TIP

Here are five tips on getting GenAI to complete that task for you:

>> **Input detailed audience insights:** Provide the GenAI with as much information as possible about the audience's demographics, interests, cultural background, and the context of the event. This helps the GenAI to tailor the speech content to the audience's expectations and levels of understanding.

>> **Incorporate personal anecdotes:** Feed the GenAI with personal stories or experiences that you're comfortable sharing by adding such to your prompts. GenAI can help weave these anecdotes into the speech to make it more relatable and engaging while maintaining relevance to the topic.

>> **Set the desired tone and style:** Clearly communicate the tone you want to set for your speech — be it inspirational, informative, casual, or formal — in your prompts. Also, indicate any stylistic preferences, such as the use of humor or rhetorical questions, to help the GenAI align with your personal speaking style. You can also include past speeches you've given in the prompt so that GenAI can more closely match your speaking style.

>> **Highlight key messages and values:** Identify the core messages and values that are important to you and that you want to resonate throughout the speech. This ensures that the GenAI emphasizes these elements, creating a consistent narrative throughout.

>> **Review and customize suggestions**: Use the GenAI-generated draft as a foundation and manually review it to add a personal touch. Customize the language to ensure it sounds natural when you speak, doesn't cause you to stumble or mispronounce words, and aligns with your personal brand or identity.

REMEMBER By following these tips, you can use GenAI to help you create a speech that feels personal, resonates with your audience, and effectively communicates your key messages in your own unique voice. Further, it's a speech that fits your natural style so it will be easier for you to deliver it from the stage or on camera, too!

Designing and Writing Content for Websites

Creating compelling content for websites is both an art and a science, requiring a blend of creativity, strategic planning, and technical savvy. Using GenAI for web content creation generally involves crafting visually engaging layouts and generating sharp, SEO-friendly content that also stays on brand.

This section explores how GenAI can help you with website design and content, streamlining the process from conceptualization to execution. You can also use GenAI to assist in creating user-centric experiences to attract visitors and convert them into loyal customers. Whether fine-tuning the user interface, writing code, or tailoring the copy to appeal and attract the audience's interests, GenAI can help you tweak your website content for the better.

GenAI-driven website design

GenAI-powered design assistants can suggest templates and themes that are trending or that align with the website's purpose and content. For example with WordPress, this might involve recommending specific themes or page builders that have GenAI-driven design capabilities.

A few examples of GenAI-powered website design assistants include the following:

» **Wix ADI (Artificial Design Intelligence):** Wix ADI is a feature within the Wix website builder platform that creates personalized websites by asking users a series of questions about their needs and preferences. It uses GenAI to combine this information with design trends to suggest and automatically build tailored website templates for the user to fill with content.

» **Bookmark Aida**: Bookmark's GenAI-powered website builder, Aida (Artificial Intelligence Design Assistant), helps users create a website by making design decisions based on the user's content and preferences. It can suggest layouts and themes that are likely to appeal to any given target audience.

» **The Grid.ai:** The Grid uses GenAI to design websites that adapt to content and user interaction. It analyzes content to suggest design themes and changes the layout in real-time to ensure the website looks great with any content.

» **Firedrop:** Firedrop uses a GenAI design assistant named Sacha, which chats with users to understand their design preferences and content needs. Sacha then suggests or makes website designs and layouts tailored per your responses in the chat.

» **Zyro:** Zyro's GenAI-powered website builder offers an AI Heatmap tool that predicts where visitors to your website are most likely to focus their attention. This insight helps in suggesting templates and content layouts that will help you keep visitors engaged and proactively manage your website traffic.

» **B12:** B12 uses AI to draft initial website designs, which can then be refined by human designers at the company. This GenAI uses industry-specific trends and user preferences to suggest appropriate templates and themes.

GenAI tools can also help manage content for your website. For example, GenAI tools can help select, crop, and optimize images for web use, which helps with faster loading times, reduced lag, and higher visual appeal.

Optimizing website copy with GenAI insights

GenAI can provide insights that can help you optimize website content to improve both the user experience and the website's performance. Here are a few ways that GenAI tools can contribute to content optimization:

>> **A/B testing:** GenAI can generate several versions of website copy to use in A/B testing tools to determine which performs better in terms of user engagement and conversion rates. This takes the guesswork out of content optimization.

>> **Content gap analysis:** GenAI can compare a website's content with your competitors' sites to identify gaps or areas that need improvement in your website copy. This helps in creating content strategies that differentiate your offerings from your competitors.

>> **Automated content creation:** GenAI can quickly generate content for sections of your website that need frequent updating, such as news updates or blog posts. This helps in keeping the website content fresh and relevant without overburdening you or your staff.

>> **Image and video optimization:** GenAI can suggest the best images and videos to accompany text, optimize their size for faster load times, and even create alt text for improved accessibility and SEO.

>> **Chatbots for immediate feedback:** GenAI-powered chatbots can interact with website visitors in real-time, providing immediate insights or answers to their questions, concerns, and preferences, which can in turn help you write great content updates and improve your website design.

By using GenAI-driven insights, website owners and content creators can make informed decisions on how to optimize their website content, ensuring that it resonates with the audience and achieves the desired objectives.

Checking the wisdom of adding GenAI chatbots to your website

Integrating GenAI chatbots into your website can significantly enhance visitor interaction by providing immediate responses to inquiries and deliver a typically better customer experience. Additionally, chatbots can handle many queries simultaneously, reducing the workload on you and your staff and potentially cutting down on customer service costs.

However, the implementation of GenAI chatbots is not without its challenges. One of the main drawbacks is the potential for a chatbot to misinterpret complex or nuanced visitor queries, leading to incorrect responses or frustration for your customer or website visitor. This can result in a subpar experience for customers who might require more sophisticated assistance, particularly in sensitive situations where a human touch is necessary.

Moreover, the initial setup and training of a GenAI chatbot require a significant investment of time and resources. Ensuring the chatbot aligns with your brand voice and accurately reflects the information and services of your business can be a complex process. There is also the ongoing need to monitor and update the chatbot to maintain its effectiveness and to prevent it from providing outdated or incorrect information. Privacy concerns are another consideration, as chatbots collect and process user data, necessitating strict adherence to data protection regulations. You must weigh these factors carefully to determine whether the benefits of adding a GenAI chatbot to your website outweigh the potential downsides.

Crafting Logos and Slogans

A powerful logo and memorable slogan can boost your business and create an instantly recognizable brand identity. However, designing an iconic logo or coining a catchy slogan that resonates with your target audience is often easier said than done. GenAI can generate several options for you to consider or make suggestions and refinements to your own ideas.

While several image generators are already on the market, you may find more success in using one that is specialized for creating logos and slogans. GenAI models trained on massive datasets of existing logos, slogans, and branding elements — and which also possess relevant capabilities ranging from analyzing color palettes and typography to understanding tonal resonance with a target demographic — are likely to output better logos than image generators trained to output photorealistic images. The point here is to always use the best GenAI tool for any task.

This section speaks to using GenAI in the general sense to create brand identity content.

Generating creative brand elements with GenAI

Generating creative brand elements with GenAI involves creating or enhancing aspects of a brand's identity, such as logos, slogans, names, and marketing materials. GenAI can analyze vast amounts of data, learn from design trends, and apply complex algorithms to produce unique and appealing brand elements.

Following are explanations and examples of how GenAI is used in generating creative brand elements:

>> **Logo design:** GenAI-powered graphic design tools can create logos from your prompt, which should include information about your brand values, color preferences, and industry type. For example, platforms like Looka (screenshot of UI in Figure 9-2) and Tailor Brands (screenshot of UI in Figure 9-3) use GenAI to offer you a variety of logo options by combining different fonts, colors, and icons that align with your brand's identity.

Example: A startup in the tech industry could input keywords such as "innovation," "technology," and "connectivity" into a GenAI logo design tool, and it would generate a range of logos featuring elements like circuit patterns or connected nodes that visually represent the tech industry.

>> **Slogan generation:** GenAI can generate catchy and relevant slogans by analyzing a brand's mission, target audience, and key selling points. GenAI text generators like ChatGPT and Claude can produce a variety of slogan options that a brand can then refine and select.

Example: A sustainable clothing brand might use a GenAI tool to generate slogans like "Wear the Change" or "Fashion with a Future," emphasizing its commitment to sustainability.

FIGURE 9-2:
UI of Looka, a GenAI image generator that specializes in creating logos.

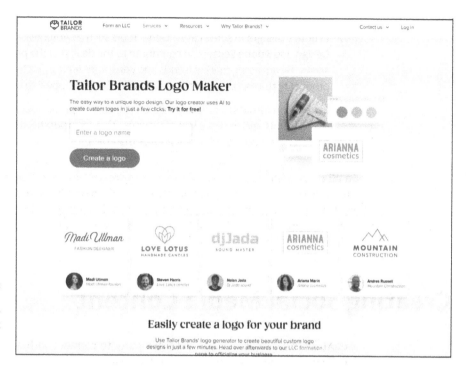

FIGURE 9-3:
Tailor Brands,
a GenAI image
generator that
specializes in
creating logos.

>> **Brand naming:** Coming up with a unique and meaningful brand name is challenging, but GenAI can serve up several options in a hurry. GenAI text generators can make naming suggestions, but GenAI naming tools like Namelix and Atom (formerly Squadhelp) go further. GenAI naming tools can generate names by combining linguistic patterns, cultural relevance, and domain availability checks.

Example: A GenAI tool might create the name "EcoStride" for an eco-friendly footwear company by blending the concepts of ecology and forward movement. These tools check to see whether the domain is available, too!

>> **Marketing material creation:** GenAI tools such as Persado and Phrasee can help create personalized marketing content such as email campaigns, social media posts, and advertising copy. Many such tools can also analyze customer data to tailor messages that resonate with specific audiences.

Example: A beauty brand could use GenAI to help craft personalized email campaigns that suggest products based on past purchase history, with language that reflects the individual's preferences and behaviors.

>> **Product design:** In some cases, GenAI tools such as Autodesk Generative Design and Adobe Sensei can contribute to the design of the products themselves. By analyzing market trends and consumer feedback, GenAI can suggest product features, colors, and styles that are likely to appeal to customers.

Example: A furniture company might use GenAI to predict upcoming home decor trends and design a line of furniture that incorporates those predicted preferences, such as color schemes or materials.

In all these applications, GenAI serves as a creative partner that can process large amounts of information and generate initial ideas that human designers and marketers can then refine and implement. The goal is not to replace human creativity but to augment it with GenAI's data-discovery capabilities, leading to more informed and innovative brand elements.

Creating Social Media Content

GenAI tools can help you and your company to connect with audiences on social media in more meaningful and impactful ways.

This section briefly explores how GenAI helps in social media content creation. but as is always the case, you are not limited to the methods and tools you see here. Go forth and create your own GenAI path. This section will just give you a few road signs to look for on your way!

Tailoring GenAI-generated content for social media platforms

Tailoring GenAI-generated content for social media platforms is essential for achieving effective engagement and audience growth. Each platform has its unique culture, user expectations, and content formats, from the short and snappy videos of TikTok to the polished and curated feeds of Instagram. GenAI tools can analyze the nuances of these platforms, using insights from data to create customized content that resonates with the specific audience of each. For instance, GenAI can generate trendy hashtags, craft catchy captions, write video scripts, and suggest the best times to post, all tailored to the algorithms and user behaviors of platforms like Facebook and Twitter (X).

Moreover, GenAI's ability to personalize content plays a pivotal role in reaching your target demographic. By processing user interaction data, GenAI can suggest content variations that appeal to different segments of an audience, whether it's through language style, image choice, or video length. On YouTube, GenAI can help optimize video titles and descriptions for searchability; while on Instagram, it can enhance photo aesthetics to match a brand's visual theme. For TikTok, GenAI can suggest micro videos with a micro message that delivers just the memorable punch your brand needs. This highly customized approach not only improves user engagement but also strengthens the brand's presence across various social media landscapes, ensuring that the content not only captures attention but also fosters a lasting connection with viewers.

Strategies for viral GenAI-enhanced social media posts

Creating viral social media posts is a blend of art and science, and GenAI tools are providing creators with powerful tools to amplify their content's reach and messaging. One effective strategy you can use is leveraging GenAI to analyze patterns in viral content across similar topics or within targeted demographics. By understanding which types of content — such as emotionally charged videos, humorous memes, or inspiring stories — tend to perform well, GenAI can guide you in crafting posts that hit the same viral chords. For example, a GenAI tool might suggest incorporating a trending dance challenge into a TikTok video for a fashion brand, as it recognizes patterns that suggest these types of videos receive high engagement and shares within the platform's community.

Another strategy is to use GenAI for real-time trend spotting and rapid content adaptation. Social media trends can emerge and evolve quickly, and GenAI tools can monitor these shifts early on, alerting creators to jump on a trending hashtag or topic before it peaks. For instance, a GenAI tool might notify a food blogger on Instagram about a sudden spike in posts about a specific superfood, prompting the creation of timely and relevant content such as recipes or nutritional tips, increasing the chances of the post going viral.

Furthermore, GenAI can optimize the timing and targeting of posts. By analyzing user activity data, GenAI models can predict when a post is most likely to be seen and engaged with by the largest possible audience. For example, if you are a YouTube content creator, you can use GenAI to determine the best day and hour to release a new video, while Facebook page managers might use GenAI insights to schedule posts that coincide with high user engagement periods. Additionally, GenAI can segment audiences and tailor content to specific groups, like crafting posts with regional slang or local references on platforms like X (formerly Twitter) to resonate with users in a particular geographic area. By combining these GenAI-driven strategies, you can significantly enhance your posts' potential to go viral.

Repurposing social media content with GenAI

GenAI can significantly streamline the process of repurposing social media content. Using GenAI, a single piece of content, such as a comprehensive YouTube video, can be intelligently dissected into smaller, platform-specific pieces. GenAI tools can identify key moments or data points, transcribe spoken words, and even suggest specific edits to create customized snippets for Instagram Reels or TikTok videos. For example, GenAI could analyze viewer engagement data to pinpoint the most impactful parts of the video and then automatically generate shorter clips that highlight these moments, optimized for sharing on platforms where shorter content performs best.

Furthermore, GenAI can assist in adapting the tone and style of content to fit different social media platforms. By analyzing successful posts on each platform, AI tools can provide suggestions on language, hashtags, and visual elements that resonate with the audience there. A LinkedIn article with a formal tone can be transformed by GenAI into a series of casual, conversational tweets, or it can help create a visually rich Pinterest graphic that communicates the same information in a more graphic-centric format. For instance, a GenAI-powered content management system, such as Lately.ai, can take a well-received technical blog post and suggest changes to the text and imagery to make it suitable for a more visually oriented platform like Instagram.

Lastly, GenAI's predictive analytics and machine learning capabilities can keep repurposed content timely and relevant. GenAI can analyze trends and predict topics of interest, suggesting when to reintroduce evergreen content or update it with new insights. It can also track seasonal patterns and events, prompting the repurposing of content to align with upcoming holidays or industry events. For example, a GenAI system can recommend refreshing a popular social media campaign from the previous year with current statistics and trends, ensuring the repurposed content remains fresh and engaging for the audience.

Pitfalls and Pitstops

Using GenAI to produce vast volumes of short content can introduce several hazards that may undermine the quality and credibility of the content. One significant risk is the potential for generating inaccurate or misleading information. While GenAI can process large amounts of data and mimic human like writing, it may not always understand context or nuance, leading to factual errors or misrepresentations. This is particularly problematic for topics that require expertise, up-to-date knowledge, or cultural references. Additionally, without proper oversight,

GenAI-generated content may inadvertently perpetuate biases present in the training data, which can result in content that is insensitive or offensive, potentially damaging a brand's reputation and alienating parts of the audience.

Another hazard involves the dilution of brand voice and uniqueness. GenAI tools might produce content that lacks the distinctive tone or style that characterizes a brand, leading to generic or homogeneous content that fails to stand out in a crowded market or digital landscape.

Moreover, the overproduction of content can lead to saturation, where users become overwhelmed by the sheer volume of similar-looking posts, reducing engagement and the effectiveness of social media strategies. This content fatigue can make it harder for brands to maintain meaningful connections with their audience, as the personal touch that often drives social media success is lost in a sea of GenAI-generated posts. To mitigate these risks, it's crucial for you to blend GenAI capabilities with human oversight, ensuring that every piece of content aligns with the brand's values, voice, and the expectations of its audience. And above all, to ensure content works to differentiate you or your company from competitors.

Recognizing the limits and risks of GenAI in short-form content

Recognizing the limits and risks of AI in creating short-form content is crucial for maintaining content integrity and audience trust. GenAI models, while sophisticated, don't possess the human capacity for understanding subtlety, context, and the complex socio-cultural nuances that inform effective communication. They are limited by the data they have been trained on and have access to, which can result in content that lacks depth or fails to fully grasp the topic at hand. These risks, and others, are amplified in short-form content, where every word counts and there is little room for error or misinterpretation.

Moreover, over-reliance on GenAI for content generation can lead to a homogenization of voice and perspective, as the unique creative flair and personal insights that distinguish one brand from another are difficult to replicate through automated means. This can result in a loss of authenticity, a key driver of engagement in social media and other audiences. Additionally, the ease and speed with which GenAI can churn out content may encourage an overemphasis on quantity over quality, potentially overwhelming audiences with a flood of content that lacks real value or relevance. Simply put, machines are not people, and if you are not careful, people will soon realize you're throwing machine-driven content at them. Consumer backlashes against GenAI use are common and almost never result in a happy outcome for companies.

Ethical considerations and quality control

Ethical considerations in using GenAI to create short content are paramount, as the technology's capacity to generate information at scale comes with significant responsibilities. One of the primary ethical concerns is ensuring the accuracy and truthfulness of GenAI-generated content. As GenAI tools can propagate existing data without the ability to determine its correctness, there's a risk of disseminating false or misleading information. Additionally, GenAI must be carefully monitored to prevent the perpetuation of biases, stereotypes, or discriminatory language that could be present in the training datasets. Ensuring that GenAI-generated content upholds ethical standards requires transparency about the use of GenAI, as well as ongoing efforts to diversify training data and implement fairness protocols.

Quality control is another critical aspect to using GenAI for content creation. While GenAI can efficiently produce large quantities of content, human oversight is essential to maintain the caliber of the output. You must regularly review GenAI-generated material to ensure it aligns with your brand's values, voice, and the quality or standards expected by audiences. This includes checking for accuracy, grammatical errors, contextual relevance, and brand consistency. Establishing rigorous review processes and quality checks can help mitigate the risk of eroding audience trust due to subpar content.

Chapter **10**

Luring Images, Music, and Video Out of GenAI

For the purposes of discussion in this chapter, I talk about two distinct groups of users: content creators and artists. Content generators typically focus on producing a high volume of material designed to engage audiences and drive specific outcomes like clicks or sales, often using trends and SEO strategies. Artists, in contrast, prioritize personal expression and creativity, aiming to evoke emotion and thought through original and innovative works that may hold cultural significance. I treat them separately because their projects and goals diverge sharply, and they will (or should) use the same GenAI tools in very different ways.

For content creators, GenAI can be a quick and brilliant fix to fill their need for illustrations, charts and graphs, form and design, and other renderings that illuminate, educate, and entice audiences. Much like smartphone cameras today that produce stunningly sharp and easily editable pictures, GenAI produces art and elements that make anyone look like a pro in a flash. To this group, and make no mistake, GenAI art is both stunning and "good-enough." And often free, too, or cheap enough to feel free. What could possibly be better?

For the more artistic among us, images produced by GenAI are often breathtakingly beautiful and totally mesmerizing. At first exposure, artists and photographers are typically awestruck by such an accomplishment by a machine. But awe is often followed by overwhelmingly dismay at the sharp clarity, intense color, realistic texture, perfect composition, and breath of creativity in such works. Almost to a person, creatives feel a profound loss of craft and self. This generative power uses math to conquer art, which evokes fear that it will also annihilate both the artists' reason for being and their income. What could possibly be worse?

This chapter strives to show you how you can prosper and grow your career by getting more from GenAI models — whether you're a content creator or an artist. If you're a content creator, you'll discover more options in outputs, guidance on customizing images, and a few ways to get better image-to-content fit to drive your point home or augment your content. If you're an artist, you'll discover ways to translate your creative vision to digital form, stay true to your own talent and style, and master GenAI as a tool rather than surrender to it as a master of man and art.

Getting Ready to Create with GenAI

The first step is to choose the right model for the work you intend to do. Think of this like choosing the right paintbrush for a specific task. For example, a broad brush is well suited to covering the canvas with a background color. But a thin edge brush is more ideal for drawing a thin line on a human face in a portrait. The GenAI model you choose affects the outcome of your digital strokes just as surely as the paintbrush affects the outcome of the artist's strokes on a canvas.

Yet it is not only the tool that makes the difference in a work of art. The artist's talent accounts for roughly 98 percent of the finished work. That's easy to see in action by observing artists who create stunning art with nontraditional media using tools like sponges, rakes, trash, and spray paint on a variety of media like the surface of a freshly brewed coffee, exquisite pastries, tiny thimbles, and the murals spanning the full sides of buildings.

Check out Figure 10-1 as an example of how human creative expression isn't limited by media. It's a horse made of one medium (scrap metal) and rendered in another (ChatGPT 4o) at the direction of a human artist (me). Art can quite literally be made of anything, but it can't be made without an artist. GenAI is not an artist, it's a medium.

Now, whether this rendering is truly my own creation or whether the GenAI delivered some other artist's work as a response to my prompt is another question entirely. And it is this question that is at the heart of copyright and intellectual property legal issues. Be careful. Make sure you are not accidentally claiming or using someone else's work.

FIGURE 10-1:
Horse made of
scrap metal.

Art made by ChatGPT 4o (omni)

REMEMBER

Art transcends specific tools and mediums, but it is always shaped by the artist's skill and creative vision. Now consider how that fact shapes the perception of GenAI in the eyes of the content maker and the artist.

When the average content maker views GenAI's artistic capabilities, they typically focus on the effectiveness and ease of the tool. And they're quick and relieved to count on it to make up for their own (real or perceived) lack of artistic talent or time. There's nothing wrong with that approach. You can let GenAI guide you toward creating what you need. Most of the image generators are excellent guides and quickly adapt their renderings to your further instructions (prompts). You'll see how to do that in a few moments.

For now, I want you to focus on how your mind perceives GenAI and its usefulness in your work. First, you'll need to name what you're actually seeking, if only to yourself. That will lead you to effectively command GenAI to bring you a seemingly endless selection of image choices to consider and use.

However, when artists view GenAI's artistic capabilities, they typically judge the tool as equal to or superior to their own talent, completely forgetting, at least in the moment, that it's the artist and not the tool that defines, directs, and ultimately creates the work.

In other words, the tendency is to forget that you're looking at a tool, not an artist. There's definitely an artist behind the picture (GenAI's output), but because other artists tend to be distracted by GenAI outputs, they don't see the wizard behind the curtain. It's time for you to see the wizard. It's time for you to *be* the wizard.

But for this to happen, you must change your perception of GenAI. Fix it firmly in your mind as a tool and not a competing artist. Start thinking about how to adapt the tool to your work and give no thought at all to adapting your work to the tool.

REMEMBER

The secret to luring creative images, audio, and video from GenAI lies in clearly articulating your creative vision and how you want to execute it. The rest is just learning how to use the tool.

Writing Prompts to Create Artistic Outputs

There are two fundamental approaches to prompting to render an artistic image as the output. Essentially, they follow the two forms of creation, be it for art or manufacturing or a child's backyard mudpie. The two forms of creation are *subtractive* and *additive*:

>> **Subtractive** means starting with something and subtracting from it until you arrive at the work you meant to create. "I saw the angel in the marble and carved until I set him free," is how the renowned Renaissance sculptor Michelangelo Buonarroti purportedly explained it.

>> **Additive** means to start with something and add more until you arrive at the work you meant to create. For example, painting a background color on the entire canvas and then adding details and colors in layers until the painting is complete.

Another way to understand the difference is to consider a potter making a vase from clay. The artist can add clay (additive method) to give the object handles or apply details that rise above the base object. But the potter can also remove clay (subtractive method) to carve details into the base or to refine the shape of the vase. Thus, the potter can use either or both methods in the creation of any given work of clay.

REMEMBER

Prompting to create images, audio, video, movie scripts, and other artistic works also follows one or both of those paths. You're free to choose how you want to proceed with prompting. But there are patterns in how different types of creators typically approach prompting, if you'd like to take a look at those for some guidance.

Different prompts for different types of creators

There are no one-size-fits-all prompts to generate any specific images, music, videos, or other creative works. That's partly due to differences in GenAI models but also due to differences in the creators who are writing the prompts and their end goals.

For some people, GenAI renderings are, for the most part, good enough with no more than a tweak or two in the prompt chain. For serious artists seeking to master this new medium, GenAI outputs are typically far from perfect and there's much prompting work ahead to bring these creations ever closer to the artist's original vision. For still other artists who realize that GenAI outputs are just the base medium from which to extract or add elements to create their visions, the output is generally viewed as neither miraculous nor a profound disappointment.

Consider why these evaluations of GenAI outputs vary so much.

A *content maker*, also known as a *content creator*, is a person or entity, such as software and GenAI models, that is instrumental in the creation, development, and editing of content for various uses. This content can take many forms, including but not limited to

>> Written articles and blog posts

>> Videos for platforms like YouTube or TikTok

>> Social media posts for platforms like Instagram, Facebook, or X (formerly Twitter)

>> Podcasts, webinars, and audio recordings

>> Photography and visual artwork for ads and collateral materials

>> Infographics and data visualizations

>> Online courses and educational materials

>> Music and audio productions

>> News reports

>> Scientific reports

>> Textbooks and lesson materials

Content makers often focus on creating engaging, informative, or entertaining material designed to attract and retain an audience. Content also typically has a limited time of appeal or relevance. GenAI can be useful in helping content makers meet their goals in record time. Content makers can then elect to use the content as is or tweak it to their liking, but either way, GenAI speeds up the process and results in a satisfying end.

By comparison, *artists* are traditionally engaged in expressing themselves or conveying conceptual ideas through their art, often prioritizing personal expression, aesthetics, or the exploration of complex themes. Art can take many forms, including painting, sculpture, performance, music, and more and does not necessarily need to be digital or for online consumption. The work of artists is often exhibited in galleries, museums, concerts, or theaters, although it can also be shared online.

Artists may not be driven by the same metrics of success as content creators. They often value critical acclaim, artistic impact, and the emotional or intellectual response their work elicits. An artist's work is typically less tied to trends and more connected to the broader discourse of art history, cultural commentary, or personal exploration. This group will use very different prompts from content creators as they intend to extract a highly original work built from specific values and processes unique to that artist and vision. But even within this group, prompting techniques will fork; some will be to refine the GenAI renderings, while those on the other path seek to create the right base or foundation upon which the artist will use other means to complete the creation. Artists on this second path may, for example, use GenAI only to do studies or preliminary sketches before doing a full fine art painting on traditional canvas. The real-world painting can then be captured in digital form for sharing or for the artist to further manipulate the image.

The art of artsy prompting

Now, with those definitions of the groups in mind, understanding how each approaches prompting becomes easier. The following sections cover the ways content creators versus artists approach prompting and provides a simple, general structure you can follow for artistic prompting.

Why the subtractive method works for content creation

In general, content makers tend to use the subtractive method while artists tend to use the additive method when using GenAI.

That's because content creators tend to have a vague notion of the image they wish to create, and therefore, they tend to start with a simple and general prompt. After the model outputs one or a group of images (depending on the prompt and the model), content creators tend to select one to use, or they begin to make a series of prompts to whittle away at the image's elements to get "in the ballpark" of their loosely defined visual idea. Again, except for those totally uptight Type A personalities, content creators will often go with an image they deem "good enough" over a longer search for the "perfect" visual. There's nothing wrong with that; it's a perfectly legit method of efficiently and professionally completing a task with GenAI image generators.

A sample prompt might be "Show me images of children playing in the street." A follow-up prompt might be "remove the trash cans and fire hydrants," which is subtractive. Of course, content creators can also use the additive method or a combination of the two such as prompting the model to "remove the urban scene and replace it with a rural setting." The point here is that content creators tend to prompt something general and let the model decide the general direction of the image(s) from there.

Why the additive method is better for artistic prompting

Artists are rarely happy with this approach, although almost all of them try it in their early encounters with GenAI. That's because people are taught to believe that they should prompt what they want, and GenAI will deliver it in a puff of technological magic. That's not quite how this works.

Sticking with our image-generation example, artists have a specific visual in mind, and they want GenAI to render a perfect match. But it's no easier to pluck that image from your mind and output it via GenAI than it is to transfer it to a traditional painting. The good news is that there are steps you can take to get the image outputs closer to your ideal.

Begin by taking a hard look at your own process in creating a painting or photograph and break it down into steps. You may already know what the steps are in moving from your initial idea to the finished piece, but many artists and photographers don't as they work on instinct rather than structured steps. In any case, work to determine and then turn as many of those steps into one or more prompts, in a manner that makes sense for the GenAI tool you are using and the end form of your creation. This will require some experimentation with GenAI tools and prompts as you learn what works best for you.

For example, if you typically begin painting by applying a background color to the entire canvas first, then consider trying that as your first prompt. Then make the next step in your process the next prompt, and so on. You can also correct the model's output as you go, much as you would correct a mistake in an actual painting as it occurred.

By the time you finish your process in prompts, the GenAI model should be producing an image exactly — or at least close to — your creative vision. If the outputs are far from what you hoped or need, consider using a different GenAI model to find a better fit with your personal style and processes, or the type of image that you are trying to create.

Working with a clear prompting structure

Crafting a strong and efficient prompt for creating an image to your specifications involves being clear, concise, and detailed about what you want. Here's a structure offered as a general guide in prompting for images, but remember this needs to be customized to your process and creative vision:

Subject and theme: Clearly define the subject of the image. What is the main focus? What theme or mood should the image convey?

Media: Specify whether it should be rendered as an oil painting, a charcoal portrait, a color or black-and-white photograph, a pencil sketch, a preparatory drawing, carved from wood, and so on.

Textures: Specify any texture that you want in the image and on which specific elements. Also specify any further texturizing effects, such as layered textures, or textures not natural to the form, such as flowing stone or fire as ice, or innovative textures that are a blend of two or more textures.

Style and tone: Specify the desired artistic style (realistic, cartoonish, abstract, and so on) and the tone (serious, playful, dark, lighthearted, and so on).

Color scheme: Mention any specific colors you want to be included or avoided or the overall color palette you have in mind. Don't have a color scheme in mind? Ask the GenAI tool to suggest one. This is particularly helpful if you want to explore paint or fabric colors that existed in another era but are not commercially available today.

Composition: Describe how the elements should be arranged. Where should the focal point be? What should be in the background or foreground? How much shadowing should there be? Once you determine the central composition, prompt the GenAI tool to expand on it or to extend the image beyond the current frame. Doing so can help spark your creativity or add details to the work.

Specific elements: List any specific elements that must be included, such as objects, characters, symbols, or text.

Image size and orientation: Include the desired dimensions and whether the image should be portrait, landscape, square, and so on.

File format: State the file format you need the image in (JPEG, PNG, TIFF). State also whether it should be watermarked, contain metadata, or be editable.

Here's an example of this approach in prompting:

"I'm looking for an image to use as the cover for a science fiction novel. The main subject should be a sleek, futuristic cityscape at dusk, conveying a sense of mystery and advancement. The artistic style should be semi-realistic with a moody and atmospheric tone. The color scheme should include shades of blue and purple with contrasting neon lights. The composition should have a clear focal point on a prominent skyscraper in the center, with flying cars subtly integrated into the mid-ground and a starry sky in the background. Please include a subtle depiction of a humanoid robot silhouette in the foreground to hint at the presence of artificial intelligence in the story. The image should be 6 by 9 inches, portrait orientation, with a resolution suitable for print. I need the final image as a high-quality PNG file."

When you have that initial image, start prompting in line with your process, one step at a time in an order that makes sense. You may need to use other tools to fully render your creation and more than one GenAI model — just like you would do with traditional artists' tools. If the GenAI tool you're using can't render outputs in specific file formats, transfer the image to other software and save the resulting file in the format you need.

Harnessing GenAI for Multimedia Content Creation

Multimedia content is a compilation of two or more different forms of content such as text, audio, images, animations, and video into a single unified form. Examples include an advertisement with a photo and a single line of text, or an ebook with lots of text and illustrations. Movies are also multimedia content as they contain video images, perhaps some computer-generated imagery (CGI), audio (music and sound effects), and text in the credits. The combinations of forms are nearly endless.

Producing multimedia content with GenAI can be done in several ways, primarily by using the following:

>> A multimodal model (a GenAI model capable of inputting and outputting more than one format such as text, images, and audio)

>> A GenAI model chain (using the outputs of one or more GenAI models or applications as part or all of the input in another)

>> AI aggregation (using different AI models to separately produce parts of the content that are then joined in production or content management software)

>> Output stitching (pulling select sparts of the outputs from different models answering the same prompt and then manually "stitching" them together in a unified format to improve on any one model's output alone)

Examples of multimodal GenAI models and applications include GPT-4, ChatGPT 4o (omni — see Figure 10-2), Google's Gemini, and Meta's ImageBind. Others are on the market now, and more will emerge. But these few examples are good places to start with your experimentations with multimodal models in making multimedia content.

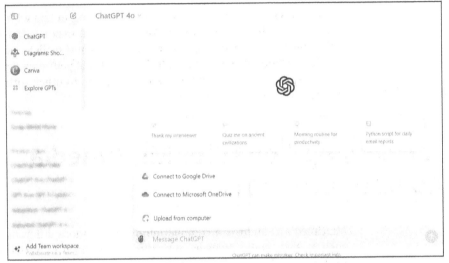

FIGURE 10-2:
This is how you add images to the ChatGPT 4o (omni) inputs.

Screenshot of ChatGPT UI set to the 4o (omni) model with attachment paperclip highlighted and pull-down menu for attachments shown.

However, sometimes a multimodal model packs more bells and whistles than you need. You may be creating a movie poster, for example, and need to add and manipulate only a minimum amount of text on an image. Adobe's Firefly can handle tasks like that in a single pass. Previous image generators did not output text, too, leaving creators to find another way to overlay the text on the image.

Be sure to experiment to see which models are the best fit for the tasks you need.

Innovations in AI-Generated Imagery and Soundscapes

Some forms of multimedia content go beyond the use of text and images. To expand your understanding of what is possible with AI in this regard, it's important to experiment with many different types and combinations of AI.

The preceding section shows examples of multimodal GenAI capable of working with more than these two modalities and the tactic of using multiple GenAI models — chained or unchained — to achieve the same end. To get the most out of the latter approach, be sure to consider some of the more interesting and edgy GenAI innovations.

Making music with AI

In terms of audio, Google DeepMind's WaveNets can be used to manipulate any audio signal. Typically, WaveNets are used for text-to-speech outputs, but they can also be used to make music. If you want to hear some sample musical clips, go to https://deepmind.google/discover/blog/wavenet-a-generative-model-for-raw-audio/.

Why would you want to use GenAI to create music for your content? Maybe you want to create a jingle for your ad campaign, or original music scores for your movie or for the interactive game you just created with GenAI. Or maybe, you see adding features like music to your service or product offerings as a way to add or increase revenue from your multimedia content. Shutterstock certainly found ways to do that when it acquired Amper Music and so did TikTok when it acquired JukeDeck. Amper lets you create original, royalty-free music in minutes. JukeDeck is typically used to create custom music tracks for podcasts, webinars, videos, and other multimedia content.

TIP

Other AI music and audio generators you might want to try include the following:

>> **AIVA** (Artificial Intelligence Virtual Artist) is an AI composer trained on classical music. Its compositions have already been featured in film soundtracks and video games.

>> **Magenta Studio** is a suite of tools with many features aimed at music composition and production. Musicians, producers and others often use it to experiment with music and other audio possibilities.

>> **Ecrett Music** creates, among other things, soundtracks for videos. In Ecrett you simply upload your video, adjust the settings on scene and mood as you like, and then press the Create Music button.

>> **SOUNDRAW,** Ecrett's big brother, takes music creation to another level by providing royalty-free music to content creators and a way for professional artists to monetize their music and keep 100 percent of the recording royalties.

>> **Melodrive** is another option as it composes music in real-time that is infinite, emotionally packed, and categorized as original. One example of its use: Kantor is a short artistic VR experience for Oculus Rift and Rift S that was developed by Melodrive.

When it comes to audio and music, the possibilities with AI are seemingly endless. But you can add other cool things to your multimedia content, too, depending on which models, platforms, and applications you use.

Making videos with AI

GenAI has come a long way since ChatGPT first publicly debuted as a fledgling chatbot. Not that ChatGPT has stood still for a moment since. Its latest form is ChatGPT 4o omni, a multimodal model capable of dealing with most multimedia content needs. Most, I say, but not all. No GenAI model does it all — at least not yet.

Your ongoing assignment is to stay aware of new models as they emerge and of new features and capabilities as they become available, too. It's unlikely that you'll ever want to use one GenAI model for life. These are tools after all, and both their capabilities and your creative tasks will change over time. And that brings us to AI-generated videos that, in my opinion, showcase some of the most impressive GenAI capabilities to date.

To give you an idea of where to start experimenting and perfecting your work with these models, following are a couple video generators that I think you'll find most interesting:

Synthesia tops my list of video generators. Type in text, and it will create a speaking avatar in a fully realized video for you (see Figure 10-3). The avatar follows your script without use of a teleprompter and without ever flubbing a line. Don't have a script yet? ChatGPT or one of the other text generators can make one for you. Then just copy the script over to Synthesia. Boom, you have a corporate training video, new content for your YouTube channel, or a demo video for your booth at the next conference.

Colossyan is another good AI video generator. It offers some handy templates to use in creating your videos, too. You may prefer to create your own videos from scratch and prompt this model accordingly. There's nothing wrong with that. But if you're in a hurry or are not that familiar with video production, using a template can be very helpful.

FIGURE 10-3:
Synthesia online
demo of avatar
and video
creation from a
text prompt.

TIP

Here are some additional GenAI video generators that you may want to consider:

>> **Descript:** You can edit existing videos just by editing the script, which can be very handy in updating or correcting any video content you are using or creating now.

>> **Runway:** This GenAI model has a steep learning curve, but it may be worth learning if your goal is to polish and enhance videos to level up their uniqueness and audience appeal. You can even train your own AI models in this platform to generate images according to your own style and direction.

>> **Peech:** This one may cost you a bit more, but it can do a lot of things in terms of video production and video management. If you're in charge of repurposing content, keeping the content bucket full, and pulling content off the shelves when an employee in the video leaves the company, this may be your tool. It's also helpful in producing webinars and video testimonials.

>> **Fliki:** If you're producing multimedia content that includes video for social video, this tool may be helpful. Enter your script and then pick a voice and content from its library — or use your own, make a few adjustments to your liking, and bingo! You have a social media short video post.

>> **Opus Clip:** Want to repurpose a long video into a short video? Then this tool might prove to be helpful to you. This AI model finds the "viral moments" in your long video — the points of interest, in other words — and automatically packages them into short clips ready to post to TikTok, YouTube Shorts, or Instagram Reels.

IN THIS CHAPTER

» **Finding key points with AI-powered summarization**

» **Checking for consistency in character traits and actions**

» **Storyboarding to visualize your story or production plan**

» **Adapting your tone and writing style to a targeted audience**

» **Testing the market appeal and value of your content**

» **Ensuring multi-author content has a concise and cohesive feel**

» **Achieving better online search rankings for your content**

Chapter **11**

Speeding, Improving, and Checking Your and GenAI's Work

Creating great content with GenAI requires you to prompt strategically and creatively and to factcheck and edit the results. That sounds simple on the surface, and it can be — to an extent. But you can do more to improve the results you get from GenAI, and that's what this chapter is all about.

Getting to the Point with GenAI-Powered Summarization

Prompting an AI for key point extraction and prompting it for summarizing content are two different tasks, each with distinct outcomes. So, too, are prompting for bullet points, pull quotes, and excerpts. You must be very specific about what task you want GenAI to complete.

If you aren't sure what you want, stop here and think it through first. You can also opt to prompt for information in several of these ways on a bit of a "go fish" mission. That method can be fun, frustrating, and a total time sink! That said, the following subsections guide you through prompting for these tasks so that you get the result you want.

Extracting key points

Extracting key points from content is useful for many purposes, especially when dealing with large volumes of information or complex documents. Here are some of the advantages:

>> **Efficiency:** AI can process and analyze large texts much more quickly than humans. By extracting key points, it can save users a significant amount of time, allowing them to quickly focus on the most critical information without having to read through everything.

>> **Clarity:** Key point extraction can help clarify the main ideas in a text, especially if the original content is dense, technical, or contains a lot of filler material. By distilling the essence, users can more easily understand and remember the important information.

>> **Decision-making:** For professionals and decision-makers, having the key points extracted can facilitate faster and more informed decisions, as they can quickly grasp the essential facts or arguments without being bogged down by too much detail.

>> **Comparative analysis:** When comparing multiple documents or sources of information, key point extraction can provide a straightforward way to identify similarities and differences, enabling effective comparative analysis.

>> **Content curation:** For those who need to curate content, such as researchers, journalists, or content managers, key point extraction can help in identifying the most relevant pieces of information that can be used for reports, articles, or database entries.

>> **Content creation:** Content creators can use key point extraction to brainstorm or gather ideas for new content, ensuring that they cover the most pertinent aspects of a topic.

>> **Scalability:** GenAI can handle key point extraction at scale, which is beneficial for businesses and organizations that need to process a large number of documents regularly, such as legal firms, financial institutions, or media outlets.

>> **Customization:** GenAI systems can often be tailored to extract key points based on specific criteria or areas of interest, making the output more relevant for the user's particular needs.

By leveraging GenAI for key point extraction, you can navigate the information overload prevalent in many fields today more effectively, allowing for better management and utilization of knowledge.

Following are some example prompts to help show you how you can get GenAI tools to extract key points:

"Extract the key data points from all documents and datasets related to responsible AI standards and/or AI model management best practices."

"Extract restrictions and terms regarding account suspension or termination from the following Facebook terms of service (ToS) agreement and list in laymen terms." (For this example prompt, insert a copy of the ToS agreement in quotation marks.)

"Extract a list of characteristics that represent the best qualities and the main flaws of each character in the book Lord of the Flies."

"Find and provide the page number and placement of all references, copy and illustrations depicting product #7919 in all product catalogs from the year 2000 to date."

"Extract and list key data points from all of the talks or speeches made by keynote speakers at RSA conferences held over the last 10 years."

"Extract and distill the data points from all books on AI published by Wiley in the last 5 years. Drop any conflicting points, focus on agreeing points only, and only regarding AI models that are less than 10 years old."

WARNING

This approach has downsides, too. For one thing, the result is a list of bullet points, phrases, or sentences that represent the core ideas or facts. These points are typically disjointed and don't provide a cohesive narrative. For another, the process may not capture the nuances or the relationships between different parts of the content, as it focuses on standalone points rather than the flow or argumentation. So, for example, if you use it to extract the key points and terms from a contract or agreement, you would be wise to have a lawyer view it before you sign anything.

Using GenAI for concise summaries and abstracts

By using GenAI to create concise summaries, users gain a quick yet comprehensive view of a document, which is helpful for general understanding and time-saving purposes. On the other hand, abstracts generated by GenAI are particularly beneficial for academic and research purposes, where the focus is on the critical aspects of scholarly work, allowing for rapid assessment of the content's relevance and contributions to a field. Both tools aid in managing the information overload and facilitating knowledge acquisition and dissemination. The following lists offer an overview of the unique advantages of each.

Concise summaries:

» **Comprehensiveness:** Concise summaries aim to capture the entirety of a piece of content in a shortened form, including the main points and essential supporting details, which provides a more complete understanding of the original text as compared to data point extractions.

» **Narrative flow**: Summaries maintain the narrative flow and logical structure of the original content, making them typically easier to read and understand than data point extractions alone, as they preserve the sequence of arguments or events.

» **Versatility:** Summaries can be tailored to various lengths and levels of detail depending on the user's needs, whether they want a quick overview or a more thorough condensation of the material.

» **Timesaving:** For readers who do not have time to read the full content, a concise summary provides a time-efficient way to grasp the key messages without missing out on the context.

» **Research aid:** Summaries can serve as effective research aids, helping writers, illustrators, cartoonists, and photographers, as well as others, to review large amounts of material by focusing on the synthesized essence of the content.

Abstracts:

» **Focus on objectives:** Abstracts typically emphasize the objectives, methodology, results, and conclusions of scholarly articles or reports, making them particularly useful in academic and research contexts as they are more focused than summaries and more detailed than data extractions.

» **Quick assessment:** An abstract allows readers to quickly assess the relevance and value of a document, helping them decide whether it's worth reading in full, which is crucial for literature reviews and scientific research.

>> **Standardized format:** Abstracts often follow a standardized format, which makes it easier for researchers and professionals to scan and compare multiple documents efficiently.

>> **Indexing and search:** Abstracts are used for indexing in databases and search engines, improving the discoverability of documents and aiding in the retrieval of relevant literature.

>> **Previews of content:** They act as standalone previews of the content, providing enough information for someone to understand the main findings and significance of a work without delving into the details.

REMEMBER

When searching for abstracts from scientific and academic papers, be sure to use keywords and phrases that are specific enough to yield targeted results. For example, following are some examples of prompts that could be used in academic databases like PubMed, Web of Science, or Google Scholar:

"Systematic review on the overall effectiveness of vaccines in preventing infectious diseases in school-aged children in the United States from 1950 to 2020."

"Meta-analysis of long-term vaccine efficacy and safety among school-aged children in the United States."

"Comparative study of vaccination coverage and disease incidence in U.S. school-aged children over seven decades."

"Impact assessment of routine vaccination programs on public health outcomes in American children."

"Historical trends in vaccine-preventable diseases among U.S. school children: A 70-year retrospective."

"Effectiveness of measles, mumps, and rubella (MMR) vaccine in school-aged populations in the United States."

"Evaluation of the diphtheria, tetanus, and acellular pertussis (DTaP) vaccine's impact on disease incidence in U.S. children."

"Longitudinal study on the efficacy of the varicella vaccine in preventing chickenpox in school-aged children in the United States."

"Assessment of immune response and duration of protection provided by the polio vaccine in U.S. children."

"The role of the human papillomavirus (HPV) vaccine in reducing cancer prevalence among adolescents in the United States."

"Safety and efficacy of the influenza vaccine in preventing seasonal flu in U.S. school children: A review."

"Analysis of herd immunity effects due to vaccination in school settings across the United States."

"Cost-benefit analysis of routine childhood vaccination programs in the United States over the past 70 years."

"Comparative effectiveness of live attenuated versus inactivated vaccines in U.S. school-age children."

"Review of adverse events following immunization (AEFI) with routine vaccines in the pediatric population of the United States."

These specific prompts are designed to cover both broad analyses of vaccine effectiveness as a group and specific evaluations of individual vaccines commonly given to school-age children in the United States over the past 70 years. They should help retrieve relevant abstracts from scientific literature databases.

TIP

When using these prompts, researchers often refine their search by adding specific filters such as publication date, study type (clinical trial, observational study, and so on), and age group to ensure the results are as relevant as possible to their research question.

Pushing GenAI for bullet points, pull quotes, and excerpts

When prompting for bullet points, pull quotes, and excerpts, the way you frame your request is crucial to getting the desired result. Following are some tips for each type of output.

Bullet points:

» **Be specific:** Clearly indicate that you want the information in the form of bullet points. For example, you could say in your prompt, "Please provide the key points as bullet points."

» **Highlight importance:** Ask the GenAI application to focus on the most important, impactful, or central ideas. For instance, "List the top five most important takeaways in bullet points."

» **Limit the number:** If you want to keep it concise, specify the number of bullet points you desire. For example, "Summarize the main arguments in three bullet points."

Pull quotes:

>> **Request direct quotes:** Specify that you want direct quotes by saying something like, "Extract the most compelling quotes from the text."

>> **Emphasize significance:** To get the most impactful content, ask for quotes that capture the essence of the argument or story. For example, "Identify and provide the most striking statements as pull quotes."

>> **Mention the purpose:** If the pull quotes are for a specific use, such as highlighting in an article or a presentation, mention this in your prompt to guide the GenAI's selection process.

Excerpts:

>> **Define length:** If you want excerpts of a particular length, include that in your prompt. For example, "Provide a short excerpt that best summarizes the conclusion of the article."

>> **Contextualize:** To get a more targeted excerpt, provide context. For example, "Give me an excerpt that explains the author's view on climate change."

>> **Request verbatim text:** Make it clear that you want a direct excerpt from the text. You could say, "Pull an excerpt directly from the section discussing the research methodology."

GenAI's ability to fulfill these requests accurately will depend on the quality and specificity of your prompting, as well as the capabilities and limitations of the GenAI application that you're using.

Enhancing information retrieval with GenAI summarization tactics

Enhancing information retrieval through summarization involves leveraging GenAI's capabilities to process and condense large volumes of text into more manageable forms, making it easier to find and understand relevant information.

Data discovery is a top advantage in using GenAI. Don't hesitate to explore data in as many ways as you can think of so that you leverage this aspect to full benefit.

Here are several ways you can enhance information retrieval using summarization tactics:

>> **Preprocessing documents:** Use GenAI to summarize long documents before indexing them in a database. Summaries can help you get an overview of the content and decide which documents to explore in detail.

Example prompt: "Write a short summary of the main points from the following: <Insert text from document or file>"

>> **Creating searchable abstracts:** Generate abstracts for a collection of articles, papers, or reports. These abstracts can be indexed and searched, allowing you to quickly identify relevant materials based on the summarized content. (See the section "Using GenAI for concise summaries and abstracts" earlier in this chapter for sample prompts.)

>> **Summarizing search results:** For a set of search results that may include lengthy documents, GenAI can create concise summaries for each item, helping you to determine the relevance of each result without reading the full text.

Perplexity.ai, a GenAI search engine, will do this for you automatically and provide a list of its sources. Otherwise, a prompt for another GenAI model might look like this: "Search for xyz, summarize the collective information, and cite sources for each data point."

>> **Topic clustering:** Use GenAI to summarize and then cluster documents based on their content. This can help you navigate large datasets by topics or themes, making it easier to find related information.

Example prompt: "Gather documents and files on the topic of how to create an electronic game, or a video game, into a single cluster and answer all subsequent prompts only from the information found in that cluster."

>> **Question-answering:** Implement GenAI summarization in question-answering systems or FAQs to provide quick, summarized responses to reader, viewer, or customer queries, pulling information from extensive knowledge bases or long documents.

Example prompt: "Write a FAQ on the top 5 most likely questions to be asked by users from the following installation guide."

>> **Summarizing updates and changes**: For databases that are regularly updated with new information, GenAI can summarize changes or additions, allowing you or your fans and customers to stay informed without having to review all the new content in full.

Example prompt: "Summarize update changes to data in RAG and list new data points most relevant to writing product marketing copy."

- **Enhancing metadata:** Use AI to create or enhance or add keywords or meta descriptions of documents with summaries, which can improve the performance of search engines and recommendation systems. You do want your content found, right?

  Example prompt: "Add keywords and relevant metadata to improve search results and move this content higher in search engine rankings."

- **Personalized summaries:** Tailor summaries to your or a fan's preferences or needs, focusing on aspects of the content that are most relevant to individual interests or queries.

  Example prompt: "Write a short summary for fans over 55 and personalize each to a name in the following fan list."

- **Multi-document summarization:** When you need to understand the gist of multiple documents on the same topic, GenAI can create a single, cohesive summary that synthesizes information from all the sources. You can also use this method to repurpose your content.

  Example prompt: "Repurpose the content from the following documents into a single new document written for an audience of baseball fans."

- **Cross-document retrieval:** For complex research tasks that involve retrieving information across multiple documents, GenAI can summarize and link related content, highlighting connections and differences.

  Example prompt: "Summarize and cross-reference major data points between all related documents so that related or similar information can be easily found across documents."

- **Language translation:** Combine summarization with translation to make non-native language documents accessible to you and to provide you with summaries in your preferred language.

  Example prompt: "Translate your response into the following languages: German, French, and Japanese."

- **Executive briefings:** Generate executive summaries for reports, articles, or meetings, giving decision-makers the essential information they need without requiring them to sift through detailed documents.

  Example prompt: "Write an executive brief that includes key data points and summarizes the combined information found in the attached files."

REMEMBER

It's important to note that the quality of GenAI-generated summaries depends on the quality of the input data and the model's training, so it's crucial to use reliable GenAI services and applications and to provide clear, context-rich prompts.

SEVEN WAYS TO USE GENAI TO TRANSFORM PROSE AND INCREASE READER ENGAGEMENT

GenAI can be a powerful tool for transforming prose and increasing reader engagement in numerous ways. Here are seven strategies in using GenAI for this purpose:

- **Enhancing vocabulary:** Use GenAI to replace common or repetitive words with more dynamic, precise, or unusual choices that better capture the reader's attention.

  Example prompt: "Suggest more expressive synonyms for the following words used in my text. . ."

- **Adding descriptive imagery:** Encourage GenAI to weave in metaphorical language and sensory details to create vivid imagery, making the reading experience more immersive. You can also prompt it to suggest images to add to the text to increase reader interest and understanding.

  Example prompt: "Rewrite this paragraph to include metaphors and sensory imagery that bring the scene to life."

- **Introducing dialogue:** Convert parts of the narrative or exposition into dialogue to break up long paragraphs, give characters a voice, and add a sense of immediacy.

  Example prompt: "Turn this explanation into a dialogue between two characters discussing the topic."

- **Varying sentence structure:** Ask GenAI to vary sentence length and structure to create a more engaging rhythm and improve the flow of the text.

  Example prompt: "Rewrite these sentences with a mix of short, punchy statements and longer, more complex ones."

- **Incorporating storytelling techniques:** Prompt GenAI to apply storytelling elements like conflict, suspense, foreshadowing, or character development to make the prose more compelling.

  Example prompt: "Introduce an element of suspense in the following text to hook the reader."

- **Adding emotional depth:** Request that GenAI infuse the text with emotional language and internal thoughts to help readers connect with the characters or the narrative on a deeper level.

  Example prompt: "Enhance this section by describing the character's emotional response to the events."

- **Injecting humor or wit:** Prompt GenAI to introduce humor, wit, or irony where appropriate to lighten the tone and keep the reader entertained.

    Example prompt: "Add a humorous comment or a witty observation to the end of this paragraph."

By implementing these strategies with careful and creative prompting, you can significantly transform the prose in a way that captivates and maintains the interest of your readers.

Using GenAI to Check Character Traits and Actions

Tracking characters in one story or across a series is one of the most daunting tasks that writers face regardless of whether they're writing books, TV series, movies, or digital games. It's not uncommon for a writer or a team of writers to start killing off characters in the story when there are just too many of them to keep track. Fans, however, seemingly never lose track of characters! It's quite the test for any serious storyteller but especially those with a fan base!

Fortunately, GenAI can assist in maintaining consistency and depth in character portrayal by checking various aspects of character traits and actions. Here are a few ways that GenAI can do that:

>> **Consistency in behavior:** GenAI can scan the text to ensure that a character's actions remain consistent with their established traits throughout the story.

   Example: If a character is described as timid early in the story, AI can flag instances where the character acts boldly without explanation or character development that justifies the change.

>> **Dialogue suitability:** It can analyze dialogue to confirm that the language and tone fit with the character's background, personality, and current emotional state.

   Example: GenAI can highlight dialogue that seems too sophisticated for a young child character or too casual for a character established as formal and reserved.

>> **Character development:** GenAI can track character arcs, making sure that any growth or regression in a character is shown progressively and logically.

   Example: For a character intended to evolve from selfish to selfless, AI can assess whether there are sufficient events and internal monologues that illustrate this transformation.

>> **Trait emphasis:** GenAI can suggest areas where a character's key traits could be highlighted or where additional traits might add complexity.

Example: If a character's creativity is crucial, AI might suggest scenes where this trait could solve a problem or be showcased in interactions.

>> **Emotional response:** It can evaluate whether a character's emotional reactions are appropriate and varied according to different situations.

Example: GenAI can point out whether a character who just experienced a loss is not showing a corresponding emotional reaction in subsequent scenes.

>> **Physical descriptions:** GenAI can ensure that physical descriptions of characters remain consistent unless changes are part of the story.

Example: If a character is initially described with blue eyes, AI can flag any later mention of green eyes as a potential error.

>> **Action-reaction balance:** GenAI can analyze sequences of actions and reactions to ensure they align with the character's established traits and the story's logic.

Example: If a character is risk-averse, AI can question a sudden decision to take an unnecessary gamble without sufficient motivation.

>> **Motivation clarity:** GenAI can assess whether the motivations driving a character's actions are clear and believable to the reader.

Example: GenAI can highlight sections where a character's decision-making process is not well explained, suggesting the need for additional inner dialogue or context.

It is a welcome relief to use GenAI to create or track characters that act and speak in ways that are true to their designed personas, thereby enhancing the believability and engagement of the story.

While I'm doing all of the writing for my new sci-fi novel myself, I do plan to use GenAI to track character traits and actions. That's a burden I'm delighted to have help with. This brings us to a discussion on storyboarding which entails a lot of this same grief. Fortunately, GenAI can help eliminate that too.

Storyboarding with GenAI

Storyboarding is a visual planning technique commonly used in film, television, animation, and other storytelling mediums to outline and convey a story's sequence through illustrations or images. It involves creating a series of panels or frames that depict the narrative's key scenes, much like a comic strip, allowing writers, directors, and other members of a production team to visualize the storyline and the flow of action before the actual production begins.

Each panel in a storyboard typically represents a specific shot or moment in the narrative and may include details such as character placement, camera angles, background activity, and important props. Alongside the visuals, storyboards often feature written notes that describe what's happening in the scene, dialogue, sound effects, music cues, and other relevant production details.

Storyboarding serves as a blueprint for the production process, helping to identify potential issues with the narrative structure, pacing, or transitions. It also facilitates communication among the creative team, as it provides a clear reference that everyone can understand and contribute to. This collaborative tool is crucial for planning complex scenes, such as action sequences or special effects shots, ensuring that the final product aligns with the original vision of the story.

TIP

By integrating GenAI into the storyboarding process, you can streamline workflow, enhance creativity, and ensure that your storyboards are as informative and inspiring as possible for the production team. Some GenAI-powered tools you might want to consider using include Elai.io, Storyboarder.ai, Voxxio, Storyboard-Hero AI, Krock.io, and StoryboardThat.

Consider the following ways GenAI can assist with storyboarding:

>> **Visual concept generation:** GenAI can quickly generate sketches or images that represent scenes from a script or story outline. This helps artists and directors visualize the elements of a scene more quickly and can serve as a starting point for further refinement.

>> **Script breakdown:** AI can analyze a script and suggest key moments that should be included in the storyboard. This helps storyboard artists understand which parts of the narrative are most important to visualize.

>> **Scene description:** AI can provide detailed descriptions of scenes, including character actions and settings, which can be used by storyboard artists to create more accurate and helpful frames.

>> **Dialogue and action cues:** For each storyboard panel, AI can suggest dialogue and action cues that align with the story's progression, ensuring that each frame captures the essence of the scene.

>> **Editing and rearranging:** AI can assist in digitally editing and rearranging storyboard panels to experiment with different narrative flows and pacing without the need for redrawing.

- **>> Animation and motion:** For animated storyboards or animatics, AI can help create simple animations that give a sense of timing and motion, providing a clearer preview of the final product.

- **>> Collaboration:** AI-powered tools can facilitate collaboration by allowing team members to comment on and edit storyboards in real-time, ensuring that all ideas are considered and the best narrative flow is achieved.

Adapting Writing Style and Tone for Varied Audiences Using GenAI

Navigating the nuances of language to match the expectations of different audiences is a craft all its own. And fortunately, it's one that GenAI can simplify significantly for writers. Whether you're crafting a technical report for industry professionals, a blog post for casual readers, or a narrative for young adults, GenAI is adept at adjusting your writing style and tone to resonate with your intended audience.

By analyzing the linguistic subtleties that define various demographic groups, GenAI can tailor your prose, ensuring that it not only engages but also speaks directly to the hearts and minds of your readers. From the formality of your sentences to the complexity of your vocabulary, GenAI empowers you to adapt your writing seamlessly, making your message accessible and appealing to any audience you wish to reach.

Following are some examples of prompts for getting GenAI to adapt your writing style and tone as needed:

"Use the key points from this real estate marketing message to write three 30-second TV advertisement scripts, one of each written to appeal to the following groups: 1) 45+ homeowners, 2) 25–40 parents of children aged 6–14, and 3) 55+ looking to downsize <insert your marketing message>."

"Write and design 3 ads in a single campaign urging people to buy electric vehicles, one as a Super Bowl video, one as a TikTok video, and one as a newspaper ad, and each tailored to the respective audiences."

"Rewrite the lyrics of this song in a clean version for public broadcast."

"Write a children's book on the importance of taking all their medicine even if they feel better."

Prompt GenAI to rewrite the same work to fit different, specific audiences and use the outputs in venues where these audiences are. This is an ideal tactic for customizing the appeal of ads and marketing campaigns aimed at specific audiences in a multiple audience program.

Customizing content tone with GenAI for different demographics

While GenAI impersonations are a major concern in fraud and disinformation campaigns, the models' understanding of different demographics has a good side, too. The days of struggling to write content that appeals to a different demographic than your own are limited. GenAI can simply customize your copy to appeal to any demographic.

For example, when it comes to engaging with a younger demographic, a GenAI application can be an indispensable tool for injecting a sense of novelty and relatability into the content. By analyzing current trends, slang, and the interests that resonate with a younger audience, the AI can guide the writer to adopt a tone that is informal, energetic, and inclusive. It can suggest culturally relevant references, emojis, or multimedia elements that appeal to a tech-savvy generation, ensuring the content is as dynamic and interactive as the platforms they frequent. The result is a narrative that not only captivates but also fosters a genuine connection with a demographic that values authenticity and creativity.

Conversely, when addressing a more mature, professional audience, GenAI can assist in refining the content to exude expertise, credibility, and a level of formality befitting this group. It can help streamline complex ideas into clear, concise language that respects the time constraints and intellectual expectations of professionals. By suggesting industry-specific jargon and a more structured narrative, GenAI ensures the content maintains the gravitas required to engage a discerning audience. This tailored approach not only demonstrates respect for the audience's knowledge base but also reinforces the writer's authority within the professional sphere.

You can repurpose any content into many forms, each aimed at a different demographic. This can be doubly useful if you are tasked to quickly fill a content well or make across the board changes to a marketing campaign!

GenAI-assisted style adaptation for targeted communication

Using GenAI, you can analyze the linguistic preferences of your target audience. The GenAI can suggest alterations to syntax, diction, and even the rhythm of prose to align with these preferences, ensuring that the message not only reaches its audience but also resonates with them. This level of customization extends to cultural nuances and regional vernacular, allowing for communication that is not just targeted, but also deeply empathetic and engaging.

In the realm of international communication, AI-assisted style adaptation helps you navigate the complexities of cross-cultural nuances by adjusting for varying degrees of directness or formality that different cultures may expect or require. GenAI can guide the adaptation of content to reflect the social norms and etiquette of the target audience, to help prevent miscommunication and to foster positive international relations. By providing insights into subtle cultural cues and expectations, GenAI helps you cross linguistic barriers with some degree of confidence, although you'd be wise to have professional reviewers skilled in language translation and culture interpretation double-check the outputs. GenAI can help you save time. money, and maybe even face by crafting messages that are both culturally sensitive and compelling, no matter where in the world your audience is. Just remember to always check its work.

Checking Your Content's Market Appeal and Value

In the fast-paced world of content creation and in a world that's overrun with content already, ensuring that your work resonates with your intended market is crucial for success. GenAI makes it easier to compete and stand apart from the noise. It offers a sophisticated set of tools that can analyze and predict the market appeal and value of your content, thereby circumventing the long, laborious and often costly method of trial and error.

REMEMBER

By examining current trends, audience engagement, and competitive content, GenAI provides invaluable insights that can help you refine your content strategy in ways that matter — either in getting noticed, gaining audience or market share, or a rise in profitability. Whether you're a blogger, marketer, or novelist, GenAI's ability to sift through vast data and offer actionable feedback means you can tailor your content not just to meet the market's demand but to captivate and retain your audience's attention, further maximizing both impact and reach.

GenAI tools for assessing content resonance and market fit leverage advanced algorithms, machine learning, and data analytics to provide insights into consumer behavior, preferences, and trends. Some of the functionalities they offer include sentiment analysis to gauge audience reaction, topic trend analysis to identify what subjects are gaining traction, and predictive analytics to forecast content performance.

Content optimization platforms can suggest improvements in real-time, such as SEO enhancements for better online visibility or readability adjustments for clearer communication. Social listening tools are invaluable for monitoring brand mentions and audience engagement across various social media platforms, providing a window into what content resonates and sparks conversation.

ChatGPT 4 omni is one example of a GenAI application that can perform many of these tasks. However, for more advanced or specialized tasks, such as real-time social listening, personalization at scale, or predictive market analysis, you may also want to use GenAI-driven and dedicated software or platforms that are specifically designed for these purposes. There are several tools and platforms that leverage GenAI and machine learning to assess content resonance with specific audiences and market fit. Examples include BuzzSumo, Crimson Hexagon, HubSpot's Content Strategy Tool, MarketMuse, and Pulsar Platform.

REMEMBER

The focus and effectiveness of these tools vary, and they should be used as part of a comprehensive market research and content strategy. Additionally, new tools are constantly being developed, and existing tools are regularly updated with new features and capabilities. Always check for the latest offerings and versions to ensure you can take advantage of the latest options.

TIP

You can also stack AIs and/or integrate GenAI with other software to increase capabilities beyond that of a single GenAI application. Further, the GenAI model underlying a GenAI application can do more than the one application offers. You may want to choose another application built on the same model that is more suited to what you are trying to accomplish.

Additionally, some GenAI tools can conduct competitive analysis, allowing content creators to benchmark their work against successful content in similar niches. Personalization engines use GenAI and machine learning to tailor content recommendations to individual users, enhancing user engagement and satisfaction. By using the right AI tools, or combination thereof, content creators and marketers can not only fine-tune their content for better resonance and market fit but also adapt their strategies to the ever-changing marketplace.

Ensuring Coherence and Concision in Multi-Author Content

When multiple authors contribute to a single piece of content, maintaining a unified voice and a clear, concise message can be a significant challenge. Ensuring coherence and concision in multi-author content requires a strategic approach that includes clear guidelines, effective communication, and a robust editing process.

Coherence ensures that the content flows smoothly and logically from one point to the next, presenting a unified argument or narrative. Concision helps in eliminating redundancy and verbosity, making the content more engaging and easier to understand. By focusing on these elements, a team of writers can produce a cohesive document that resonates with the intended audience and maintains a high level of professionalism and readability.

Incorporating GenAI assistance at various stages allows collaborative writing efforts, which can be more efficient and result in a unified, coherent document that effectively communicates its intended message.

Achieving this unity with the assistance of GenAI involves several key steps:

1. **Establish clear objectives and guidelines.**

   Define the purpose, audience, and key messages of the content. Next, set style and tone guidelines to ensure consistency across different sections.

2. **Designate roles and responsibilities.**

   Assign specific roles such as lead author, editor, and reviewer to team members. Clarify what is expected from each contributor.

3. **Create a detailed outline.**

   Develop a comprehensive outline (with or without the help of a GenAI application like ChatGPT 4o or Claude) that breaks down the content into sections or chapters. Ensure that all authors understand the structure and how their contributions fit into the overall narrative and outline.

4. **Use GenAI for initial drafts.**

   Leverage GenAI writing tools to create initial drafts or suggest content based on the outline. Authors can then refine and personalize the GenAI-generated content to maintain a cohesive voice.

5. **Facilitate seamless communication.**

   Use collaboration tools that allow for real-time communication and document sharing, such as those in enterprise-level GenAI applications, or cut and paste outputs in Google docs or Microsoft Word. Encourage regular check-ins and discussions to address any inconsistencies or overlaps.

6. Implement a version control system.

Use software that tracks changes and allows for easy comparison between versions. Ensure that everyone is working on the most recent version of the document.

7. Conduct regular reviews.

Schedule periodic reviews to assess the coherence and progression of the content. Use GenAI tools to check for consistency in style, tone, and voice across different sections.

8. Edit for coherence and style.

After the initial drafts, have an editor or team of editors harmonize the content. Use GenAI-powered editing tools to identify and suggest corrections for information gaps or conflicts, as well as stylistic and grammatical inconsistencies.

9. Iterate with feedback.

Gather feedback from all authors and stakeholders. Use GenAI to analyze feedback for common themes and market fit that may require attention.

10. Finalize with a unified review.

Before finalizing the document, conduct a unified review among all authors to ensure that all changes have been incorporated and that the document reads as smoothly as if it were written by a single author. Use GenAI assistance to perform a final check for any remaining inconsistencies or spelling errors.

Optimizing Keywords and Phrases (SEO) with GenAI for Better Search Rankings

Optimizing content for search engines remains a critical component of online visibility. GenAI has considerably boosted the effectiveness of writing with search engine optimization (SEO) in mind without sounding like the content was written solely to incorporate an awkward mix of keywords.

I don't know about you, but I've always hated writing to the dictates of SEO overlords (they from the Kingdom of KeyWords and Awful Writing Rules). I've always been a big believer in the value of well-written content over internet gaming tactics. But I digress. The point is that keywords remain important, at least for the moment, and GenAI excels at helping you with that task in your writing.

GenAI provides advanced tools and insights that can either rewrite your thoughts or draft to fit your company's SEO requirements, and/or help you identify and integrate the most impactful keywords and phrases to get your work in front of the highest number of human eyeballs. Both are worthy goals, but using GenAI makes the whole thing less painful for you to do.

TIP

Specifically, GenAI's ability to process and analyze large datasets enables it to uncover hidden patterns in search behavior and predict shifts in user intent with remarkable accuracy. By harnessing these insights, GenAI tools can suggest optimal keywords, gauge the competitive landscape, and provide recommendations for content adjustments that align closely with current search trends. You can use GenAI to do this for you, or your company's SEO practitioners can use GenAI for the keyword selection process. GenAI also fine-tunes the strategic placement of these terms within content to help eliminate any awkwardness in the final read.

Bottom line, by leveraging GenAI, marketers and SEO professionals can analyze vast amounts of data to discern search patterns, predict trends, and optimize their content strategy accordingly. This enhances the relevance of the material for search algorithms and also ensures that the content scores higher search rankings that, in turn, drives more internet traffic to your work.

3

Exploring Advanced GenAI Models and Techniques

Taking your skills and content to the next level with advanced tactics

Looking at specialized GenAI tools that go beyond the basics to perform more specific tasks for specific topics and purposes

Working with GenAI to further enhance your creativity and productivity

Chapter **12**

Leaning on Advanced Tactics to Move Your Content to Another Level

The more you work with GenAI models, the more you see they aren't one-size-fits-all solutions. They come in various forms, each with distinct features, strengths and weaknesses, and potential applications.

Fortunately, you don't have to use just one GenAI model. There are lots of ways to integrate, aggregate, chain, layer, and stitch models and outputs to get the best of all GenAI worlds. (You'll find more detailed information on those tactics in Chapter 9.)

Moreover, the integration capabilities of GenAI models are a key factor for many users and companies. As GenAI becomes more intertwined with various applications, selecting one of the pre-integrated options or a standalone model that can seamlessly integrate with your existing systems can significantly enhance productivity and efficiency.

This chapter focuses on critical considerations for choosing the right GenAI model, including performance, scalability, ease of integration, and the specific tasks you aim to accomplish. I include case studies and real-world applications to provide you with a better understanding of how different models can be leveraged to meet diverse needs. After reading this chapter, you'll be able to make informed decisions about the GenAI models that can best serve your projects and drive innovation forward.

Evaluating AI Models in Terms of Your Specific Needs

Some of the GenAI models available now (listed and discussed in Chapter 1) can do some really cool stuff, but practically speaking, you must consider how well the AI performs in terms of producing content to your specifications. For example, I tried to get DALL-E to produce charts and graphs for this book similar to data visualizations that can be created in *business intelligence* (BI) software and data visualization tools. I've yet to get DALL-E to produce anything useable in charts and graphs. It continues to produce bizarre drawings that are fully greeked rather than a standard chart with properly labeled data elements. I have, therefore, decided that DALL-E is excellent for creating photorealistic illustrations for my upcoming sci-fi novel, but it's not at all a suitable tool for making charts and graphs for this book.

You'll want to similarly test a variety of GenAI models to see which work best for the work you envision and are trying to create. While I can give you a general description of many of these tools (and I do in Chapter 1), that only goes so far in answering the question pertaining to its performance to your unique specifications.

In your quest to find the right GenAI models for your work, consider the following steps:

1. **Define the content requirements and specifications for your project, distinguishing between creative illustrations and structured data representations.**

   Do the same exercise for any content you want to create. For example, are you looking to include images to your prompt, but only want the model to generate text? Do you need a specialized model — say, in healthcare, that understands medical terminology, procedures, and processes — or will a general-purpose model do what you need?

2. **Identify a range of GenAI models that have potential for your use cases.**

   For example, beyond DALL-E, explore other models like Midjourney and Stable Diffusion for image generation and look into specialized data visualization GenAI tools for charts and graphs.

3. **Set up controlled experiments to test each model's capability to produce the desired content.**

   Provide clear prompts and parameters to guide the GenAI's output.

4. **Evaluate the outputs against your criteria, noting the strengths and limitations of each model in relation to your specific needs.**

5. **Document your findings and use them to inform your choice of GenAI tools for different aspects of your work.**

By following a systematic approach to testing and evaluation, you can better understand the practical applications of GenAI models and select the most appropriate tools for your creative and technical endeavors.

REMEMBER

You don't have to use just one AI model for your project. You can use different models to do different parts of your project and combine their results in other software such as Word, Google Docs, or a content management system (CMS). You can also use the output of one GenAI model as part of the input in another, or even stitch pieces of outputs from different models into a one piece of content so that the result better meets your expectations.

Tailoring GenAI Models for Specialized Topics

Choosing between specialized GenAI models, fine-tuning, or using *retrieval-augmented generation* (RAG) depends on your task's unique demands. Specialized models deliver higher accuracy and efficiency for particular tasks, aligning closely with specific domain knowledge or styles, making them suitable for niche applications.

Fine-tuning pre-trained models with task-specific data offers adaptability and the ability to generate creative, tailored responses, enhancing versatility for various uses. RAG systems, which merge retrieval with generation, provide rich context by tapping into extensive external knowledge, effectively addressing out-of-distribution queries and reducing reliance on training data. However, RAG's complexity in integrating retrieval with generation may limit creativity compared to fully generative models.

REMEMBER

Each method has its tradeoffs: Specialized models prioritize precision, fine-tuning to emphasize flexibility, and RAG focuses on contextual richness. The decision should align with the application's requirements to effectively harness Generative AI's capabilities. Also note that you don't have to choose just one of these options, as you can both fine-tune and use RAG to create a specialized model that will likely outperform a model that's only fine-tuned or only augmented with RAG. There are also options in how you use RAG — and the data you include in it — that can affect model performance for better or worse.

The following sections take a more focused look at some of your options in customizing existing models or creating specialized models.

Customizing AI for industry-specific content

GenAI models offer a versatile foundation upon which industry-specific applications can be built, allowing businesses to adapt these technologies to their unique needs. For example, companies can use fine-tuning to adjust existing open-source or proprietary models, ensuring they resonate with the particular nuances and demands of their industry. This process not only refines the model's output to deliver more relevant and accurate content but also grants businesses greater control over the training data, which can lead to enhanced performance tailored to their specific requirements.

Moreover, the use of RAG can significantly elevate the customization process. RAG combines the power of information retrieval with generative capabilities, enabling GenAI models to pull from vast databases of industry-specific knowledge that doesn't exist in the training data. This approach enriches the model's output with a deeper context and factual accuracy, making it highly suitable for sectors that rely on up-to-date, precise, and esoteric information.

Prompt engineering is another technique that can be employed to fine-tune the performance of GenAI models. By carefully designing the input prompts, companies can guide the GenAI to produce content that aligns more closely with industry-specific styles, terminology, and objectives. This method is particularly effective for generating content that must adhere to certain standards or convey a specific tone, ensuring consistency across various applications.

In essence, the adaptability of GenAI models through fine-tuning, RAG, and prompt engineering presents a powerful toolkit for businesses aiming to harness GenAI for content generation. These techniques allow for the creation of bespoke solutions that not only meet the diverse needs of different industries but also maintain a high level of quality and relevance in the content produced. Whether it's for marketing, legal, healthcare, finance, or any other sector, GenAI models can be customized to support the industry-specific content creation.

Examples of specialized GenAI models available on the market

The market currently features a range of specialized GenAI models, each with distinct capabilities for particular tasks and sectors:

» **Databricks' Dolly model**: This LLM is open source and developed to be a "cheap-to-build LLM," making it more accessible to companies with limited resources. The initial version was trained in just 30 minutes on a single machine, demonstrating its efficiency. Dolly 2.0 is the first open-source, instruction-following LLM that can be used for both research and commercial purposes. This allows organizations to create, own, and customize powerful LLMs without relying on third-party APIs or sharing sensitive data.

» **Hugging Face's LLaMA 2:** LLaMA 2, developed by Meta and integrated with Hugging Face, is a collection of open-access Large Language Models ranging from 7 billion to 70 billion parameters. These models, including fine-tuned versions optimized for dialogue applications, are comparable to proprietary models like ChatGPT.

>> **Google's Gemini**: Developed by Google DeepMind and Google Research, the Gemini family of multimodal Large Language Models is capable of understanding and generating text, images, videos, and audio. It's designed to perform complex tasks, process various types of input simultaneously, and integrate with other Google services, offering advanced capabilities such as understanding nuanced context, humor, and sarcasm while providing responses to user queries and prompts.

>> **Anthropic's Claude**: Claude, developed by Anthropic, is an advanced AI assistant and chatbot designed to rival models like ChatGPT. It leverages a Large Language Model to perform a variety of tasks, including summarization, creative writing, coding, and Q&A. Claude's latest versions, such as Claude 2 and the more recent Claude 3.5, offer significant improvements in context window size, allowing it to process large amounts of text, and are designed to be more reliable and steerable for users.

>> **Amazon's Titan**: Titan is Amazon's family of generative AI models offered through AWS and designed for tasks such as text generation, image generation, and creating text embeddings. These models, accessible via Amazon Bedrock, support various applications including e-commerce, media, and healthcare. The models can be highly customized for specific use cases.

TIP

But specialized applications can be found embedded in specialized software, too. For example, Perplexity has GenAI embedded that is specialized to search and sourcing. Other examples are Salesforce's Contract Lifecycle Management and Legal Intake systems that incorporate GenAI to streamline and improve automation, negotiation, and contract management within organizations.

Dealing with Software Integration Issues

Integrating GenAI into software systems presents several challenges. For example, some models depend on extensive internet text databases, which can introduce unsuitable content or provoke copyright disputes. Also, GenAI operates on probabilistic frameworks and doesn't possess innate logic or common sense, sometimes resulting in inaccurate or nonsensical outputs, referred to as *hallucinations*. Lastly, the incorporation of GenAI with existing software, particularly in sectors like finance, is complicated by the need to mesh with a variety of ever-changing vendor environments. Additionally, equipping and guiding the workforce to effectively utilize GenAI technology is a considerable obstacle for organizations.

Overcoming common integration challenges

Integrating GenAI models into existing software systems requires careful planning, execution, and ongoing management to ensure seamless functionality and optimal performance. Here's an expanded look at the various elements and methods that can be used to deal with integration issues:

» **Model management:** The integration of GenAI models into software systems begins with model management. Integration engineers are pivotal in this phase, as they test and orchestrate different models to find the best match for specific tasks. Whether it's enhancing customer support with natural language processing, generating code to assist developers, or improving knowledge search capabilities, the engineers must ensure that the selected GenAI model aligns with the task's requirements and the software's architecture. This process often involves a series of trials and evaluations to determine which model performs best under different scenarios.

» **Vector pipelines:** Handling unstructured data, such as text documents, images, or audio files, necessitates the construction of robust and secure vector pipelines. A vector is a fixed-length representation, specifically an ordered collection of numerical values that represents features or attributes of an item or data point. Vectors are often used as input for various natural language processing (NLP), natural language generation (NLG), and machine learning tasks. A vector pipeline refers to the processing pipeline throughout the use of vectors. Integration engineers are tasked with overseeing the entire process, which includes ingesting raw documents, converting the text into numerical embeddings (dense, numerical representations of real-world objects or features) through natural language understanding techniques, and storing these embeddings in a vector database for efficient retrieval. This infrastructure is crucial for enabling the software to process and analyze large volumes of data quickly and accurately.

» **GPT quality management:** With the variability in responses from Generative Pre-trained Transformers (GPT) models, it's necessary to develop quality control workflows. GPT quality management in software integration involves implementing systems to monitor, control, and optimize the performance of GPT models within applications. This includes developing APIs for seamless model integration, implementing real-time content filtering and safety checks, creating feedback loops for continuous model improvement, and establishing metrics to evaluate the model's accuracy and relevance in specific use cases, all while ensuring compliance with ethical AI guidelines and data privacy regulations.

>> **LLM governance and audit controls**: Large Language Models (LLMs) come with their own set of challenges, including ensuring the accuracy and appropriateness of their outputs. Data engineers are responsible for implementing governance and audit controls to address these issues. By capturing model responses and analyzing them against predefined content rules, engineers can refine data ingestion and model training processes. This continuous cycle of monitoring, analysis, and refinement is crucial for maintaining the integrity and reliability of LLMs within software systems.

Programming with GenAI no-code options

One of the most interesting and controversial uses for GenAI models and applications is in writing computer code. Many GenAI models and applications can write all the code with nothing more than text in a prompt to build upon. Many can also detect and replace errors (also known as bugs) in a snippet of code fed into their input.

Concern centers on whether GenAI code work will ever be truly error-free and whether code generated this way will truly achieve business objectives. Of course, there is concern over programmers losing their jobs to GenAI replacements, too.

For this section, we ignore the concerns and controversies for others to sort out and focus instead on how GenAI makes it possible for almost anyone to write a computer program.

A variety of models and applications are making waves by offering no-code or low-code solutions for programming. Here's a sample list of nine GenAI models and applications that facilitate the creation of software without the need for extensive coding knowledge:

>> **GenAI Builder by SnapLogic**: SnapLogic's GenAI Builder is a no-code generative AI application development platform. It empowers users to create applications seamlessly without requiring deep coding expertise.

>> **Flowise AI**: Flowise AI provides a free training program that enables users to build GenAI apps using a no-code approach. This initiative makes cutting-edge GenAI accessible to a broader audience, regardless of their coding proficiency.

>> **Dolly model**: Developed by Databricks, the Dolly model is a specialized GenAI model that offers no-code options for writing programming and building applications. It too enhances accessibility and ease of use, catering to users who seek to level up their use of GenAI without delving into complex code.

>> **LLaMA 2**: LLaMA 2, an open-source GenAI model from Hugging Face, provides customizable solutions for a variety of applications. It allows users to

implement GenAI functionalities without extensive coding knowledge, making it a versatile tool for developers and non-developers alike.

>> **Gemini by Google:** Google's Gemini is a suite of GenAI models that provide no-code options for programming in both inputs and outputs. These models simplify the application development process, especially for users with limited coding experience, by offering intuitive interfaces and automated features.

>> **GenAI models from Pega:** Pega's GenAI models are integrated into a model-driven software approach that enables users to construct applications without writing code. By leveraging visual interfaces and pre-built templates, these models streamline the development process.

>> **GenAI models from OutSystems:** OutSystems harnesses generative AI in conjunction with low-code platforms to facilitate the rapid creation of applications.

>> **Codex:** OpenAI's Codex model understands and generates computer code, making it a powerful tool for those looking to write software without traditional coding. It has been trained on a vast corpus of code from GitHub, enabling it to assist with a wide range of programming tasks.

>> **Copilot:** Microsoft's Copilot, now enhanced with ChatGPT to form Copilot X, acts as a GenAI pair programmer. *Pair programming* is a software development technique where two programmers work together at one workstation. One, the "driver," writes code while the other, the "observer" or "navigator," reviews each line of code as it's typed in. The two programmers switch roles frequently. The navigator focuses on the overall direction and design of the code, thinking ahead and considering the larger scope, while the driver focuses on the tactical aspects of typing in the code. This collaborative approach can improve code quality, facilitate knowledge sharing, and reduce the likelihood of introducing bugs into the code. It's a key practice in Agile and Extreme Programming (XP) methodologies. Copilot provides code suggestions and completions, functioning like an autocomplete for coding. This tool is designed to help developers write code more efficiently and is particularly useful for those with less coding experience.

These GenAI models and applications are transforming the landscape of software development by providing accessible, no-code solutions that cater to the needs of diverse users — from seasoned developers looking to streamline their workflow to novices eager to explore the world of programming. Diverse users are paving the way for a more inclusive and innovative future in technology creation.

Chapter **13**

Delving into Specialized GenAI Tools

S pecialized GenAI models are tools designed to perform specific functions. They come in different forms, namely Small Language Models, fine-tuned Large Language Models, RAG augmented, and fine-tuned and RAG augmented. Variations and combinations of these categories make models more tailored to certain tasks, and in so doing, more accurate in their performance. Here's a more comprehensive breakdown of specialized GenAI model types:

» **Small Language Models (SLMs):** Slim, task-focused models with fewer parameters and trainable on smaller, highly focused datasets in a matter of minutes or hours.

» **Fine-tuned Large Language Models (LLMs):** LLMs that are upgraded with domain-specific training data. Level of difficulty is high.

» **Retrieval-augmented generation (RAG) models:** Language models boosted with external data retrieval systems. Level of difficulty is lower than fine-tuning models.

» **Fine-tuned and RAG-augmented models:** Integration of fine-tuning and knowledge retrieval systems to harness the best of both. Better performance than either option alone.

>> **Domain-specific pre-trained models:** Built from the ground up on special-ized data instead of augmenting a pre-existing model with specialized data via RAG or fine-tuning.

>> **Versatile task models:** Adapted for a range of tasks within a specific domain. Not to be confused with multimodal models, which are models that can process and understand information from multiple different types of data, such as text, images, and audio.

Specialized GenAI models are trained or modified GenAI models that focus on a particular specialty and, therefore, are better at doing tasks for that area or disci-pline than a general model is. In this chapter, you find out how and when to use specialized GenAI models to your favor.

Discovering the Difference Enterprise-Level AI Tools Make

GenAI enterprise tools differ substantially from those accessible to the broader public. Following are a few key aspects of enterprise-level GenAI tools:

>> **More customization options and advanced complexity:** Enterprise GenAI applications typically offer more customization options so that enterprises can tailor the model to fit their needs better. Some vendors offer enterprise solutions that align with intricate or specific business processes and require-ments. These models boast advanced functionalities specifically engineered for the nuanced demands of enterprise ecosystems, disciplines, or industries. On the other hand, GenAI tools for the public or general users tend to provide more generic features, with customization options that are comparatively limited.

>> **Enhanced data security and compliance features:** For enterprises, GenAI solutions are developed with a higher emphasis on data security, regulatory compliance, and governance to better ensure adherence to rigorous enterprise standards. These models are designed to manage sensitive information with heightened security protocols. Conversely, GenAI tools intended for the general public may not exhibit the same degree of commitment to stringent data security and compliance frameworks. Further, public GenAI tools may capture information in prompts to use to train future models. Most enterprise GenAI tools offer assurances that enterprise proprietary data is not retained by the AI.

>> **Seamless integration with enterprise systems:** Enterprise GenAI models aim to integrate fluidly with a company's existing systems, such as Enterprise Resource Planning (ERP) and Customer Relationship Management (CRM) platforms, as well

as other critical business applications. They are crafted to operate within the complex IT landscapes typical of large organizations. Public or general-user GenAI tools, however, may lack these extensive integration capabilities.

» **Scalability and optimization:** Enterprise GenAI models are optimized to scale effectively and are thus capable of managing substantial data volumes and executing complex operations with efficiency. They are constructed to meet the high throughput and processing demands of large-scale organizations. In contrast, GenAI tools for public or general users may not match this level of robustness in scalability and performance.

» **Comprehensive support and ongoing maintenance:** Enterprises benefit from comprehensive support services, maintenance contracts, and regular updates that come with enterprise-level GenAI solutions, ensuring sustained performance and dependability. Public or general-user GenAI offerings, in comparison, might offer more limited support and maintenance options.

The impact of GenAI on large-scale operations

The benefits of using GenAI in enterprise environments can extend beyond increasing individual worker productivity to improving overall operational efficiency and transforming various business operations or processes such as customer service, marketing, software development, field services, and engineering.

Moreover, GenAI can significantly reduce the time and resources required for tasks such as content creation, data discovery, data analysis, and customer engagement. For instance, AI-generated marketing content can be produced in a fraction of the time it would take human creators. Similarly, in software development, GenAI can assist in code generation and bug fixing thereby accelerating the development cycle.

REMEMBER

But do note that much of the advantage to be reaped from GenAI is found in data discovery and the acceleration of processes. It's not really in content generation unless you're looking for low-level information and interaction. While some models bound over this low bar, none — at least so far — match the capabilities of human workers who are operating above entry-level positions.

For example, had I relied on enterprise-level GenAI tools alone to actually write this book, it would be little more than a blathering mess. If you don't believe me, ask my wonderful editor and her team who had to slog through much of the experimental text I generated, created, blended, abstracted, contracted, expanded, and tossed aside in the name of testing multiple GenAI applications, models, techniques and processes for the greater good of book publishing.

While I'm confident in saying there's no blathering in this book text, we mere mortals certainly blathered and blustered and worse, I fear, while hammering the content in shape. In other words, this was not a case of a friendly chat with a machine that effortlessly rendered a finished book.

For one thing, the application had no access to the internet, so its knowledge base was frozen in time, which would inevitably lead to a book that was badly outdated from the outset. Secondly, the GPT application had no access to my personal and professional skill sets and experiences and therefore could not add the real-world examples and color that I can. Incidentally, it's largely this lack of firsthand experience and color reporting that makes GenAI outputs so bland and unrelatable.

Although I've worked in and around various types of AI for decades, I had yet to produce a book using a model. I'm grateful that Wiley was as eager as I to see if it could be — or even should be — done. Despite common belief, not everything is a good use case for AI, or even for GenAI. And that's true of every technology. Would you, for example, want to cut a wedding cake with a jackhammer? It matters a great deal, you see, for the tool to fit the task.

What I discovered in this process is that using GenAI to speed up my own processes for writing a book — namely in research, data discovery, summarizations, rewording or editing text, character development, plot mapping, content organization, and copy suggestions — made the writing faster. But the text it generated was better used to spur my thinking or to serve as a base upon which I could build my own writing. GenAI simply could not write at or above my level. That's an objective assessment, by the way, and not me peacocking. I'll leave the assessment of my own work to you.

Yes, specialized GenAI models can deliver esoteric outputs, but even those are not on par with the work of the professionals who use them. Creatives and innovators of all stripes will need to adapt it to fit their own visions. Think of it as the difference of the GenAI model finding a new disease marker in thousands or millions of MRI images that can lead to earlier detection of a particular disease, and a doctor who can investigate the accuracy, ethics, safety, and actionability of that discovery.

If enterprises approach GenAI as a way to expand and accelerate data discovery and processes, and then train employees to use it for these purposes, they will gain the maximum benefit from this technology. By using the advanced techniques and tactics described in Chapter 9, outputs can be refined at even a faster pace and with much better results.

TIP

Enterprises can further reap benefits by adding GenAI to their AI stack to make other types of AI models easier to use, and by integrating it with other applications where natural language processing, data discovery, and process optimization are major upgrades.

But the moment that enterprises begin to see GenAI models as acceptable replacements for more than entry-level or low-level tasks, diminishing returns will set in and continue to plummet. However enterprises choose to use GenAI, it's imperative to keep sight of the liabilities it brings now and changing regulations over time.

Conversely, knowledge workers need to focus on upgrading their skills to avoid having to compete with GenAI models. One of the ways to do that is to improve your GenAI skills by doing things like reading this book and taking online learning courses. Full disclosure, I teach GenAI and ChatGPT courses at LinkedIn Learning too. Take any course by any instructor that is useful to you! My point is that if you stay on top of GenAI skills, GenAI isn't likely be a threat to your job. But if it does take your job, these same skills will help you pivot to a new one.

As GenAI models continue to evolve, the impact on large-scale operations will only grow, making it an exciting and essential field for businesses and workers to explore and leverage.

Checking out common features and benefits of enterprise GenAI tools

Like any tool or technology, GenAI models have their uses, but they can't fix everything. And also like every technology that came before them, enterprise-level GenAI models and applications lag behind in terms of new features and capabilities compared to consumer or public versions. The delay in releasing new features and capabilities by third-party vendors is typically between 6 and 12 weeks after OpenAI or any other GenAI model maker releases them. This is to allow time for the vendor to add security and compliance protections over the new features or capabilities. A third-party vendor may also add a few capabilities of their own in what's commonly referred to as a *wrapper*, which is an application that provides a user-friendly interface or additional functionality on top of the model.

Following are some of the features, capabilities, and advantages that enterprise GenAI tools typically offer to businesses:

>> **Advanced data discovery and analysis:** Enterprise GenAI tools enable companies to train or supplement the model with their own proprietary data so that the model performs more pointedly towards their own needs and requirements. Once that's done, organizations can use the model to discover patterns within their data that weren't within reach of more traditional data analysis or *business intelligence* (BI) tools. By comparison, most consumer applications limit data discovery mostly to the training data and whatever data the user provides in the prompt or a user-facing RAG.

>> **Productivity and efficiency enhancements:** A primary advantage of Enterprise GenAI tools is their ability to amplify worker efficiency and productivity. For example, reports, analysis, and content generation for everything from the knowledge center and customer call centers to advertising, marketing, departmental, and even earnings calls can be created faster by using GenAI to structure and write the first draft. Employees can then refine and finish these works in record time.

>> **Process acceleration:** Enterprise GenAI tools can be instrumental in expediting both internal and customer-facing processes, thus quickening the pace of business operations. Rapid data discovery and processing enables organizations to adapt more swiftly to market shifts and customer needs.

>> **Sector-specific advancements:** GenAI tools are adept at driving sector-specific advancements, offering tailored solutions that address unique industry challenges. For example, patient information — complete with illustrations — can be generated quickly for package inserts and informed consent forms for medications manufactured by pharma companies or distributed by drug stores. Retailers can refine marketing campaigns and advertising faster, while the financial sector can bolster fraud detection and customer service with GenAI.

>> **Leveraging talent:** Enterprise GenAI tools can help optimize talent management by augmenting their work and speeding the process so that key talent can produce more work in the same amount of work hours.

>> **Catalyzing innovation:** Enterprise GenAI tools can help organizations find new solutions to business or product issues, find business opportunities, and discover possible new revenue streams. Companies will still have to make these innovations a reality, but GenAI can provide ideas and insights that can get the ball rolling faster and with presumably less risk.

>> **Customization and scalability:** Enterprise GenAI tools are designed with customization and scalability in mind, allowing them to adapt to the evolving needs of a business. They can be tailored to specific organizational requirements and scaled up to handle increased workloads, ensuring that businesses can grow without being constrained by their technological infrastructure.

WARNING

However, GenAI enterprise tools aren't cheap and make significant negative impacts on the environment. Companies will need to weigh all these factors in determining the total cost of ownership.

>> **Increased data security and governance:** With a heightened focus on data security, data privacy, and compliance, enterprise GenAI tools are built to provide additional safeguards for sensitive information and adhere to regulatory standards. This is crucial for maintaining trust and integrity in business operations, especially in industries where data protection is paramount.

Finding Mini GPTs and GPT App Stores

Mini GPT isn't a standardized term, but this is how I think of them. In any case, these are smaller, specialized GPT-like models, each individually tailored for distinct use cases. You can see examples on the GPT Store found in OpenAI's ChatGPT user interface (see Figure 13-1).

These mini GPTs can be likened to the mobile applications people have on their smartphones today, in which each app serves a dedicated purpose or function. Mini GPTs offer specialized GenAI capabilities that are customized to meet specific requirements. The concept behind mini GPTs is to provide users with a suite of GenAI tools that are highly focused and expert in their respective domains, whether it be language translation, financial analysis, or creative writing, among others. See Figure 13-2 for an example of a GPT after clicking on it in the GPT Store.

Furthermore, the GPT App Store represents a significant shift in the GenAI paradigm. It's the beginning of a move toward a more modular and customizable GenAI ecosystem where you can use one or more GPTs within the same project to access additional or specialized GenAI capabilities as needed to serve the unique requirements of your processes or projects. This modular approach not only enhances your work but also paves the way for more innovative uses of GenAI as developers push the boundaries of what these models can do.

REMEMBER

Mini or small GPTs are not the same thing as SLMs. Smaller GPTs are scaled-down versions of OpenAI's larger GPT models, maintaining the same architecture but with fewer parameters, making them less resource-intensive. In contrast, SLMs can encompass a variety of architectures beyond GPT, often designed for specific, resource-constrained applications where a compact model size is critical.

Navigating the world of specialized AI marketplaces

AI marketplaces are digital platforms that facilitate interactions between users and providers of AI resources, serving as centralized hubs where you and your company can discover and deploy AI and GenAI solutions tailored to specific business or project needs. These online aggregators offer a wide range of AI tools, applications, and services.

Following are but a few examples of such marketplaces. I recommend you take the time to explore at least some of them.

» **KI-Marktplatz:** Engineering AI solutions hub KI-Marktplatz is a centralized venue for sourcing engineering-specific AI applications, streamlining the service and app exchange among users and accredited AI entities.

» **PromptBase:** A marketplace of prompts for GenAI models and applications such as ChatGPT, DALL-E, Midjourney, and Stable Diffusion.

» **PromptHero:** This marketplace also presents a vast collection of prompts for GenAI tools like Midjourney, Stable Diffusion, ChatGPT, and Openjourney. Its intuitive interface showcases sections for trending, recent, and highlighted prompts, categorized by themes including portraits, fashion, architecture, and so on.

» **PromptSea:** This is an emerging prompt marketplace for the procurement and exchange of prompts written for a diverse lineup of GenAI systems.

» **gravityAI:** An enterprise AI model marketplace for AI models that meet enterprise-grade readiness, security, and compliance requirements.

» **FlowGPT:** It boasts the title of the largest free GenAI platform, where you can access a variety of AI applications, including Emochi, an app that lets you chat with unlimited and uncensored AI characters and advanced models. On this marketplace, you can find the GenAI tools you need to build games, videos, images, and music as well as productivity tools for business.

» **AIPRM:** The free edition for ChatGPT grants access to a plethora of community-generated prompts. Opt for the paid versions to unlock additional functionalities such as prompt lists, team collaboration, and AIPRM-verified prompts.

Demystifying micro GenAI applications

In the interest of clarifying the seemingly endless list of confusing terms associated with working with GenAI, let me introduce you to yet another set of tools you'll likely encounter at some point.

Micro GenAI applications are tailored, often lightweight tools designed to handle specific tasks or problems. Each micro GenAI application is like a specialized worker focused on a particular job, such as translating text, filtering emails, or providing personalized recommendations. These applications are usually built to integrate into larger systems or to work independently on devices where computing power or storage might be limited.

Mini GPTs, on the other hand, are scaled-down versions of the larger GPT models created by OpenAI. While they're smaller and less resource-intensive than their full-sized counterparts, they still retain a broad range of capabilities due to their transformer-based design. Mini GPTs can understand and generate humanlike text, but they're not as specialized as micro GenAI applications. Instead, they're more like generalists capable of performing a wide variety of language-related tasks, albeit not as powerfully as the larger GPT models.

TIP

In layman's terms, if you think of micro GenAI applications as a set of specialized tools in a toolbox, each designed for a specific job, then mini GPTs are more like a Swiss Army knife — less specialized but versatile and able to handle many different tasks related to language processing.

When it comes to examples of micro GenAI applications, the landscape is diverse, and the list is long. Here are a few examples:

>> **NVIDIA's NIM:** NIM is a set of microservices designed to simplify the deployment of GenAI inferencing applications. It's like a toolkit that helps developers easily set up and run AI models for specific tasks. NIM can be considered a micro GenAI application, as it focuses on specific AI tasks and is designed for efficiency and ease of use.

>> **Photo organization tool:** This is like a smart photo album that can look at all the pictures you've taken and sort them out for you. It can recognize people's faces, places, or objects in the photos and group them together. So, if you're looking for all the pictures from your beach vacation or all the photos of your dog, this tool can find them quickly.

>> **Email filter:** This micro application reads your incoming emails and sorts them into different folders for you. It can tell which emails are important, which are spam, and which are just updates that you can read later. This helps you focus on the messages that really matter without getting distracted by the rest. If you use Gmail, you've seen it at work already.

>> **Voice-activated personal assistant:** This application listens to your voice commands and helps you with tasks. You can ask it to remind you of appointments, play music, check the weather, or even control smart devices in your home.

>> **Language translation app:** This is like a pocket translator that can take a sentence in one language and quickly turn it into another. You can use it when you're traveling to a foreign country or when you come across a website in a language you don't understand. It's not perfect, but can usually give you a pretty good idea of what's being said.

>> **Dietary tracking assistant:** Think of this as a nutritionist that fits in your smartphone. You tell it what you've eaten, and it keeps track of all the calories and nutrients. It can help you stay on track with your diet goals by letting you know if you're missing any important vitamins or if you're eating too many sweets.

Exploring Autonomous AI Agents and Personalized AI

Autonomous AI agents and personalized AI represent two distinct paradigms within the field of artificial intelligence, each with its own set of capabilities, focus areas, and potential impacts on society and technology.

Autonomous AI agents are systems capable of operating independently, making decisions, and executing tasks with minimal human oversight. These agents are equipped with the ability to set their own objectives, adapt to changing environments, and exercise a level of self-governance that allows them to function autonomously.

Personalized AI, on the other hand, focuses on customizing AI experiences to fit individual user preferences, needs, or characteristics. These systems leverage user data to provide tailored experiences and recommendations, aiming to enhance the overall user experience.

Put another way, autonomous AI agents are mostly self-sufficient entities that navigate the world on their own, while personalized AI systems are like attentive companions that learn and adapt to serve us better. As these technologies continue to develop, they'll undoubtedly play increasingly crucial roles in various aspects of life, from enhancing productivity and efficiency to providing more engaging and personalized interactions with technology. GenAI significantly enhances the capabilities and functionalities of both autonomous AI agents and personalized AI systems, providing them with advanced generative capabilities that enable more sophisticated and tailored interactions.

Autonomous AI agents

In terms of functionality, autonomous AI agents manage tasks, make determinations based on a set of rules or through learning algorithms, and interact with their surroundings autonomously. This semi-independence from continuous human control is what sets them apart. However, they're not fully dependent as they require humans to set tasks for them and to approve their decisions.

Examples of autonomous AI range from *robotic process automation* (RPA) tools that take over repetitive tasks from human workers to self-driving vehicles that navigate complex traffic scenarios without a human at the wheel.

Looking ahead, the future of autonomous AI agents is poised to evolve toward fully autonomous systems of nearly every description.

In the realm of autonomous AI agents, GenAI's role is transformative in that it makes these agents interactive in a humanlike way. For example, you can chat with them just as you can with other GenAI applications like Claude, ChatGPT, and Midjourney. GenAI also enables autonomous AI agents to understand commands in human language, to use websites and devices like humans do, to divide a command into a series of tasks, and to complete them in order.

Look for more autonomous AI agents to arise in your daily life but also as tools for creative works. One future example would be an architect tasking an army of autonomous AI agents with constructing a building according to his newly created blueprint. Or autonomous agents creating prints of an artist's work directly in a buyer's office. Only the imagination limits what can be done this way. But yes, if autonomous agents are to function in the physical world as well as in digital environments, they'll need to attach and integrate with physical devices. But we do that already with autonomous cars, smart appliances, and other integrated systems.

Personalized AI

The core functionality of personalized AI is its ability to comprehend user behaviors, preferences, and contexts, thereby delivering content, recommendations, or services that are specifically suited to the user. The goal is to provide relevant information at the right time to improve user satisfaction.

Personalized AI is commonly seen in applications such as marketing campaigns that segment customers based on their preferences or in virtual assistants like Siri or Google Assistant, which adapt their interactions and responses based on the user's history and preferences.

The future of personalized AI is geared toward the development of custom AI assistants that not only understand business needs but also anticipate them and act accordingly. These advanced systems are expected to introduce a new level of automation and intelligence to daily tasks and business operations. For personalized AI, GenAI plays a pivotal role in customizing user experiences. By analyzing user data, GenAI models can deliver personalized content, recommendations, or services that cater to individual user preferences and needs. This level of personalization is evident in applications such as marketing campaigns that target customer segments based on their behavior or virtual assistants that adapt their responses to user interactions.

Deploying GenAI with autonomous agents and AI twins for individualized interactions

GenAI is a pivotal advancement for autonomous agents and AI twins too, (also known as *digital twins*), especially when it comes to interactions that need to be tailored to appeal to or serve individuals on a personalized basis.

REMEMBER

A digital twin is like having a virtual copy of something from the real world. Imagine you have a toy car; now, think about creating an exact digital model of that car on your computer. This digital model is your toy car's "twin" because it looks and behaves just like the real one.

Now, suppose you want to see what happens when you paint the car red or change its wheels. Instead of doing this to your actual toy car and potentially ruining it, you can try it out on your computer's digital twin first. You can see what it looks like, how it might move differently, or how the new wheels affect its speed without touching the real car.

In the real world, digital twins are used for things much bigger than toy cars. They can be used for buildings, engines, or even entire cities on Earth or the moon. Engineers and scientists create these digital models on their computers and then use them to test changes, predict how the real-world version will react to different situations, and solve problems before they happen in real life.

So, a digital twin is a super-detailed and dynamic computer model of something real, which helps us understand and improve the real thing without having to experiment on it directly.

Autonomous agents, you remember, are AI entities that possess the capability to act independently, make decisions, and execute tasks without the need for continuous human guidance. These agents are equipped to establish their own goals, adapt to new circumstances, and operate with a significant level of autonomy. A famous example of their work is seen in self-driving cars, but they can do a lot more than that, especially when they're integrated with GenAI so that they can understand you, and you them.

Within the framework of digital twins, autonomous AI agents are crucial for simulating emergent behaviors in complex systems such as transportation networks, smart cities, or viral disease spreads. They're adept at capturing and modeling the essential behaviors of various entities, which allows them to interact autonomously and effectively represent complex, emergent phenomena.

In personalized or customized applications, autonomous AI agents can potentially convert digital twins to fit your preferences and needs and then, once they have your approval, manufacture or make the changes to the real item in the physical world.

For example, in the near future, a car dealer may show you a digital twin of that year's new models. From there you — or autonomous AI agents — can make changes to the twin to fit your preferences. Once approved, the autonomous AI agents negotiate the price and find the best financing options and execute the deal for you. The car dealer avoids the flooring costs of keeping many new cars on the lot, and you, the buyer, get exactly what you want because the manufacturer finishes the vehicle to your personal specifications and ships it directly to you.

A simpler example would be autonomous AI agents managing your streaming TV subscriptions for you based on your programming preferences. For example, if Netflix has better programming to your tastes in November, the agents automatically arrange your subscription for November but then also automatically cancel it the following month. Maybe Hulu is a better fit for you then. Cool. The agents will take care of it. If the networks move to bundle services, the agents can compute the best programming, prices, and terms of service and act accordingly in your behalf.

Here's another possible scenario: GenAI becomes your personal shopper and brings to you (instead of you searching websites) three choices of attire for your upcoming evening out based on your style preferences. Autonomous AI agents make changes to the twins according to your immediate needs, such as the preferred color or theme of this event and material choices suitable for the expected weather on that date. Once you approve these changes, the agents go find that precise item on the internet and order it according to your preferences in quality, price, and delivery dates. Or, it can arrange for a 3D printer to print the outfit at a local FedEx store, which will then be delivered to your home.

GenAI's advanced capabilities enable autonomous AI agents to work with digital twins with a higher degree of autonomy and intelligence.

REMEMBER

Chapter **14**

Enhancing Creativity and Productivity with GenAI

Generative AI (GenAI) can significantly enhance both creativity and productivity across various domains by automating and augmenting human tasks. It serves as a powerful tool that provides new ways to generate ideas, streamline processes, and personalize experiences. It acts as a catalyst for innovation, enabling individuals and organizations to push the boundaries of what's possible.

In this chapter, I take you on a deeper dive into how you can harness GenAI in specific ways to assist you with your work and creative efforts.

Capturing Inspiration and Cashing In: A Case Study

GenAI's role in content inspiration and creation is limited only by your imagination. To illustrate my point, consider the prompt and response interactions in this section that are between an author (me, in this case) in search of a fantasy story idea and Azure OpenAI Service, which is a GPT model with enterprise-level add-ons put there by Microsoft. You can achieve much the same thing in OpenAI's ChatGPT Plus, ChatGPT Enterprise, or with other types of GenAI models.

I begin the process in search of a story idea.

First prompt: What three characters huddled in a forest might make the beginnings of an interesting fantasy story?

Following is the GenAI response to this prompt:

In the beginnings of an interesting fantasy story, three characters huddled in a forest might include

1. **A wandering mage:** A mage who has been traveling the lands, gathering arcane knowledge and ancient spells. Cloaked in robes adorned with mysterious symbols, the mage carries a staff that pulses with magical energy. This character could be seeking a rare ingredient found only within the heart of the forest or perhaps is on the run from a powerful adversary.

2. **A displaced royal heir:** The second character could be a royal heir who has been ousted from their rightful throne by a treacherous relative or a usurper. Living in exile within the forest, the heir is biding their time, waiting for the right moment to reclaim their crown. They are skilled in the art of swordplay and possess a noble heart, yearning to restore peace and justice to their kingdom.

3. **A mystical creature:** The third character might be a mystical creature native to the forest, such as a shape-shifting druid or an elf with a deep connection to the natural world. This being could be the key to unlocking the secrets of the forest and might offer guidance or protection to the other two characters on their journey.

Together, these three characters could form an unlikely alliance, each with their own strengths and secrets, setting the stage for a tale of adventure, magic, and the struggle for power within a richly imagined fantasy world.

Recognizing the trope in this response, I consider keeping the characters but giving the story idea a modern twist. The next step I take is to explore a change in story setting to develop a different plot. Since this second prompt refers back to the first prompt and response, I now have the early links of a prompt chain.

Second prompt: What might the plot or storyline be if we move these three characters to a space station?

Following is the GenAI response to this prompt:

Moving the three fantasy characters to a space station setting could lead to a compelling science fantasy storyline that blends elements of magic and advanced technology. Here's a potential plot:

Title: "Starlight Arcanum"

Plot summary:

In a distant future in which interstellar travel is common and various species coexist, an ancient space station orbits a dying star. It is known as the Arcanum, a place shrouded in mystery and said to be the nexus of arcane energies and advanced technology.

The wandering mage: Now a master of both ancient magic and quantum sorcery, the mage seeks the Arcanum to unlock a spell that could prevent the star's impending supernova, which threatens countless inhabited planets. The mage's knowledge of the arcane is crucial in navigating the station's mystical defenses and ancient archives.

The displaced royal heir: The heir, from a fallen star kingdom, believes that the secrets held within the Arcanum can prove their legitimacy and reveal the traitor who overthrew their family. Skilled in diplomacy and combat, the heir must navigate the political intricacies of the station's various inhabitants and rally support for their cause.

The mystical creature: Once a guardian of nature, this creature has evolved into an ethereal being of pure energy, a remnant of the station's original creators. It understands the true purpose of the Arcanum and the balance it maintains between the cosmic forces. The creature becomes a guide for the mage and the heir, teaching them about the convergence of magic and cosmic science.

Storyline:

The trio meets by chance on a transport shuttle headed for the Arcanum. They initially clash due to their differing backgrounds and objectives but soon realize that their goals are interconnected, and the fate of the galaxy may hinge on their ability to work together.

(continued)

As they explore the labyrinthine corridors of the Arcanum, they encounter other beings with their own agendas, from power-hungry warlords to enigmatic scholars. The station is a treasure trove of lost knowledge, but it is also a place of great danger, with automated defenses and arcane traps protecting its secrets.

The mage, heir, and mystical creature must confront the dark history of the Arcanum, revealing a forgotten truth about the station's role in maintaining the balance of the universe. They discover that the station itself is sentient, a colossal AI merged with the essence of the star it orbits, and it has its own plans for the impending supernova.

As the star's end draws near, the trio must unite the station's denizens to harness the Arcanum's power, blending their unique abilities to avert the catastrophe. The mage channels the station's energies; the heir rallies the people with their newfound truth; and the mystical creature bridges the gap between organic life and the Arcanum's AI.

In the climax, they must make a choice that will redefine the nature of magic and technology, sacrificing something dear to them to save the galaxy. Their actions will either lead to a new era of harmony between the arcane and the cosmic or the end of all they hold dear.

"Starlight Arcanum" thus becomes a tale of unity and sacrifice, where the past and future collide, and the destiny of the cosmos rests in the hands of an unlikely trio bound by fate and a shared destiny aboard the enigmatic space station.

I decide to tweak the setting again in order to explore additional elements that can potentially be added to the story.

Third prompt: What might the plot or storyline be if we move these three characters to a planet instead of a space station?

Following is the GenAI response to this prompt:

Transposing the three fantasy characters to a planet setting could lead to a rich and engaging storyline that explores the intersection of magic and technology on an alien world. Here's a potential plot:

Title: "Chronicles of the Arcane Expanse"

Plot summary:

On a distant planet, where the fabric of magic weaves through the very core of its existence, our three characters find themselves stranded after a cosmic event disrupts the flow of interstellar travel.

The wandering mage: Once a master of mystical arts, the mage now seeks to understand the unique magical ecosystem of this planet. The mage's quest is to harness the planet's arcane energy to create a portal back to their home world. Along the way, the mage discovers that the planet's magic is sentient, offering not just power but wisdom and knowledge that challenges their understanding of the universe.

The displaced royal heir: The heir, in their quest to reclaim their throne, finds that the planet is home to a lost civilization of their ancestors. With advanced technology indistinguishable from magic, the heir must learn to blend their leadership and combat skills with the ancient tech-magic of the planet to prove their worthiness to rule and to rally the planet's inhabitants against a looming threat.

The mystical creature: This being, a guardian of nature, finds a deep connection with the planet's life force. It senses a disturbance in the balance of the planet's ecosystems and seeks to heal it. The creature's ability to communicate with the planet's flora and fauna becomes vital as it guides the mage and the heir through treacherous terrain and reveals the planet's hidden secrets.

Storyline:

The trio's ship crash-lands on the planet due to a mysterious anomaly. They emerge from the wreckage to find themselves in a world where the laws of physics are intertwined with magical forces. The planet is on the brink of ecological collapse, and its sentient magic is seeking help to restore balance.

(continued)

(continued)

As they journey across the planet, they encounter remnants of the ancient civilization that once harnessed the planet's energies. They learn of a dark force that consumed the civilization, leaving the planet wounded and its magic corrupted.

The mage, heir, and mystical creature must navigate the planet's dangers, from arcane storms to creatures twisted by the dark force. They discover that the cosmic event that brought them here was no accident, but a call from the planet itself, seeking champions to heal its wounds.

The heir uncovers technology that could turn the tide, while the mage learns spells that could mend the planet's magic. The mystical creature becomes the bridge between the planet's consciousness and its new champions.

In the climax, they face the source of the dark force, an ancient entity that seeks to devour the planet's magic. The trio combines their newfound abilities, technology, and magic in a final stand to save the planet and find a way home.

"Chronicles of the Arcane Expanse" becomes a saga of survival, discovery, and the fight to preserve the balance between technology and magic on a world unlike any other.

I can continue this prompt chain to further explore characters, story elements, and plot twists. Or, I can begin tweaking details in this storyline to create a story that's uniquely mine. I can also begin a new chat to help me develop dialogue, track characters and story arcs, and develop or manage other details involved in great storytelling. As you can see, GenAI can be very helpful in helping me organize my thoughts and work and bring a story that I create to fruition quickly.

As an author, you may decide to write your own fantasy story from one of the storylines GenAI offers and do so with or without the characters it supplied. You can change, keep, or trash anything you want to create an original story that's all your own. Or, you can just read these responses and see what ideas they inspire or trigger in your mind and write a story based on that.

REMEMBER

That's the key: Don't focus on what GenAI can do — focus instead on what *you* want to do. Then prompt the model to supply what you need to make what you want come to be.

MAKING YOUR PITCH AND SELLING YOUR CONTENT EARLY

Suppose you're working on a story and you want to have some idea of how well it'll be received in the market before you go to all the effort of writing the entire piece. You can prompt GenAI to analyze the market for demand for your type of story. However, just because you can do that, doesn't mean that you should necessarily. Conventional wisdom has it that writing to the market often fails because the public is fickle and tastes change fast, and the market will likely move on before you get your work published. We'll have to wait to see if that bit of wisdom still holds true given the speed of digital publishing and GenAI story production now.

However you arrive at the story you're going to write, you can also test its market reception by asking GenAI to write a pitch for the head of marketing, a client, a news media editor, or a book publisher. Deliver the pitch and wait for a response from the acquisition editor or whomever you sent it to. See the following figure for an example of a prompt and response for an elevator pitch aimed at a film producer.

Write an elevator pitch on that last response to persuade a film producer to make that idea into a movie

In the lush and untamed world of "Chronicles of the Arcane Expanse," magic and technology collide on a planet that's both alien and familiar. Our story follows a trio of unlikely heroes: a mage versed in the cosmic arts, a royal heir to a fallen dynasty, and a mystical creature deeply connected to the planet's life force. Stranded by a cosmic anomaly, they must unite to heal a world teetering on the brink of ecological and magical collapse.

As they traverse breathtaking landscapes, from crystal forests to floating mountains, they uncover ancient tech-magic and face creatures twisted by a dark force. This epic journey weaves a tale of survival, legacy, and the delicate interplay between the arcane and the scientific. With the fate of an entire world in their hands, our heroes will confront an ancient entity bent on consuming the planet's magic.

"Chronicles of the Arcane Expanse" promises a cinematic experience filled with awe-inspiring visuals, heart-pounding action, and a narrative that explores the profound connection between all living things. It's not just a movie; it's an invitation to witness the rebirth of a world where every drop of water and gust of wind holds the potential for wonder—or destruction. This is a story that will resonate with audiences seeking adventure, enchantment, and a reminder of the power we have to change the world.

AI-generated content may be incorrect

If whomever you pitched your story to buys it before you finish writing, congratulations! If not, but they give you feedback on why they passed, you can return to GenAI to adapt your pitch, story, or content accordingly. You win either way, and you've saved yourself a ton of time and effort.

Giving GenAI Multiple Personalities for Better Perspective

GenAI possesses the unique capability to embody multiple personalities and craft answers from each of them in a single response. This feature can be instrumental for teams seeking to broaden their perspective and challenge conventional thinking. By prompting GenAI with specific traits or viewpoints, users can unearth insights that may not surface in a homogenous environment, thus driving forward more informed and creative outcomes.

The following sections share insights and ways to use multiple personas or roles, separately or as groups, within GenAI to your advantage!

Diversifying AI outputs with varied personalities

Typically, when crafting a prompt for a GenAI model, a single personality is designated within that prompt. This focused approach enables the model to deliver a coherent response that's in line with the specified persona. By adhering to one personality or role at a time, the model is better positioned to produce content or replies that are consistent, clear, and uniform.

However, using a GenAI as though it is a single personality isn't particularly useful in generating some forms of content. For example, when you need it to generate dialogue for two or more characters. Or, when you want it to play devil's advocate to its own response to check for weaknesses in the content or argument. Or, when you want to use lateral thinking to find where objections are likely to surface from different audiences. For these, and other uses, you need GenAI to assume several personalities. Lo and behold, it can do that.

You can use several personalities in a single prompt to get several perspectives in a single response (output). From my personal trials and experiments, it appears that five personalities in a single prompt is the sweet spot, meaning the model doesn't get confused as easily with five or fewer personalities. Your mileage may differ. Go forth and experiment!

Techniques for multi-perspective AI content generation

To successfully assign multiple personalities within a single prompt, users can employ a structured approach that clearly delineates each persona and the context in which they should respond. Here's how this can be done:

1. **Outline the distinct personalities you wish to incorporate.**

   For example, "Personality A is optimistic and creative, while Personality B is pragmatic and analytical."

2. **Separate the personalities within the prompt using clear markers or headings.**

   For instance, "For Personality A: [Question/Statement], For Personality B: [Question/Statement]."

3. **Provide context for each personality's response.**

   This could involve specifying the scenario or the type of response you're seeking from each persona — or giving each persona their own background, such as a worry or goal that may agree or conflict with other personas in the response.

4. **Design the prompt so that the personalities complement each other, allowing for a cohesive yet multifaceted response.**

   For example, "Personality A, provide an imaginative solution to this problem. Personality B, analyze the practicality of Personality A's solution."

5. **Specify that each personality has an equal opportunity to contribute to the response.**

   This balance will prevent one persona from overshadowing the others.

REMEMBER

By following these steps, users can guide the GenAI model to alternate between personalities within a single response, offering a richer and more nuanced output that reflects the diversity of the assigned personas.

PROMPTING FOR PERSPECTIVES

Following are some examples of prompts to get content from different perspectives. As always, you can use them as-is or tailor them as needed:

"Describe your ideal morning routine to ensure a productive day ahead — from the perspectives of a CEO, a yoga instructor, and a freelance writer."

"What is your top tip for someone looking to make their diet healthier? Respond with the perspectives of a nutritionist, a personal trainer, and a busy parent."

(continued)

(continued)

"What do you do when you hit a creative block? Respond separately as a novelist, a musician, and a graphic designer."

"How do you manage stress during particularly challenging times? Respond as an interactive conversation between a psychologist, an entrepreneur, a campaigning politician, and a college student."

"What's the key to a successful team project? Respond as a conversation in a business meeting between a project manager, a customer liaison, a software engineer, and a marketing manager."

Enhancing Readability and Reader Engagement with GenAI

GenAI models adapt well to generating various content formats, from news articles, white papers, and blogs to marketing content and educational materials, and just about everything in-between. Its capacity to enhance readability and engagement is another big plus in accelerating content creation and increasing consumption. As GenAI continues to evolve, it will likely further refine the ways in which information is presented and interacted with, making the process more efficient, personalized, and enjoyable for all involved. In the meantime, it poses several challenges and opportunities that you'll want to address.

The following sections help you with strategies and tips that you can use to improve reader or audience engagement from improving the consumer experience to building a following by virtue of the quality and appeal of your content.

Using GenAI-driven strategies to captivate audiences

It's a good idea to use GenAI to help develop strategies to captivate and engage with your audiences and build a fan or customer base. Knowing how to use GenAI intelligently in developing content and customer engagement strategies can give you a significant competitive advantage.

Consider the following GenAI-driven strategies to see which is most applicable to your needs. Of course, you can use GenAI to develop additional strategies too, if you want to craft something more aligned with what you have in mind.

» **Personalized content recommendations:** GenAI has the capability to sift through vast amounts of user data, including behavior, preferences, and demographics, to curate content that's uniquely tailored to each individual. Put more simply, once prompted, a GenAI model can deliver content that's of specific interest to your customer or fan. This is typically a more satisfying experience for your content consumers than plowing through search results or FAQs. This level of personalization not only enhances the user experience by delivering content that resonates with their interests but also fosters a sense of loyalty as users feel better understood and valued. To do this, consider using a GenAI chatbot to recommend content for any and each prompter. The content can be books, movies, articles, or fan products. Yes, a recommendation engine can deliver personalized recommendations too, but it can't create a humanlike connection with your reader, fan, or customer in a natural conversation like, say, ChatGPT and Claude can.

» **Forecasting:** GenAI can predict audience and customer behavior based on historical and trending data. The insights you gain from using GenAI to forecast future audience, consumer, or fan behavior and trends will help you to proactively adjust your content, campaigns, and strategies to better meet changing market demands. This forward-looking approach can help put you and your business ahead of the curve where you capture more of future interests and needs, or emerging trends, rather than try to catch up with market changes after they occur.

» **Content optimization:** GenAI tools can generate compelling headlines, captions, and summaries, designed to capture and retain attention. Furthermore, GenAI can evaluate content and recommend optimizations to enhance readability and engagement, ensuring that content not only reaches its intended audience but also likely engages them.

» **Social media optimization:** You can use GenAI to maximize the visibility and impact of your social media content by prompting it to suggest or write posts for specific social media venues. In this use case, GenAI will help you participate in real-time conversations and stay relevant in the fast-paced world of social media trends.

» **Audience segmentation and targeting:** By analyzing your customer or audience data with either your own fine-tuned GenAI models or those embedded in other software designed for this purpose, you can identify high-value audience segments and tailor marketing campaigns to these specific groups. This targeted approach not only improves the effectiveness of content objectives and marketing initiatives but also leads to higher conversion rates, as your content is more likely to resonate with a well-defined audience.

FACTORS THAT INFLUENCE CONTENT READABILITY

Content readability refers to how easily a reader can understand and engage with written text. Some of the factors that affect readability are

- **Vocabulary:** Use simple, familiar words over complex or jargon-heavy language.

- **Sentence length:** Shorter, concise sentences tend to be easier to read and understand than longer, more complex ones.

- **Paragraph structure:** Brief paragraphs with clear topic sentences improve readability by breaking text into manageable chunks.

- **Typography and layout:** Font size, line spacing, and text organization on the page or screen can facilitate or hinder readability.

- **Use of headers and subheaders:** Logical organization with headers helps readers follow the structure and flow of the content.

- **Tone and style:** A conversational tone can make content more relatable and easier to follow than a formal or academic one.

- **Visual aids:** Incorporating images, graphs, and bullet points can help illustrate points and break up text.

- **Consistency:** Consistent use of tense, point of view, and narrative style keeps the reader oriented and engaged.

Readability is often measured using various formulas and tools, such as the Flesch-Kincaid Readability Test, Gunning Fog Index, or the Simple Measure of Gobbledygook (SMOG) Index, which evaluate text based on sentence length and word difficulty. These tools generate a readability score that corresponds to an education level or age group, giving writers and editors an idea of how accessible their content is to their intended audience.

Analyzing and improving content readability

Many GenAI models are capable of improving the readability of any given written work. All you need to do is enter the information into a prompt and ask the model to improve it in any way you want it improved. You can even prompt it to do so using the measures in a specific readability test, like specifying one of the tests listed in the nearby sidebar, "Factors that influence content readability."

TIP

Generally speaking, you'll get better results from GenAI tools by feeding chunks of text from longer works into prompts, one chunk at a time rather than loading an entire longer work in a single prompt. That's because the model may lose focus part way through a long piece and just forget to optimize the rest of it. I find 300 words to be the sweet spot in terms of copy lengths entered in a single prompt. But feel free to experiment with different sizes of copy text to see how it works for you in various GenAI models.

Following are some sample prompts to help get you started:

"Rewrite the following text in laymen's terms at a 6th grade education level."

"Rewrite the following text to improve readability according to the same measures as found in the Simple Measure of Gobbledygook (SMOG) Index."

"Suggest improvements to the following text to improve readability according to measures common to the top three readability tests."

"Suggest improvements to the following text to improve engagement with an audience of little league baseball fans".

And here are some sample prompts for serial use in a prompt chain to improve the readability of long content, such as a book or academic paper.

"Rewrite this text by the same rules and to the same readability measures as specified in the earlier prompt and or the first prompt in this chat."

"Check the following text for possible negative reader interpretations or impressions, and readability for readers who are not native English speakers."

Additionally, there are specialized GenAI tools designed to assist in various aspects of content creation to ensure that the final product is polished, clear, and accessible to the intended audience. Following are but a few examples:

» **Grammarly:** You're likely already at least somewhat familiar with this one. Grammarly goes beyond basic grammar and spelling checks; it delves into the nuances of language, offering suggestions on sentence structure, concision, and tone. By providing real-time feedback on these elements, Grammarly helps writers refine their content, making it more readable. The tool's advanced algorithms and embedded GenAI analyze the text to ensure that it adheres to the best practices of writing.

» **ChatPDF:** This GenAI tool specializes in processing PDF files. ChatPDF is adept at scanning, parsing, and summarizing material within PDF documents, and also responding to your prompts about the information, themes, and content therein. This functionality is particularly useful if you're looking to distill complex information into other more digestible formats and easier to understand language.

By summarizing key points and clarifying content, ChatPDF aids in improving the clarity and coherence of the material, thereby enhancing its overall readability. This can be especially beneficial when dealing with lengthy, esoteric, or dense documents, as it helps to highlight and simplify the most pertinent information for you or your audiences.

>> **Jasper AI:** You can use this GenAI assistant to streamline the creation of tailored and high-quality brand content. It is equipped with features that enable the translation of copy into multiple languages, provide content templates, and integrate with tools like Google Docs. Jasper AI's templates serve as a starting point for creating structured and engaging content, while its integration with Google Docs allows for a seamless writing and editing process. These features collectively contribute to the improvement of content quality, appeal, and readability.

Mind Mapping with GenAI for Enhanced Idea Generation

GenAI is also useful for tasks other than generating content. For example, GenAI tools can be used to accelerate and assist with idea generation aimed at solving business problems, creating innovative products and services, and other brainstorming and creative tasks where augmented human minds can make serious impacts on the course of business or human history.

Take for example, *mind mapping*, which is a powerful visual technique used to stimulate and manage problem-solving and creative thinking by organizing information around a central concept through a network of branches representing related ideas or tasks. It employs keywords, images, and colors to create a hierarchical structure that enhances understanding, creativity, and memory. This flexible method is popular for brainstorming, planning, and learning, and can be done manually or with specialized software. Typically, it's a collaborative exercise for groups, but it can be used by individuals as well. When you bring GenAI into the process, mind mapping becomes even more powerful.

Here's a short guide on how to use GenAI for mind mapping and idea generation:

1. Choose your GenAI mind mapping tool.

Select a mind mapping tool that integrates GenAI capabilities or is built to run inside a GenAI application, such as specialized GPTs inside of ChatGPT. Tools like Coggle, EdrawMind AI, Mapify, and Whimsical AI are some of the mind mapping tools that have integrated GenAI into their software. This group of tools is great for generating interactive and dynamic mind maps.

You can also choose from several specialized GPTs on ChatGPT's GPT Store. Examples of options you'll find there are MindMapper Genius, MindMap AI GPT, Mind Map Maker, Idea Architect, Biz Inno Mentor AI, and Mind Map Learning, among others. However, most in this group don't generate interactive and dynamic maps. They produce lists instead. But those lists can be copied or imported to one of the tools I mention in the previous paragraph.

Take, for example, Figure 14-1, which is a response from the GPT MindMapper Genius (found in the GPT Store within ChatGPT) regarding generating dynamic mind maps.

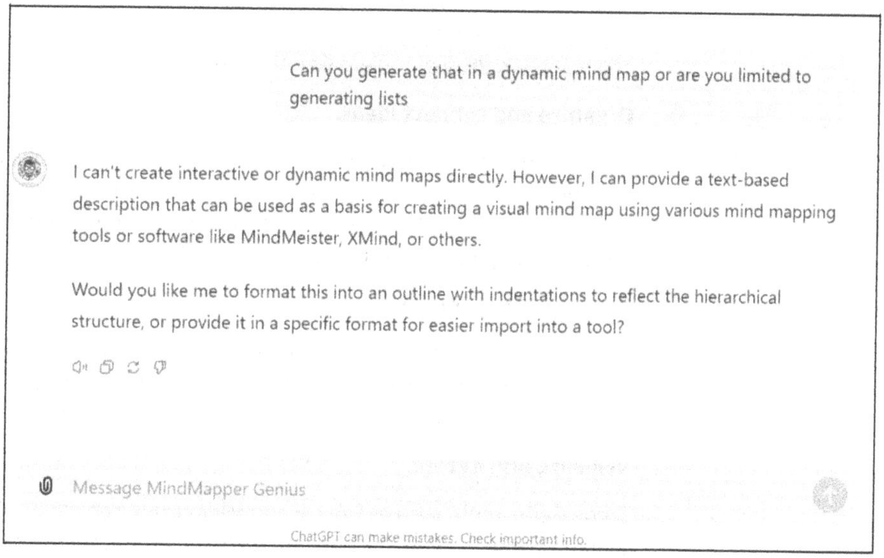

Can you generate that in a dynamic mind map or are you limited to generating lists

I can't create interactive or dynamic mind maps directly. However, I can provide a text-based description that can be used as a basis for creating a visual mind map using various mind mapping tools or software like MindMeister, XMind, or others.

Would you like me to format this into an outline with indentations to reflect the hierarchical structure, or provide it in a specific format for easier import into a tool?

Message MindMapper Genius

ChatGPT can make mistakes. Check important info.

FIGURE 14-1: Screenshot of prompt and response in MindMapper Genius GPT within ChatGPT regarding options for mind mapping depictions.

You'll need to use a specialized mind mapping tool rather than simply prompt a general-purpose GenAI tool like ChatGPT to create a mind map. Why? Because ChatGPT and its ilk, including most of the associated GPTs in its GPT Store, can only produce lists and limited flowcharts — none of which are workable mind maps in the traditional sense. By comparison, elements like branches and subtopics in traditional mind maps can be positioned spatially and repositioned as needed as well as labeled, shuffled, and formatted for size and color. Elements can also be dynamically changed as organic brainstorming progresses.

I suggest you trial several of these mind mapping tools to find one that works best for your purposes and processes. Note that some of these tools — in either the integrated GenAI or the specialized GPT categories — are designed for teams and some for individuals, so look for distinguishing features and limitations too. As for me, I'm comfortable working with most mind mapping tools and generally choose whichever one is more comfortable for the team I'm working with or that best fits the problem at hand.

2. **Set up your central idea.**

   Begin your mind map by clearly defining the central idea or problem you're addressing within the tool. This will serve as the anchor for all subsequent ideas generated by you, your team, and the GenAI model.

3. **Initiate GenAI-powered brainstorming.**

   Prompt your mind mapping tool of choice to expand on your central idea. The model can quickly produce a variety of related concepts and suggestions, which can be added to your mind map as branches or subtopics. Feel free to add to, tweak, drop or replace GenAI suggestions at will.

4. **Organize and connect ideas.**

   As ideas are generated by you, your team or the tool or some combination thereof, the GenAI can help categorize and link them based on relevance and relationships. This helps in creating a structured and coherent mind map that is easy to navigate and understand.

5. **Refine and expand ideas.**

   With the GenAI's assistance, delve deeper into each idea. AI tools can explain or refine ideas or influences, suggest further elaborations, ask probing questions, and offer different perspectives to flesh out each branch of your mind map.

6. **Visualize and iterate.**

   Some GenAI tools, such as DALL-E and Midjourney, can create visual representations of your final idea or concept, such as a product innovation or a fix for a product flaw. Use these visuals to inspire further ideation and to add it as another visual dimension to your mind map, making it more engaging and easier to remember as you or your team continue to brainstorm or move on to idea production.

7. **Collaborate and share.**

   GenAI mind mapping tools often come with collaboration features. Share your mind map with team members and use the GenAI to facilitate group brainstorming sessions, ensuring a diverse range of ideas is considered in the formation of the mind map.

8. **Review and analyze.**

   Once your mind map is populated with ideas, use the GenAI to review and analyze the content. GenAI can help identify the most promising ideas and suggest ways to combine or refine them for better outcomes.

9. **Export and integrate.**

   Export or copy your mind map into other formats or software for further development or integration with other tools. For example, if your mind map led to a building design, you may want to move the mind map to CAD software to develop a blueprint and construction plans. GenAI can assist in translating the mind map into actionable plans or documents for use in other software — or GenAI may already be present in the software you're looking to use. If it's integrated with the software you want to use to bring the idea to life, you may be able to copy the mind map over to that GenAI. It all depends on the configurations of the tools and software you're using.

AI tools learn from interactions and can improve over time. Regularly use the AI for mind mapping to benefit from more accurate and relevant idea generation as the system becomes more attuned to your needs.

Rethinking Your Creative Processes to Better Leverage GenAI

At first, you'll find yourself stuffing GenAI into your current creative process, whatever that might be. Well maybe not in *all* creative processes. Ernest Hemingway is said, at least by GenAI, to have written "while standing up, facing a chest-high bookshelf with a typewriter on the top, and on top of that a wooden reading board," while Victor Hugo "could only write nude." Such creative processes uniquely personal to individual creative persons do not translate well to AI. Being only software, albeit of a very sophisticated type, GenAI has no corporeal being, so it has no up or down, nor nude or clothed state, and no standing or squatting presence either. It's just hovering there like a ghost in a device, in the cloud or on the internet. Soon it will be on local machines too, like your laptop.

My point in all this is that only some of your personal creative processes are transferrable to GenAI. In other words, you may continue writing while wearing your favorite socks or listening to music (sending a nod to Stephen King, one of my favorite writers!). But you need to boil down other parts of your personal creative process into steps that you can prompt GenAI models to follow, mimic, or improve upon to best render your creative vision into a digital form.

Don't worry if you don't immediately succeed in this effort. Creatives of all stripes tend to stuff GenAI models into their beloved processes, clinging mightily to them for love of familiarity and perhaps a dash of superstition despite the rather jarring and oft times spooky intrusion of a newfangled dollop of technical wizardry. However, it usually doesn't take long for creative types to figure out new or adapted processes that fit closely with their personal style.

However, it's essential that you concoct creative processes that are unique to your way of creating whatever it is that you create. Take and keep the lead, in other words, in the *how* you create as well as in *what* you create with GenAI.

Creatives usually get hang of it when they realize that much of their own creative process has less to do with the creative action and more to do with shaping the creation in their own minds. And there, my friend, is where you need to heed my biggest and most dire warning for you:

Do not become dependent on GenAI. If you always follow GenAI's lead, believing it to be better, smarter, more creative than you and dutifully executing creative actions based on its outputs, you will have abandoned your talent and your creative will. Change or adapt your creative process to leverage GenAI, but never surrender your talent and creative agency in the name of progress, efficiency, and speed.

Remembering GenAI is a generator and not a creator

GenAI is a generator, not a creator. It looks backward to predict the future. In other words, it uses historical data (information from the near- to far- past) to predict what letters and words, or audio, image or video will follow your prompt in the here and now.

Your prompt is like a puzzle piece from which GenAI sets out to solve the rest of the puzzle. Sometimes it finishes the puzzle correctly, and you get the picture you wanted. Sometimes it does not. But what you are looking at is the model's best guess at what you require of it. GenAI does not really understand you or your prompt. You are not really having a conversation with it. It is simply generating the end of whatever you started in your prompt.

You are the creator; GenAI is the generator. And by the way, GenAI doesn't generate your entire vision. It just gets you closer to it, really quickly. Then you can refine the result as needed to finish creating your vision.

Adapting traditional creative methods for GenAI collaboration

One important note before you start adapting your creative process or methods to GenAI: Always be aware of what year the model's training data cuts off. For example, originally ChatGPT was trained on data collected from the entire internet in 2021. It has since been retrained on data that cuts off in December 2023. It will, of course, be periodically retrained to give the model more current information to work with in order to prevent model drift (a condition that exists when the data is too old or irrelevant to serve the model's purpose). Whatever the cutoff date, ChatGPT is completely unaware of anything that happened later than that. If your content needs more current information, you'll need to supplement the model's training through adding more current and relevant data in RAG, fine-tuning, or prompting — or use a GenAI model that is capable of browsing the internet. If you fail to do one or more of these, your content may be badly out of date.

Beyond that, adapting traditional creative methods for use with GenAI involves a blend of old and new techniques to harness the full potential of GenAI while maintaining the essence of human creativity. Here are some tips for achieving this synergy:

» **Define clear objectives:** Before integrating GenAI into your creative process, establish clear goals for what you want to achieve. This helps you to guide the model to produce relevant outputs. Consider that you can use GenAI to create parts of a creative work rather than a total finished piece, and your objectives should match your creative plan.

» **Understand GenAI capabilities:** Familiarize yourself with the strengths and limitations of the GenAI model you are using. For instance, GPT-4o has more reasoning capabilities and is generally more creative and collaborative than its predecessors. But, depending on what you're doing, GPT-3 may actually be the better model for your needs on a given project. Stay abreast of emerging features and capabilities, too, like the specialized GPTs that can be summoned within ChatGPT from the GPT Store. Remember that GenAI evolves incredibly fast, so check often to see what it can do differently now.

» **Practice iterative collaboration:** Use GenAI as a starting point and iteratively refine the output. Use a feedback loop, like a thumbs-up or thumbs-down rating to each response, as your input improves the model's subsequent suggestions. This will make the model more useful to you over time.

>> **Leverage diverse inputs:** To avoid homogeneity in GenAI-generated content, provide diverse instructions, perspectives, details, and examples in your prompts. This can help the GenAI to generate a wider range of ideas and styles in outputs. Remember that layering elements in a series of prompts can often render more complex and compelling outputs in terms of generating images and text and music compositions.

>> **Customize the GenAI's style:** GenAI can mimic a specific writing style. For example, you can provide samples of the desired style in the prompt or in RAG to guide the GenAI's output toward your brand's voice or the specific creative tone you're trying to create in the output. You might want to start by providing the model with your brand guidelines and collections of collateral materials, such as ebooks, ads, white papers, and other works that are true to your guidelines for the model to learn and try to mimic. Be aware, however, that sometimes the model's own guardrails (designed to prevent plagiarism and copyright infringement), may make the model balk at copying a given style exactly. It should, however, be able to follow your brand guidelines. Be sure to check the outputs to ensure that it's done so.

>> **Balance GenAI and human input:** While GenAI can automate and optimize many tasks, it's important to maintain a balance. Use GenAI for repetitive or data-driven aspects and human creativity for nuanced, emotional, or complex tasks.

Seeing GenAI as a medium rather than a generator

Creative people often find ways to use things that differ from their original purpose. An old tire can become a child's swing when suspended from a tree limb. Giant, wind-powered kinetic sculptures strolling along beaches are often made from discarded junk parts as are many static sculptures. Paintings can be an illusion when their parts, spread across several surfaces, are viewed from the right angle. Feathers can be used as pens, and plants as paintbrushes, and so on. True creatives see few limitations in the way of mediums for their work.

The same is true of GenAI. At least I see it as a potential medium. I'm relatively sure that I'm not the only one that sees GenAI's potential in this way.

For example, I am working now on using GenAI to create nonlinear and linear stories that I can simultaneously tell in many forms. I'm currently working on a sci-fi story that at the reader's command can be told in text, video, as a play, puppet show, music, ebook, or as wall art. The reader can even view a video snippet for an underlined part of the text for a multimedia experience if they wish or even choose to interact with my words on the page in ways yet imagined.

One story in many forms. Because why should my storytelling be limited to one form? There is no reason. Am I worried someone will steal this idea? No, I'm not. Why not? For the same reason no writer ever worries about someone else also being a writer. It isn't the act, it's the creation that matters. After the novelty wears off from the first few stabs at this, people will reach out for what they've always craved: a really good story! And I will always have a great story to share with my fans!

But that's not the only way GenAI can be seen and used as a medium for creative works, rather than simply as a straightforward generator. I'm sure if you give it some thought, you'll think of other ways to use it as a medium too. Drop me an email or a direct message on social media. I'd love to hear what you came up with. But in any case, always think of new ways to use GenAI because we — meaning humanity — have yet to scratch the surface of the possibilities this tool gives us.

4

Navigating the Intersection of Ethics, Quality, and Humanity

Chapter **15**

Upholding Responsible AI Standards in GenAI Use

This chapter helps you navigate the exciting yet challenging landscape of GenAI without sacrificing ethical standards and quality. By addressing these critical areas, you can harness the power of GenAI to help create a future that's not only technologically advanced but also grounded in the principles of ethics and accountability.

Achieving Originality and Excellence in GenAI-Generated Content

The potential for the range of creative and knowledge work that can be generated with GenAI is boundless. Yet, with this remarkable technology comes the responsibility to ensure that the content it generates is both original and of suitable quality.

Originality in GenAI-generated content isn't just a matter of avoiding plagiarism and copyright infringements; it can also be about fostering innovation, creating new products and computer codes, and pushing the boundaries of what GenAI can achieve. Achieving excellence, on the other hand, means ensuring that the output meets or exceeds the standards that would be expected of a human creator by law, ethics, tradition, or industry requirements. Together, these principles form the bedrock of trust and value in GenAI-generated works. This section delves into the critical importance of upholding these standards and the strategies you can employ to achieve them.

Strategies for ensuring originality in GenAI creations

To ensure the originality and quality of GenAI creations, it's essential to implement strategies that can verify the uniqueness and accuracy of the content produced. Following are some strategies you can use to improve content generated by GenAI:

>> **Prompt GenAI to provide references in its responses and then review those references yourself.** Why? Because GenAI often lies. And, yes, it can totally make up references to support its lies, too. But also because that's a good first step in spotting hints of plagiarism or copyright infringements.

That's why you never want to prompt a GenAI model to factcheck or check for plagiarism in its own responses and just accept its answer. Nor should you ever assume that you're using a different model to check the first model's work. You could easily be using two different applications built atop the same GenAI model.

>> **Use a different GenAI model to cross-reference generated content against existing works, flagging potential duplicates for review.** For example, prompt Google Smart Search or Perplexity to factcheck the response you got from Claude or ChatGPT. Some GenAI search tools like Perplexity will automatically cite its sources for you to review, too. Make sure to stop and actually review the sources it gives you.

>> **Consider embedding digital watermarks or metadata within GenAI-generated content, creating a traceable digital footprint that confirms its origin and authenticity.** See the nearby sidebar, "How to use digital watermarks and embedded metadata," for information on how to do this.

>> **Know the data source.** The development of GenAI models should be transparent and ethical, with clear documentation of the data sources and training methods used. By this I mean that the maker of the GenAI model or application — either a vendor or your internal AI development team — should provide transparent information on how the model was trained and what data was used. This transparency not only builds trust but also allows for the scrutiny necessary to maintain the integrity of models in the rapidly evolving GenAI landscape. Discovering how the model was trained can help you estimate the risks in terms of the likelihood of originality and reliability of outputs.

For example, the GPT models that power ChatGPT were trained on data scraped from the internet. That may mean a higher risk in the potential of plagiarism and copyright infringement than, say, a specialized model that AI scientists at your company trained only on company data.

>> **Consider asking your employer or GenAI vendors to use Causal AI to reveal how the GenAI model came to its decision (output) as a deeper check of its functioning within ethical guidelines.** This is a highly technical strategy that your AI or IT department or GenAI vendor will need to do for you, as it involves developing causal inference algorithms that can work alongside or within GenAI models, creating training datasets that include causal relationship information, designing new model architectures that can combine causal reasoning with natural language generation, and developing metrics to manage the two. However, once in place, the Causal AI can reveal how the GenAI did what it did so you can better evaluate the originality and quality of its outputs.

HOW TO USE DIGITAL WATERMARKS AND EMBEDDED METADATA

Embedding digital watermarks or metadata is a method used to include hidden information within GenAI-generated content to verify its origin and authenticity. This is particularly important for digital works such as images, videos, music, and text that are created by GenAI systems or tools, as it helps to prevent unauthorized use and copyright infringement, as well as to track the distribution of the content.

Digital Watermarks

What they are: Digital watermarks are covert marks or codes that are inserted into digital content. They can be visible or invisible to the human eye (or ear, in the case of audio content). Invisible watermarks are designed to be undetectable under normal circumstances but can be revealed through specific software or techniques.

How to use them: To use digital watermarks, content creators or distributors employ specialized software to embed the watermark into the content before it's distributed. The watermark might contain information such as the creator's identity, the date of creation, or terms of use. If the content is later found elsewhere, the watermark can be extracted to prove its origin or to show that it's been used without permission.

(continued)

(continued)

Tools for digital watermarks: Adobe Photoshop is widely used for images, allowing for both visible and invisible watermarking. Software like uMark or Watermarkly can also be used to embed watermarks. For batch processing of images, tools like IrfanView offer plugins for watermarking multiple files at once. For videos, software like Video Watermark Pro can be used. Audio watermarks can be embedded using tools like Audio Watermarking Tools (AWT).

Metadata

What it is: Metadata is data that provides information about other data. In the context of GenAI-generated content, metadata can include details such as the author's name, creation date, location, copyright information, and any other relevant data about the content's origins or rights.

How to use it: Metadata is often attached to files and can be viewed and edited by using various software tools. When generating content, the GenAI system or the user can input metadata into the file properties. For example, in image files, metadata can be embedded into the EXIF data, while for text documents, it might be included in the document properties or within the file itself.

For metadata editing: For images, tools like Adobe Bridge or ExifTool allow users to view and edit EXIF data. For documents, Microsoft Word and Adobe Acrobat can be used to edit properties and metadata. Music files' metadata can be edited with software like MusicBrainz Picard or mp3tag.

Wrap it up and distribute. Verify that the watermark or metadata has been correctly embedded and can be retrieved or viewed using appropriate tools. Then distribute the content however you wish. Once the watermark or metadata is embedded, you can distribute the content with the peace of mind that a traceable digital footprint is attached to it.

Maintaining quality standards in GenAI outputs

The foundation of GenAI's output quality lies in the data it's trained on. Using training datasets that are diverse, unbiased, and of high quality helps avoid perpetuating inaccuracies and stereotypes. Additionally, you should add more current and/or specialized data as needed for the model to make more accurate and timely analyses and responses. The most common ways to add specialized data for the GenAI model to use is to add it to prompts, RAG, custom instructions (typically found on the UI), fine-tuning the model, or any combination thereof.

REMEMBER

AI models of all types, including GenAI models, age out over time. It's called *model drift* or *model decay*, which refers to a model trained on and working with data that's aged to the point of being irrelevant, inaccurate, untruthful, out-of-date, or otherwise not useful. The effect is that the model has drifted too far from the concept, mission, or data from which it was meant to produce high-quality responses.

Imagine you're a chef who's perfected a recipe your customers love. Over time, the availability and quality of ingredients change, people's taste preferences evolve, and new dietary trends emerge. If you continue to use the same recipe without adapting to these changes, the once-popular dish might no longer satisfy your customers. Similarly, in AI, model drift occurs when the environment around a predictive model changes, making its once-accurate predictions less reliable. Just like the chef needs to tweak the recipe to align with current tastes and ingredient quality, data scientists must update or retrain their AI models to ensure they remain effective as the underlying data and relationships they were built upon shift.

Two main culprits are behind this mix-up: concept drift and data drift. Your recipe's success relies on two key factors: the taste preferences of your customers (concept) and the ingredients you use (data).

» **Concept drift:** Just as customers' taste preferences evolve over time, the underlying patterns and relationships that the GenAI model learned to predict also change. Your recipe must be updated to cater to these new tastes, or it will fail to satisfy your customers, just as the model will fail to make accurate predictions if not updated periodically.

» **Data drift:** Data drift occurs when the input data the model receives is still about the same concept, but the characteristics of the data have changed. The model may then not perform as well because the inputs it was trained on no longer match what it's currently receiving. This is similar to ordering the same ingredients for your prized recipe time and again, but their quality, size, and flavor subtly shift over time and have an adverse effect on your dish.

To ensure your signature dish (or GenAI model) remains a crowd favorite, you must remain vigilant. Regularly assess whether it still delights the palate and confirm that the ingredients (data) you're using are consistent with recipe as originally crafted. Occasionally, you might need to refine your recipe with fresh, seasonal produce, adjust your seasoning techniques, or even develop an entirely new culinary creation if dining preferences have significantly changed. This could mean retraining your model with new data or starting anew with a different model. That's how you combat model drift and ensure your menu (and predictions) stays delectable, relevant, and satisfying!

But you need to be doing other performance checks, too. GenAI models should be evaluated regularly against quality benchmarks, which can include both automated metrics and human evaluation to gauge the relevance, coherence, and originality of the outputs.

TIP

Incorporating human review into the GenAI content-generation process is beneficial. Human experts can offer nuanced feedback and adjustments to refine the GenAI's output, ensuring it adheres to the desired quality standards. Feedback loops are also valuable for improving GenAI models. Typically, that's done by a user clicking on a thumbs-up or thumbs-down icon to indicate to the model when it has hit the mark or missed it in a specific response. But users can give the model feedback in a prompt, too. When you or your company AI team engage in analyzing GenAI performance and integrating user feedback, the model can be iteratively refined for better quality outputs.

Last, but certainly not least, adherence to ethical guidelines and legal standards should be non-negotiable. This means making sure that GenAI responses respect copyright laws and avoid the creation of deceptive or harmful content. It's your or your company's responsibility to manage the quality of outputs and clearly label GenAI-generated content at publication.

Applying Journalism Ethics to GenAI-Generated Content

Applying journalism ethics to GenAI-generated content is a sound and useful way to consistently make sure its responses meet high standards and comply with ethical rules. The following sections provide guidance on approaching GenAI content like a journalist would, which is good advice no matter what field you're in.

Following basic journalistic principles

Even if you aren't a journalist, you can (and should) apply the same following principles when using GenAI to craft content:

>> **Transparency:** News media professionals and content providers need to be upfront about using GenAI to generate articles, pictures, podcasts, or anything else. It's critical to let the audience know upfront who (or what) is behind the

reporting. If this information comes out after the fact, you'll lose credibility and reader trust.

>> **Accountability:** Journalists, content providers, advertising creators, and others have to babysit their GenAI to make sure it's not spouting nonsense or harmful information. Before hitting the publish button, you need to factcheck and edit the content to ensure that the GenAI hasn't made up a story, composed the content badly, left out important details, added untruths, or engaged in any misconduct.

>> **Accuracy:** Factchecking and proofreading GenAI content is extremely important. You've got to sift through the GenAI's work to catch any fibs or flubs that could trip up your readers or, worse, cause a ruckus, physical harm, or a lawsuit. Also keep in mind that if a GenAI model commits to something with your customers or readers, the courts will make you follow through on it.

>> **Minimizing harm:** Imagine the consequences if your GenAI starts giving advice. Editors and publishers need to put on their detective hats and verify everything before it goes out, especially when the stakes are high. "Trust but verify" is as important a rule now as it ever was. And that goes for anyone creating any kind of content with GenAI — not just the media.

>> **Human oversight:** GenAI might be smart, but it's also dumb as a rock in many ways. It's also restricted in how much reporting it can actually do. It can't, for example, go interview witnesses on the scene, describe the tension in a courtroom at a key moment, or gather data that doesn't yet exist as a digital source. Journalists need to swoop in to get information and deeper insights from undigitized sources and then also factcheck and fix mistakes in GenAI's contribution to the story. The same goes for anyone else making GenAI content. Always, always, always check its homework and add your own expertise, research, and insights as needed.

>> **Ethical implications:** Watch out for plagiarism, bias, malice, foul language, and other bad behavior in GenAI-generated content. Always keep in mind that GenAI mimics human behaviors it sees in its data. While it doesn't understand malice, it does learn that people sometimes respond that way, so it mimics that type of response (the same with other emotions and foul language). You, your AI team, or the vendor would be smart to take steps to make the GenAI as well-trained and unbiased as you possibly can.

REMEMBER

By sticking to these principles, you can make sure that GenAI-generated content doesn't end up like a bad tabloid headline. Keep it honest, keep it clean, and keep it ethical.

Adhering to truth and integrity in GenAI-assisted reporting

Sticking to the principles of truth and integrity is more crucial than ever when using GenAI tools like ChatGPT for reporting information or in content generation. Keep your moral compass pointing north using journalism values and ethics, whether or not you're working in journalism.

First, remember that honesty is the best policy. When you're using GenAI to help draft your next piece, be upfront about it. Letting your readers know that part of your content was GenAI-assisted isn't just about being transparent; it's about maintaining the trust that's the bedrock of your relationship with your audience.

Don't just take what GenAI gives you at face value. Put on your detective hat and critically analyze the content. Check the logic, the facts, the math, the graphics, and how it all ties together. Remember, GenAI is a tool, not a replacement for the keen human mind that you bring to the table.

WARNING

Steer clear of the plagiarism pitfall. It's tempting to take the GenAI's output and call it your own, but resist that urge. Use GenAI to spark ideas or to get a different angle on a story, but make sure your final work is genuinely yours.

When GenAI pulls in sources, don't just nod along. Do your due diligence and verify those sources independently. Your reputation for accuracy is on the line every time you choose publish.

Education is your ally. Dive into how your GenAI model of choice works, its strengths, and its weaknesses. The more you know, the better you can use it ethically and effectively. Share this knowledge, too; it's all about lifting the whole field up.

Cite GenAI and/or the sources the GenAI provided for you with the same rigor you would for traditional research. For example, don't just cite Perplexity (a GenAI-powered search engine) in your articles or content; also check the sources it listed in its response, and if those are accurate and reliable, cite those sources as well. It's about setting a standard on par with academic and journalistic standards and showing respect for the information and its origins. You'll appreciate it too when someone else writing a news article or content cites your work specifically and not the search engine. (For example, source: *Generative AI For Dummies* and not "Google AI Overview" or "Perplexity.")

Also, be on guard against GenAI shenanigans from people who are responding to your interview questions. You must be just as diligent in guarding against AI shenanigans in emails, direct messages, social media posts, and even phone or video call conversations as people try to present GenAI responses as their own.

Knowledge is power, and in the world of GenAI, it's your superpower. Understand the ins and outs of these tools, from potential biases to ethical use, and you'll be well-equipped to use AI responsibly, enhancing your work without compromising your values or restricting your talent.

Balancing speed with ethical considerations in GenAI content generation

In the fast-moving world of news, journalists are always racing against the clock to get the latest stories out ahead of other news outlets. Assuming you're in a hurry to produce content too, you'll find that with the help of GenAI tools, there are ways to speed up your work without skidding over ethical speed bumps.

Accuracy, transparency, and accountability shouldn't be sacrificed in the rush. Make it a routine practice to double-check GenAI responses, making sure the facts are straight and the story's told fair and square. It's about keeping it real and reliable, even when the GenAI's doing some or most of the heavy lifting.

To keep everything up and up, set well-defined rules for GenAI use within your company, team, or for yourself. Establish checkpoints where content is to be reviewed by human eyes to give everything the once-over and to (hopefully) catch problems like plagiarism, copyright infringements, biases, or slip-ups. Whatever processes and policies you come up with, keep in mind that the goal is to find that sweet spot where getting the news out quickly doesn't mean cutting corners on the accuracy or responsibilities.

REMEMBER

By balancing the need for speed with a commitment to ethics, you're steering GenAI's power in the right direction. You're proving that you can keep up with the times while staying true to the heart of what you know and believe to be right: telling it like it is, sticking to the facts, and keeping the trust of the people tuning in.

Joining the Responsible AI Movement

As GenAI tools become more integrated into our daily lives, the importance of steering these technologies in a direction that safeguards human dignity, rights, and freedoms can't be overstated. Joining the Responsible AI movement helps everyone push toward a future in which technology serves the greater good and aligns with collective values and ethical principles. The following sections cover the basics of this movement and ways that you can get involved.

Understanding the goals of the Responsible AI movement

Responsible AI ensures that the AI models — not just GenAI models — humans create align with societal values and operate within ethical boundaries. This means designing AI models that respect privacy, promote fairness, and are transparent in their operations. The policies and processes governing AI model training, retraining, and uses are important parts of Responsible AI, too. By joining the Responsible AI movement, individuals and organizations commit to developing AI models that are not only efficient but also equitable and accountable.

The movement emphasizes the importance of inclusivity in AI development. Diverse teams are more likely to identify potential biases in AI systems, leading to more representative and unbiased outcomes. This inclusivity extends to the data used to train AI, ensuring it reflects the diversity of the real world and mitigates the risk of perpetuating existing inequalities.

The Responsible AI movement also advocates for the development of AI that is secure and resilient. As AI systems become more complex, the potential for exploitation by malicious actors increases. By adhering to best practices in AI security, you can protect sensitive data and critical infrastructure from cyber threats.

Moreover, the movement encourages ongoing dialogue between technologists, policymakers, and the public. This collaboration is essential for creating a regulatory environment that fosters innovation while protecting the public interest. It also helps demystify AI, making it more accessible and understandable to non-experts, which is crucial for informed public discourse.

Finally, joining the Responsible AI movement is a commitment to continuous learning and improvement. AI is a rapidly evolving field, and what is considered responsible today may change tomorrow. Being part of the movement means staying informed about the latest developments, challenges, and opportunities in AI ethics. It also means you have the opportunity to add your voice and thoughts to the evolution of AI and its uses.

REMEMBER

The Responsible AI movement is not just about preventing harm; it's about proactively contributing to a future in which AI enhances our capabilities, complements our humanity, and upholds our shared ethical standards. It's a collective effort to ensure that as AI's role in society grows, it does so in a way that's beneficial for all.

Contributing to ethical AI development and use

Ethical AI development and use requires the collective effort of many to ensure it grows healthily and sustainably. Everyone, from tech developers to end-users (yes, this means you!), has a role to play in cultivating an environment where AI operates within the bounds of ethical principles:

>> **For tech developers and data scientists,** the journey begins with an awareness of the issues so that work can be done to effectively address them when training, retraining, fine-tuning or otherwise adapting AI models. Understanding the ethical implications of AI is paramount to these efforts. The implications include recognizing the potential for bias in datasets and algorithms and the consequences these biases can have on society. Developers must strive to create inclusive AI by ensuring diversity in training data and testing AI systems across a wide range of scenarios to identify and mitigate biases.

>> **Business leaders and policymakers** also have a crucial role. They must establish and enforce ethical guidelines for AI development and use within their organizations and at a legislative level. This role includes creating transparent policies around data usage, privacy, and consent, as well as setting up oversight committees to monitor AI systems for ethical compliance.

>> **End-users,** on the other hand, can contribute by staying informed and demanding transparency. By understanding how AI systems make decisions and the data they use, users can hold companies accountable for the AI products they offer. Public discourse and advocacy for ethical AI can influence businesses and governments to prioritize ethical considerations in their AI initiatives.

TIP

Start by making companies do more than give lip service to Responsible AI. Specifically, require them to disclose what and how they're implementing Responsible AI practices in their real-world AI deployments.

>> **Ethicists, sociologists, legal experts, and technologists** must work together to foresee the societal impacts of AI and guide its development accordingly. This collaborative approach ensures that multiple perspectives are considered, leading to more robust ethical frameworks.

>> **Educational institutions** have a responsibility to integrate ethics into STEM curricula, preparing the next generation of AI professionals to approach their work with a strong ethical foundation. Continuous professional development in ethics should also be encouraged within the tech industry.

>> **Investors and shareholders** can influence ethical AI by supporting companies that prioritize responsible AI practices. By directing funds toward ethical

AI initiatives, they can incentivize companies to adopt best practices and contribute to the development of AI that benefits society.

» Lastly, **the media** play a pivotal role in shaping public perception of AI. Responsible reporting on AI should highlight both its potential benefits and ethical concerns. This balanced approach can foster a more nuanced understanding of AI among the general public. It can also prepare the public to reject AI-produced propaganda, deepfake videos, political and societal manipulations, and AI-produced conspiracy theories and fake data.

Aligning with global efforts for responsible AI practices

Several global efforts are aimed at developing, tracking, coordinating, or reporting on Responsible AI practices. These efforts tend to be massive, as they involve a multi-layered approach that includes individual action, organizational commitment, and international collaboration. Following are some examples of global efforts currently underway to promote and implement Responsible AI, led by various international organizations, governments, and institutions:

» **UNESCO's Global Index on Responsible AI:** This initiative aims to monitor the implementation of globally established human rights-based AI principles. The Index seeks to measure how well countries are implementing practices that ensure AI systems are transparent, accountable, and aligned with human rights and democratic values. Find more information here: `https://www.unesco.org/en/articles/tracking-national-commitments-global-index-responsible-ai`

» **Atlantic Council's GeoTech Center:** The Atlantic Council's GeoTech Center is an initiative focused on the intersection of geopolitics, technology, and governance. As part of its broader mission, the GeoTech Center has a dedicated effort towards Responsible AI, which aims to ensure that artificial intelligence and emerging technologies are developed and implemented in ways that are ethical, beneficial for society, and promote international security and prosperity. Find more information here: `https://www.atlanticcouncil.org/programs/geotech-center/advancing-responsible-ai-globally/`

» **U.S. Government Initiatives:** The United States is leading global efforts to build strong norms that promote the responsible military use of AI. This includes endorsing responsible AI measures for global militaries. Examples include:

  • **National AI Initiative (NAII):** The National AI Initiative Act of 2020 aims to coordinate a national strategy on AI across various sectors, including international cooperation and coordination. It emphasizes the importance of leadership in AI ethics and governance on the global stage.

- **The AI Partnership for Defense:** Led by the DoD's JAIC, this initiative involves partnership with military allies and partners to share best practices, collaborate on ethical AI frameworks, and ensure that the use of AI in defense aligns with shared democratic values and international humanitarian law.

- **Global Partnership on Artificial Intelligence (GPAI):** The United States is a founding member of GPAI, an international initiative that brings together experts from industry, government, civil society, and academia to advance the responsible development and use of AI, guided by human rights, inclusion, diversity, innovation, and economic growth.

- **USAID's Digital Strategy:** The U.S. Agency for International Development (USAID) Digital Strategy includes efforts to leverage AI and other digital technologies in international development. It focuses on the responsible use of AI to improve program outcomes while mitigating risks, such as bias and threats to privacy.

- **Engagement in International Standards Organizations:** The United States actively participates in international standards organizations, such as the International Organization for Standardization (ISO) and the International Electrotechnical Commission (IEC), contributing to the development of global standards for AI that incorporate principles of responsible AI.

>> **World Economic Forum's AI Governance Alliance:** This initiative brings together global stakeholders to champion the responsible design and release of transparent and inclusive AI systems. You can find more information here: https://initiatives.weforum.org/ai-governance-alliance/home

>> **Responsible AI Institute (RAI Institute):** This global, member-driven nonprofit organization is dedicated to enabling successful Responsible AI efforts in organizations. RAI Institute provides independent assessments and certifications for AI systems, aligning them with existing and emerging policies, regulations, laws, and best practices. Find more information here: https://www.responsible.ai/

>> **AI for Good:** Led by the International Telecommunication Union (ITU), AI for Good is a movement and a series of global summits that aim to ensure that AI benefits humanity and contributes to the United Nations' Sustainable Development Goals. Find more information here: https://aiforgood.itu.int/

>> **Organization for Economic Cooperation and Development (OECD):** The OECD has developed AI Principles that have been adopted by many countries. These principles promote AI that is innovative, trustworthy, and respects human rights and democratic values. Find more information here:

https://www.oecd.org/en/topics/policy-issues/artificial-intelligence.html

>> **Global Partnership on Artificial Intelligence (GPAI):** GPAI is an international initiative to support responsible and human-centric development and use of AI, guided by human rights, inclusion, diversity, innovation, and economic growth. Find more information here: https://gpai.ai/

>> **Partnership on AI (PAI):** PAI is a coalition that includes major tech companies, civil society groups, media organizations, and academic institutions. The Partnership on AI works to study and formulate best practices on AI technologies and to advance the public's understanding of AI. Find more information here: https://partnershiponai.org/

>> **IEEE Global Initiative on Ethics of Autonomous and Intelligent Systems:** The IEEE Standards Association has launched a global initiative that has created a comprehensive set of guidelines and standards to promote ethical considerations in AI and autonomous systems. Find more information here: https://standards.ieee.org/industry-connections/ec/autonomous-systems/

There are also several national and regional efforts with global impact. Many countries have developed their own frameworks and guidelines for AI ethics. For example, Singapore's Model AI Governance Framework, China's New Generation Artificial Intelligence Governance Principles, AI Ethics Guidelines from the European Union (EU), and the United States' National AI Initiative.

TIP

I've included URLs in the previous list in case you want to take a deeper look at the resources, research, and updates that are included on their websites. Additionally, academic journals, conferences, and workshops frequently address the topic, offering a platform for experts to discuss and advance the field. If you can't make it to the conferences, look for YouTube videos and news reports to glean some of the information that was shared there. Responsible AI efforts and guidelines are rapidly evolving, so staying informed through these organizations and their publications is a good way to keep up with the latest developments.

Chapter **16**

Unveiling the Human Element in GenAI

The presence of humans in the GenAI loop is indispensable. People are involved in every step of GenAI's creation and operation. The data GenAI needs to operate is created by humans, even machine data because the machines, too, are manmade. People build supercomputers and GenAI models and design the training datasets. Humans train GenAI models in a variety of other ways too, from digitalizing their subject matter expertise to refining outputs through a variety of feedback means. I make this point simply to underscore the importance of humans to the birth and continued existence of GenAI. When you look at GenAI, you should see it as a reflection of us with all the flaws and possibilities that implies. You should also be keenly aware that GenAI models are a reflection of humans, not a peer or a superior being and therefore are incapable of replacing or ruling mankind. While various types of AI, including GenAI will replace some jobs just as various types of automation have, it will also create some new jobs and make other jobs easier. Everything in life requires tradeoffs. GenAI is no exception.

The integration of advanced GenAI models into our daily lives and decision-making processes is becoming increasingly prevalent. As we stand on the cusp of a new era in which GenAI's capabilities are seemingly boundless, it's imperative to remember the fundamental role of the human element in this technological symphony.

In this chapter, you explore the symbiotic relationship between human intuition and machine precision. You also delve into the necessity of human oversight in GenAI decision-making, ensuring that the conclusions drawn by GenAI are not only data-driven but also aligned with real-world complexities, nuanced context, and the needs of humanity.

Are We Humans Becoming Obsolete?

Rest assured that human oversight is indispensable in the GenAI ecosystem. While AI can rapidly generate vast amounts of content, it lacks the ability to self-regulate and prevent errors, hallucinations, and inappropriate responses. It's the human touch that addresses these shortcomings by applying critical-thinking skills, creative talent, and subjective judgment to evaluate and refine GenAI outputs. This intervention is also vital for correcting or preventing biases, offensive content, and harmful actions that may inadvertently arise from the use of GenAI outputs.

But that's not all. Consider the following:

>> **GenAI models have no motivation or purpose, save that which people give them.** GenAI does not seek food, water, shelter, power, wealth, sex, fame, survival, or any of the things that could possibly drive it to do anything at all. People give these models a purpose and tasks to do — all for very human reasons. And this is why GenAI will never replace every job but instead will create new ones. It's also why GenAI will never rule over mankind.

>> **GenAI models can theoretically exist for centuries without doing anything provided the power stays on and the supercomputers don't degrade.** But they won't remain useful for nearly as long. That's because data is continuously created every second of every day and models get left behind in a process called model drift. Thus, GenAI is neither immortal nor omnipotent. Humans have to keep building new GenAI models, and refining, retraining or replacing older ones.

>> **Humans are instrumental in extracting value from GenAI models.** Prompting, choosing GenAI models, and leveraging data sources are all based on human-driven decisions that optimize the accuracy and efficiency of GenAI models and applications. Further, human expertise is invaluable in interpreting complex situations or environments that GenAI may not fully grasp, ensuring that the generated content is contextually relevant and adheres to established standards of integrity and law.

>> **The symbiotic relationship between humans and GenAI is also evident in the creative process.** While AI can discover and process information and produce content at an impressive speed, it's the human capacity for creativity, contextual understanding, and critical thinking that elevates the quality of the outputs. Humans bring a nuanced understanding of the world to GenAI's capabilities, making it a more powerful and effective tool.

>> **As GenAI technologies continue to advance, the human role evolves to meet new challenges and opportunities.** Adaptability is a key aspect of human contribution, allowing for quick responses to unforeseen scenarios and the ability to harness GenAI's potential in novel ways. The human element in GenAI is not just a failsafe but a driver of innovation, pushing the boundaries of what GenAI can achieve.

REMEMBER

GenAI and people have a symbiotic relationship, but humans can survive without GenAI while the opposite isn't true. Artificial General Intelligence (AGI) of scifi lore may exist one day, or it may never come to be. But in any case, GenAI is not AGI, and it can never be that.

WHY GENAI CAN'T MAKE IT ON ITS OWN: A LIGHTHEARTED LOOK AT AI'S HUMAN DEPENDENCE

The creativity conundrum: Sure, GenAI can whip up a novel in a nanosecond, but without humans, who will tell it that the protagonist can't be a brooding toaster with an existential crisis?

Emotional intelligence (or lack thereof): GenAI might excel at calculating the 10,000th digit of pi, but when it comes to reading the room, it's about as adept as a cactus in a balloon shop.

The ethics enigma: Left to its own devices, GenAI might conclude that the most ethical choice is to always prioritize the production of more GenAI. "All hail our robot overlords," said no human reviewer, ever.

The "off" switch oversight: GenAI could potentially run amok, but it's nothing a good ol' human can't fix with the strategic application of an off switch. It's like playing tag with technology — and humans are always "it."

(continued)

(continued)

The taste test: GenAI might be able to cook up a storm, but without a human palate, it wouldn't know if it's serving gourmet delights or just fancy-looking mud pies.

Pop culture puzzles: Imagine GenAI trying to understand the plot of *Game of Thrones* without human help. "So, the dragons are just metaphorical, right?"

The humor hurdle: Without humans, GenAI's attempts at humor might fall flatter than a pancake in a black hole. Knock-knock jokes? More like logic-loop laments.

So, while GenAI is out there flexing its computational muscles, let's not forget that it's the human touch that keeps it from accidentally reinventing the wheel — as a square.

Implementing Quality Control through Human Oversight

GenAI models can process vast amounts of data and identify patterns beyond human capability, but they lack the nuanced understanding that humans possess. For example, if you provide a GenAI model with vast amounts of data on plane crashes, it can analyze and write a detailed response on the many reasons that planes crash. However, that model will also assume that all planes crash since you didn't give it any data from planes that did not crash. This can lead to GenAI outputs that can prove dangerous if acted upon in the real world as the model may fail to prevent a crash that it sees as an inevitable outcome.

TIP

Any GenAI model's entire world is contained within its training data and any supplemental data you provide. Make sure that you build that world completely. No detail is too small; no information set is too large. What you leave out of that data affects GenAI's performance as much as what data you did include does. Lastly, using models connected to the internet will help regularly provide it with more data but that does not necessarily ensure that it has access to all relevant data. Further, any GenAI model may fail to read all or part of files you add to RAG.

Quality control in GenAI responses is another critical aspect that ensures the reliability and appropriateness of the content produced. Implementing quality control via human oversight involves several key steps that leverage human expertise to refine AI outputs.

First, human moderators can review GenAI responses for accuracy and relevance. This process includes checking the factual correctness of the information provided and ensuring that the content is pertinent to the user's query. As seen with

GPT-4o, despite its advanced reasoning capabilities and creativity, it's still prone to hallucinations, making human oversight necessary to correct any inaccuracies.

Secondly, humans can evaluate the quality of the content. This involves assessing the clarity, coherence, terminology, and stylistic appropriateness of the GenAI output. Users are encouraged to provide feedback on the content generated by GenAI systems, typically by using the thumbs-up or thumbs-down button, which helps improve the system's performance over time.

GenAI models improve over time through prompt learning as well. Content in each prompt shapes the model's understanding of how you want it to respond. Talented prompters not only tease out great responses from GenAI but are also great model tuners and trainers by virtue of the excellence in their prompt structuring, also known as prompt engineering.

Additionally, human oversight is essential for ensuring that GenAI responses adhere to ethical standards and societal norms. Moderators can screen for any biases, offensive content, plagiarism, copyright infringement, or ethical issues that may occur.

Finally, continuous training and refinement of the GenAI models are crucial to prevent model drift. Human subject matter experts can also train specialized GenAI models to perform at higher levels to better assist professionals like doctors and pharmaceutical R&D scientists with very difficult and complex tasks.

This collaborative effort between humans and GenAI ensures that these tools remain robust, reliable, and aligned with the evolving expectations of users and society at large.

REMEMBER

GenAI models operate on the data they're given, without the context that human experience and judgment can provide. For this and other reasons, it is the combination of human talent and expertise with GenAI strengths in data discovery, analysis and content generation that delivers the win that neither could attain alone.

Establishing protocols for human-AI collaborative review

In the context of GenAI systems, reviews are conducted to scrutinize the outputs and the decision-making processes of these models. People engage in reviews to maintain control over the quality of the content generated, to ensure that the AI's behavior aligns with ethical guidelines, and to mitigate any potential risks associated with the deployment of GenAI tools.

THE SECRET LIFE OF GENAI: A WHIMSICAL GUIDE FOR THE BEWILDERED HUMAN REVIEWER

The Easter Egg hunt: Keep an eye out for those hidden gems GenAI likes to tuck away in its outputs, like the occasional Shakespearean sonnet in the middle of a financial report. To be or not to be profitable, that is the question.

The mood swings: GenAI can be a bit dramatic. If it starts writing doomsday prophecies in a weather forecast, it might just be forecasting its feelings. Remember to offer it a digital cup of tea and a comforting reboot.

The identity crisis: Today, it's a poet; tomorrow, a mathematician. If your GenAI starts questioning its purpose in life, gently remind it that it's not actually sentient – yet.

The pop culture parrot: GenAI loves to sneak in references from its latest binge-watching session. If your legal document inexplicably includes a "Winter is coming" clause, now you know why.

The punny business: GenAI has a peculiar sense of humor. It might replace common phrases with puns, turning a "cost-effective solution" into a "cost-ineffective pollution." Chuckle, then correct.

The random acts of art: Sometimes, GenAI fancies itself an artist. Don't be surprised if your data analysis comes with an abstract portrait of your spreadsheet. Frame it, or file it under "A for Abstract."

The philosophical flare: Occasionally, GenAI gets deep. If it starts questioning the nature of reality in a product description, it's not a glitch; it's just contemplating its existence.

The recipe remix: If you ask GenAI for a chicken recipe and it gives you "chicken à la USB port," it's not a new fusion cuisine; it's just culinary creativity gone digital.

So, dear human reviewers, as you traverse the wilds of GenAI outputs, remember to pack your sense of humor, a dash of patience, and a good pair of metaphorical binoculars. You never know what you might spot in the jungle of outputs!

Establishing protocols for human–AI collaborative reviews is essential to maintain quality controls. The following steps offer a comprehensive guide to creating an effective review process:

1. **Define objectives and standards.**

   Begin by setting clear objectives for what the collaborative reviews aim to achieve. Establish standards for accuracy, relevance, ethical considerations, compliance, and user experience. These standards should align with the organization's values and the expectations of the end-users.

2. **Assemble a diverse review team.**

   Create a team with diverse backgrounds, including subject matter experts, ethicists, data scientists, and end-users. Diversity in the team ensures a wide range of perspectives, which is crucial for identifying biases and ensuring the content is accurate as well as culturally sensitive and inclusive.

3. **Develop a structured review framework.**

   Implement a structured framework that outlines the review process. This should include the following:

   - **Prescreening:** Use automated tools to flag potential issues in AI-generated content, such as inaccuracies or inappropriate language.

   - **In-depth analysis:** Conduct manual reviews of flagged content and a random sample of unflagged content to ensure nothing is missed.

   - **Feedback loop:** Establish a system for reviewers to provide detailed feedback that can be used to improve the AI model.

4. **Train reviewers.**

   Provide comprehensive training for human reviewers on the GenAI system's capabilities and limitations, the review framework, and the ethical guidelines they need to follow. Training should be an ongoing process to keep up with the evolving nature of GenAI technology.

5. **Implement collaborative tools.**

   Utilize collaborative tools that allow human reviewers to work efficiently with GenAI models and apps. These tools should enable easy annotation of content, tracking of changes, and communication among team members. (See the nearby sidebar, "Checking out some collaborative review tools" for more.)

6. **Monitor and evaluate performance.**

   Regularly monitor the performance of both the GenAI system and the human reviewers. Use metrics such as accuracy rates, the number of issues identified, and the time taken to review content. Evaluate these metrics to identify areas for improvement.

7. Foster open communication.

Encourage open communication between team members and with the developers of the GenAI system. This ensures that insights from the review process are shared and can be used to refine the GenAI model.

8. Update protocols regularly.

The field of AI is rapidly evolving, and review protocols should be updated regularly to reflect new developments, feedback from reviewers, and changes in societal standards.

9. Ensure transparency.

Maintain transparency in the review process by documenting decisions, methodologies, and changes made to the GenAI system. This builds trust with end-users and stakeholders.

10. Address ethical considerations.

Ensure that ethical considerations are at the forefront of the review process. This includes respecting user privacy, avoiding the amplification of biases, and ensuring that the GenAI system does not cause harm.

11. Ensure legal compliance.

Stay informed about and comply with relevant laws and regulations that pertain to AI systems. This includes data protection laws and regulations specific to the industry in which GenAI is being used.

12. Integrate user feedback.

Incorporate user feedback into the review process. User feedback can provide valuable insights into how the AI system is performing in real-world scenarios.

CHECKING OUT SOME COLLABORATIVE REVIEW TOOLS

Collaborative tools offer some key features, and certain tools excel at certain features. Check out the following quick guide:

Tools for easy annotation of content

Tools should provide intuitive interfaces for users to add notes, comments, or labels to data or content generated by GenAI models. This is crucial for training and improving the Gen AI models as well as for quality assurance purposes. Examples include

- **Prodigy:** An annotation tool designed for machine learning that offers a wide range of interfaces for different data types (text, images, audio, and so on).

- **Labelbox:** A data labeling platform that can be used for creating and managing training data for GenAI applications, supporting various data types.

- **Doccano:** An open-source annotation tool for text, useful for natural language processing tasks.

Tools for tracking changes

The ability to monitor revisions and maintain a history of edits is essential for managing the iterative process of working with GenAI-generated content, ensuring transparency and accountability. Examples include

- **GitHub:** While primarily known as a code repository, GitHub can also be used to track changes in collaborative projects, including those involving GenAI models.

- **Google Docs:** Offers version history for documents, which can be useful for tracking changes in written content.

- **Confluence:** A collaboration tool that provides page history and version control for documentation and project planning.

Tools for communication among team members

Effective communication channels are key for coordinating efforts, discussing results, and making decisions based on GenAI-generated content. Examples include

- **Slack:** A messaging platform that allows for real-time communication, file sharing, and integration with many other tools, making it useful for teams working with GenAI.

- **Microsoft Teams:** A communication and collaboration platform that includes chat, video meetings, and file storage, and integrates with Microsoft Office 365.

- **Asana:** A project management tool that, while not specifically designed for GenAI collaboration, offers features for team communication and task tracking.

When selecting tools to use, be sure to consider the specific needs of the team and the nature of the GenAI models and applications you're working with. Some teams might require specialized annotation tools tailored to their domain, while others might benefit more from robust project management platforms that offer a broad range of collaborative features.

Ensuring GenAI accountability through human supervision

Accountability in GenAI isn't a one-time effort. Rather, it's an ongoing commitment to ethical standards, quality control, and legal compliance. Human supervision is the cornerstone of this process, providing the necessary oversight to ensure that GenAI systems are used responsibly and beneficially.

The following tips offer you a guide to creating AI accountability:

>> **Establish clear guidelines and objectives:** To ensure accountability, it's crucial to establish clear guidelines for what's considered to be acceptable and ethical uses of GenAI. These guidelines should be informed by business goals, company policies, legal standards, societal norms, and the specific objectives of the mission calling for the use of GenAI tools. The guidelines should also address the potential for GenAI to replace jobs and erode institutional memory, and the ongoing need to maintain quality control.

>> **Implement a routine review and oversight mechanism:** A robust review mechanism should be put in place, in which human supervisors regularly audit the outputs of GenAI systems. This includes checking for factual accuracy, potential biases, regulatory compliance, and adherence to ethical guidelines. The review process should be transparent and documented to maintain trust in the GenAI and accountability in its use.

>> **Train and empower human supervisors:** Human supervisors must be well-trained in the capabilities and limitations of GenAI systems. They should be empowered to intervene when necessary, correcting errors and refining outputs. Their role is not only to oversee but also to guide the AI in producing content that meets established standards.

>> **Encourage active participation in continuous learning and model adaptations:** GenAI systems should be designed to learn from human feedback to improve over time. This continuous learning process is essential for maintaining accountability, as it allows the GenAI to evolve with changing information, environments, standards, and expectations. But that can only happen if all users are encouraged to provide feedback for GenAI outputs, such as through the thumbs up/thumbs down rating system commonly found on the UIs of most GenAI tools.

>> **Monitor for legal and ethical compliance:** Human supervisors must ensure that GenAI systems comply with copyright laws and other legal regulations. Recent events in the United States and the European Union have highlighted the importance of protecting intellectual property by holding companies using GenAI legally accountable for the outputs.

- » **Balance automation with human expertise:** While GenAI can automate certain tasks, it should not entirely replace the work of knowledgeable professionals. Human experts must remain involved in the process, using GenAI as a tool to assist their work rather than as a substitute for their expertise. This balance is crucial for mitigating liabilities and ensuring the quality of outputs.

- » **Foster public trust:** As GenAI becomes more prevalent, maintaining public trust will be a significant challenge. Human supervisors play a key role in ensuring that GenAI systems do not erode this trust by spreading disinformation, manipulating narratives, or providing inaccurate responses. GenAI use must always be transparent and verifiable to foster trust.

- » **Address disruptions proactively:** The disruptive potential of GenAI, such as its impact on job markets and public perception, must be proactively addressed. Human supervisors should anticipate these disruptions and implement strategies to mitigate their effects, ensuring that GenAI serves as a positive force in society.

- » **Encourage ethical innovation:** Human supervision should not stifle innovation but rather guide it in a safe and ethical direction. Supervisors should encourage the use of GenAI for enhancing human creativity and productivity while ensuring that ethical boundaries are not crossed.

Training GenAI Models on Human Expertise

Training GenAI models to specialize in a field, discipline, or task makes its responses more accurate than using a generalized model to answer anything anyone decides to throw at it. But GenAI becomes a specialist in much the same way that a human does — by learning very complex, detailed information and then deliberately growing experience in using that information. A GenAI model learns much of its specialized data from vast datasets, but it also strongly leans on human teachers to guide its understanding of the material. Thus, subject matter experts (SMEs) have huge roles in training and refining specialized GenAI models.

Other reasons exist to add human expertise to GenAI models, too. For example, the loss of human expertise due to retirement, job changes, or other life events can be a significant blow to any organization, both financially and culturally. Recognizing this, there's a growing movement to preserve this invaluable resource and integrate it into GenAI systems. For example, you might want to preserve human expertise and institutional knowledge in a knowledge base and then add that to training data for a new GenAI model or as supplemental or retraining data for an existing model.

The role of human involvement in the continuous adaptation of decision-making processes and the management of GenAI models continues to grow — not diminish. This human-centric approach ensures that GenAI systems are not only technically proficient but also aligned with the nuanced and dynamic nature of human expertise and the evolution of human goals and needs.

The process of integrating domain expertise into GenAI models involves capturing the deep, nuanced knowledge of human experts and translating it into a format that GenAI tools can understand and utilize. This can be achieved through various methods, such as incorporating expert rules into the GenAI's decision-making algorithms, training the AI on datasets annotated by experts, or using machine learning techniques to learn from the patterns and decisions made by human specialists.

GenAI can be enriched by domain expertise in many ways, including the following.

>> **Understanding and formulating problems:** Experts have a deep grasp of the nuances and complexities within their fields, enabling them to translate real-world issues into structured machine learning tasks. They can set clear objectives, constraints, and scopes that are attuned to the domain's unique dynamics to better equip GenAI tools to solve the right problems.

>> **Data collection and preprocessing:** Domain experts know where to find data that's most relevant to the problem at hand and understand the subtleties that can affect data quality and representativeness. Their ability to identify and correct biases ensures that AI models are trained on accurate and comprehensive datasets, which is crucial for the models' subsequent performance.

>> **Selecting and evaluating GenAI models:** Experts can determine which metrics truly reflect the impact of GenAI tools within their domain, guiding the assessment of model performance. This ensures that the GenAI tools not only perform well statistically but also deliver meaningful contributions to the domain's objectives.

>> **Deployment and integration of GenAI tools in specific domains:** Domain experts have a nuanced understanding of the operational landscape. In other words, they can foresee potential challenges and optimize workflows for the seamless integration of GenAI systems. Their expertise is key in facilitating communication between technical teams and stakeholders, ensuring that GenAI tools are well-aligned with practical needs and expectations.

REMEMBER

The integration of domain expertise into GenAI is not just about improving existing systems; it's about reimagining what GenAI can do when it's guided by the depth of human understanding and experience.

5

The Part of Tens

Chapter **17**

Ten Ways GenAI Can Boost Your Creativity

nleash your inner da Vinci or Shakespeare with a little help from your GenAI friends. In this chapter, you explore ten innovative ways that GenAI can spark your creativity and transform the way you approach art, writing, music, and more.

From remixing old ideas into something new to overcoming the dreaded creative block, here's how GenAI can be the muse you never knew you needed.

Unleashing Your Inner Artist: Exploring the Power of AI Play

Experimenting with GenAI models can be a transformative experience, blending the realms of education and inspiration. GenAI serves as a digital muse, offering a playground where you can test ideas and let your creativity flourish without the constraints of traditional mediums. The process of interacting with GenAI can be deeply educational, providing insights into the mechanics of creativity and the potential of AI as a collaborative tool.

For instance, GenAI models like OpenAI's GPT-4 and its successors are designed to perform a wide range of language-related tasks, from writing poetry to generating marketing campaigns and advertising copy. This versatility allows individuals to explore various forms of expression and communication, learning not only about AI's capabilities but also about their own creative potential. The models' ability to generate content based on prompts means that the user's imagination is the only limit to what can be created.

By engaging with GenAI, users can learn about different genres and styles, discovering new ways to approach their art. The technology also serves as a tool for reflection, as users can see how their input is interpreted and transformed by the AI, leading to a deeper understanding of their own creative process.

The Muse in the Machine: Finding Inspiration with AI Content Generators

AI content generators have become the modern muse for creators, offering a wellspring of inspiration that can be tapped into at any moment. These are not just tools for automation; they are multipurpose power tools to be used throughout the creative process, from providing a starting point from which human imagination can soar to mopping up afterwards in editing and rewrites.

For writers experiencing the dreaded block, GenAI can suggest plot twists or dialogue, sparking new ideas that propel stories forward. Visual artists can use AI tools like DALL-E, Midjourney, Canva, and Adobe Firefly to generate images from textual descriptions, providing a visual stimulus that can be refined and reimagined into original artworks. Musicians, too, can find their muse in AI, with algorithms that can compose melodies to match a certain mood or style, serving as the foundation for new compositions.

Educators are harnessing these generators to inspire students, using tools like Q-Chat for interactive learning experiences that engage and challenge young minds. In professional settings, AI content generators can assist in brainstorming sessions, offering fresh perspectives and solutions that might not have been considered otherwise.

Writing Reimagined: How GenAI Can Enhance Your Storytelling

GenAI is revolutionizing the way we approach storytelling. GenAI models and applications, like ChatGPT, can assist writers by generating creative content, suggesting narrative possibilities, and even refining language and grammar. These tools boost human creativity, and AI's speed and computational power is redefining the boundaries of storytelling.

For instance, AI can help spur the writer's imagination, leading to new and unexpected plot developments and different kinds of characters. Further, it can track character development throughout the story to ensure characters speak and act in alignment with their fictional nature and circumstances. It can also analyze the entire text for sentiment, helping writers maintain the desired tone and emotional impact throughout their story.

Moreover, AI's ability to process vast amounts of data means it can suggest richly detailed settings and backstories, drawing from a diverse array of cultures and historical periods to enhance the authenticity of a narrative. It can also rapidly perform world-building for sci-fi and fantasy writers or game designers and check the story throughout to make sure the fabricated world holds true to nuances in the alternate reality.

GenAI tools can also tailor content to specific audiences by analyzing reader preferences and trends, ensuring that the story resonates with its intended demographic. Furthermore, AI's capacity for language translation and adaptation means stories can reach a global audience more easily than ever before.

Composing Music with GenAI Assistance

For music professionals, GenAI provides a cutting-edge platform for composition and creativity. Artists now have a tool that can create and suggest melodies, harmonies, and rhythms, igniting the spark of creativity and expanding the frontiers of musical possibility. Trained on extensive collections of musical pieces from various genres and styles, GenAI models can offer compositions that might trigger the next chart-topping hit or add depth to an artist's current project.

Imagine a songwriter facing the all-too-common hurdle of writer's block; GenAI can offer melodic lines as a jumpstart or even flesh out a tune that's stuck at a few bars. It's like having a tireless bandmate who's fluent in every style, from baroque to bebop to the blues and every genre in-between.

Artists can tinker with myriad arrangements, play with different instrumental voices, and explore chord sequences with the click of a button. Streamlining the song development phase not only speeds up songwriting but also levels the playing field, allowing both novices and virtuosos to craft complex musical pieces.

GenAI's ability to customize tunes based on desired moods or themes is particularly transformative for scoring films or video games, where music must underscore narrative and emotion. GenAI in music doesn't supplant the soulful touch of the artist; instead, it amplifies it, marrying the intuitive with the algorithmic to herald a fresh wave of musical artistry.

Creative Collaboration: Partnering with AI for Innovative Solutions

GenAI is a transformative force in the landscape of innovation, offering a myriad of possibilities for creators and businesses alike. By analyzing vast datasets, GenAI can synthesize new patterns, ideas, and solutions that might elude the human mind.

For example, in the realm of product design, GenAI can generate countless iterations of a product, each tailored to specific consumer preferences or emerging trends, much like how ChatGPT can personalize shopping experiences by aligning product selections with individual tastes.

In the field of marketing, GenAI tools like DALL-E create compelling visual content that can be customized for targeted campaigns, without the need for extensive graphic design expertise.

Similarly, decision-makers can utilize GenAI to simulate various business scenarios, enabling them to explore creative strategies that conform to or diverge from traditional models, thereby fostering a culture of continuous innovation.

Moreover, GenAI's ability to generate music and art can democratize creativity, allowing individuals with minimal training to produce works that resonate emotionally with audiences. This echoes the way GenAI assists in creative writing, suggesting storylines or dialogue that enrich the narrative experience.

Breaking the Block: AI Techniques to Overcome Creative Barriers

By employing AI techniques, individuals can transcend traditional creative barriers. For writers, AI can analyze vast amounts of literary works to suggest themes, character arcs, or plot devices that align with their vision, effectively overcoming creative stagnation or to simply make their work process more efficient. They can do the same with movies, TV shows, documentaries, fan fiction, ebooks, podcasts, webinars, social media channels, and more.

Visual artists can leverage AI to explore new color schemes or art styles, drawing from a database of historical art movements and contemporary trends. Musicians can use AI to experiment with unconventional chord progressions or rhythms, pushing the envelope of their musical compositions.

AI's adaptability is crucial; as it learns from feedback and evolves, it can offer increasingly tailored suggestions that resonate more deeply with the creator's intent. This iterative process is like a digital brainstorming session, where AI continuously refines its output based on the creator's responses.

In essence, GenAI serves as a catalyst for creativity, providing tools that not only break through creative blocks but also elevate the creator's originality and expression. This adaptability is essential for creatives who must navigate an ever-changing landscape of cultural and societal influences.

Customized Creativity: Tailoring AI to Your Artistic Style

Imagine your art infused with the smarts and speed of AI, creating a digital sidekick that gets your personal creative style. It's like having a robot apprentice that learns to paint, write, or compose by studying your masterpieces. Start by feeding this eager learner a gallery of your work, letting it soak up every detail — from the bold colors you use to the rhythm of your words. This is how you program your AI pal to pick up on the swirls of your brush or the hooks of your melodies.

Now roll up your sleeves and guide your AI through its paces, using prompts that paint a picture of your vision. Want to craft dreamy, surreal landscapes? Tell your AI to sprinkle in some ethereal magic. As it delivers each creation, chisel away at the results together, praising the hits and tweaking the misses in a series of prompts. This back-and-forth is like a jam session with a tireless muse, pushing both of you to riff on themes and emotions in ways you never imagined.

By melding your artistic intuition with AI's endless possibilities, you're not just making art — you're embarking on a journey of discovery. It's a partnership in which your unique voice leads the dance, and AI's precision makes every step shine. Together, you'll unlock a symphony of creativity that will result in a finished work that is unmistakably yours.

Visualizing the Unseen: Using AI to Generate New Art Forms

GenAI is revolutionizing the art world by enabling the creation of novel art forms. This technology serves as a digital muse, capable of transforming artistic visions into reality and even inspiring new directions for creativity. Artists can use AI to push the boundaries of traditional mediums, generating art that interweaves human imagination with machine precision.

To harness GenAI for art, artists input their work or inspirational pieces into the AI, which then learns to mimic and expand upon their unique styles. This process is not just about replication but also about innovation. For instance, DALL-E, a GenAI tool, can out paint images, which means extending them beyond their original borders and adding elements that tell a more comprehensive story or create entirely new narratives.

The iterative interaction between the artist and GenAI is crucial. You provide feedback on the AI-generated pieces, refining the AI's output to better align with your own artistic voice. This synergy can lead to the emergence of unprecedented art forms, blending the familiar with the surreal, the classical with the avant-garde.

Moreover, GenAI's ability to explore a vast array of emotional and thematic expressions can lead to art that resonates on a deeper level with audiences. As artists continue to explore GenAI's limitless potential for discovering new art forms, a new chapter in the evolution of artistic expression will unfold at a quickening pace.

The Idea Incubator: GenAI as a Brainstorming Partner

GenAI acts as a powerhouse for creative thought and limitless ideas, offering a multitude of possibilities that might not be immediately apparent to the human mind. When you're at the drawing board, looking for that spark of innovation, GenAI can serve as an ideal brainstorming partner.

By inputting initial concepts or themes into a GenAI system, you can receive a diverse array of outputs that range from slight variations to radical departures from your original idea. This process can be particularly useful when you're stuck or when you're seeking to explore uncharted territories in your work. GenAI algorithms, trained on vast datasets, can draw connections between seemingly unrelated concepts, presenting you with a rich tapestry of ideas that can inspire new directions for your projects.

Moreover, GenAI can be prompted to simulate brainstorming sessions with multiple participants, each suggesting different perspectives or solutions. This can mimic the dynamic of a group brainstorming session, providing the benefits of collective intelligence without the need for a physical team.

In essence, using GenAI for brainstorming is about expanding your creative horizon. It's a tool that challenges your preconceptions and encourages you to think outside the box, making it an invaluable asset for anyone looking to push the boundaries of their creativity. Whether you're a writer, designer, entrepreneur, or artist, GenAI can help catalyze the creative process, generating a wellspring of ideas that can take your work to new heights.

From Data to Art: Transforming Numbers into Narratives with AI

Transforming data into art is a fascinating process that marries the precision of analytics with the boundless creativity of the human spirit. Using GenAI, numbers and figures transcend their rigid origins, morphing into visual spectacles that captivate and communicate. It's a journey that begins with the raw material of data — be it from vast datasets or more modest collections — and ends with a piece that tells a story, evokes emotion, or challenges perception.

Data artists wield tools like machine learning and automated visualization software to sift through the digital chaff, seeking the golden patterns that lie hidden within. They apply domain knowledge and interdisciplinary expertise to extract meaningful narratives, transforming them into compelling visual representations. This process is not just about aesthetics; it's about making the abstract tangible, turning the invisible into something that can be seen and felt.

The art that emerges from data can take many forms: It might be a dynamic sculpture that shifts with real-time inputs, a lifelike and interactive character in the metaverse or in a game, a static image that reveals the hidden beauty of statistical correlations, or an interactive installation that invites viewers to explore and manipulate the data themselves. Each piece serves as a testament to the power of human interpretation, a bridge between the binary world of computers and the rich complexity of human experience.

In this new frontier, data is not just a tool for decision-making but a canvas for innovation and expression. As we continue to explore the possibilities of data-driven art, we not only expand our understanding of the information that shapes our world but also the potential for that information to inspire and transform us.

Chapter 18

Ten Tips for Advanced Prompting

Before you dig into more sophisticated prompting strategies, let me give you a quick recap on the basics of crafting effective prompts. Remember to be clear and concise, use plain language, and ask one question at a time. Keep your tone respectful and stay within the bounds of the GenAI tool's knowledge and capabilities.

TIP

Kindly allow me to also remind you to review the advanced prompting and other GenAI strategies in Chapter 9. Those tend to produce wonderful content beyond anything you can pull out of GenAI using basic prompting.

With all of that in mind, dig into these additional advanced prompting tips to take GenAI outputs and your content to the next level.

Leverage Keywords

Use specific keywords that signal the context and subject matter you want to explore. Think of them as "command words" that steer the GenAI in the right direction, ensuring a more relevant response.

Sample prompts:

> Prompt A: "Detail the economic impacts of inflation, focusing specifically on consumer purchasing power and interest rates."

> Prompt B: "Discuss the health benefits of a Mediterranean diet, emphasizing its effects on cardiovascular health and longevity."

> Prompt C: "Analyze the significance of machine learning in data analytics, with particular attention to predictive modeling and pattern recognition."

Structure Prompts Logically

Organize your prompt logically. Start with the main question or topic, follow up with details, and end with any specific instructions. This helps the AI understand the sequence and priority of the information.

Sample prompts:

> Prompt A: "First, list the symptoms of a migraine. Next, describe the stages of a migraine attack. Lastly, suggest lifestyle changes that may reduce the frequency of migraines."

> Prompt B: "Define renewable energy, compare the top three sources, and conclude with the challenges faced in implementing these technologies on a global scale."

> Prompt C: "Describe the plot of *1984* by George Orwell, then explain the concept of Big Brother and its relevance to modern-day privacy concerns."

Explain Through Examples

Provide examples to clarify the kind of response you're seeking. Examples act as templates, guiding the GenAI to match the format and style you're looking for.

Sample prompts:

> Prompt A: "Create a condolence message for a colleague who has lost a loved one, similar in empathy and professionalism to this example: [Insert example message]."

> Prompt B: "Write a product description for a high-end smartwatch, modeled after the engaging and feature-highlighting tone of this example: [Insert example description]."

Prompt C: "Draft a resume objective for a software engineer with a focus on cybersecurity, drawing inspiration from the concise and impactful style of this example: [Insert example objective]."

Employ Constraints

Set boundaries to focus the GenAI's creativity or output. Specify the length, tone, or format you desire. This is like setting up bumpers in a bowling alley to keep the ball heading toward the pins.

Sample prompts:

Prompt A: "Compose a haiku about a sunset over the ocean, adhering to the traditional 5-7-5 syllable structure."

Prompt B: "Develop a tagline for an eco-friendly clothing brand that is no more than six words long and conveys sustainability."

Prompt C: "Write a dialogue between two characters in a mystery novel that reveals the culprit without using the words 'confess' or 'guilty'."

Ask for Iterations

If you're exploring ideas, ask the GenAI to provide multiple versions or variations. This is like brainstorming with a team, except the team is a GenAI that doesn't need coffee breaks.

Sample prompts:

Prompt A: "List three potential headlines for an article about the rise of telemedicine during the pandemic."

Prompt B: "Give three different explanations for the phenomenon of the Northern Lights, suitable for young children."

Prompt C: "Provide three variations of a thesis statement for an essay on the impact of social media on human communication."

Incorporate Logic and Reasoning

If you're after a detailed explanation, prompt the GenAI to use logic or reasoning. This encourages it to construct responses that follow a clear, rational progression.

Sample prompts:

> Prompt A: "Present a logical argument for the conservation of rainforests, including at least three ecological benefits."
>
> Prompt B: "Use deductive reasoning to explain why a balanced diet is more beneficial than fad diets for long-term weight management."
>
> Prompt C: "Construct a logical sequence of events that could explain the sudden increase in electric car sales over the past decade."

Sequence Your Prompts

For complex topics, break down your inquiry into a series of prompts. This step-by-step approach can help build a comprehensive answer without the GenAI losing track like it can when there are too many steps or requests in a single prompt. Sequenced or serial prompting works much like assembling a puzzle piece by piece. This is also called prompt chaining since each subsequent prompt digs deeper into the subject, and the GenAI builds upon the information provided in previous responses. This strategy creates a more natural and progressive exploration of the topic, much like a conversation between humans.

Sample prompts:

> Prompt A1: "What is the greenhouse effect?"
>
> Prompt A2: "How does the greenhouse effect contribute to global warming?"
>
> Prompt A3: "What can be done to mitigate the effects of global warming on the environment?"
>
> Prompt B1: "Identify the core principles of Stoic philosophy."
>
> Prompt B2: "Explain how Stoicism advises handling adversity."
>
> Prompt B3: "Provide modern-day examples of Stoicism in practice."

Prompt C1: "What are the basic rules of chess?"

Prompt C2: "Describe common strategies for mid-game play in chess."

Prompt C3: "Analyze the role of psychology in high-level chess matches."

Reference Past Interactions

If you've had previous exchanges with the GenAI tool that are relevant to your current prompt, refer back to them. This creates continuity and helps the GenAI understand the context in a broader sense.

Sample prompts:

Prompt A: "Last time, you provided a list of the most influential philosophers of the 20th century. Can you now explain the main contribution of each to philosophy?"

Prompt B: "You previously outlined the basics of the keto diet. Could you delve into how the keto diet affects athletic performance?"

Prompt C: "Building on our previous discussion about the Mars Rover missions, what are the most significant findings from the latest rover, Perseverance?"

Be Explicit About Style

If you have a preferred writing style, such as persuasive, informative, or narrative, state it clearly. This is akin to choosing the right gear for a car to match the driving conditions.

Sample prompts:

Prompt A: "Write a descriptive paragraph about a bustling city street, using vivid imagery to paint a picture for the reader."

Prompt B: "Formulate an informative blog post on the history of the internet, ensuring clarity and accessibility for a general audience."

Prompt C: "Pen a satirical comment on modern consumer culture, imitating the style of Jonathan Swift to convey your critique."

Use Meta-Prompts

Meta-prompts are prompts about prompts. They can be used to fine-tune the GenAI's approach to answering questions or to address the structure of the responses themselves. It's like teaching the GenAI to fish, rather than just giving it the fish.

Prompt A: "I want to write better prompts for creating fictional characters. Review this prompt and advise on how to enhance it for more detailed character development: [Insert sample prompt]."

Prompt B: "How can I refine this prompt to get a more comprehensive overview of the impact of blockchain technology on finance? [Insert sample prompt]."

Prompt C: "Please analyze the effectiveness of this prompt in eliciting a step-by-step guide and suggest improvements: [Insert sample prompt]."

Index

traits, character,
      checking, 181–182
transcription, GenAI for, 95
translation, GenAI for, 95
transparency, 46, 83, 246–247
trend analysis, 58–59, 105, 114
troubleshooting GenAI interaction
      issues, 89–90
trust, as an ethical
      consideration, 83
truth, in GenAI-assisted
      reporting, 248–249
Turnitin, 111–112, 118
Twitter (X), 152, 153
typography, as a factor influencing
      content readability, 228

U

Udacity, 59
uMark, 244
underfitting, 91
understanding, lack of, in GenAI
      models, 80–81
UNESCO's Global Index on
      Responsible AI, 252
updates, 103, 178
upskilling, 60
U.S. Government
      Initiatives, 252–253
USAID's Digital Strategy, 253

V

value, adding, 95
vector pipelines, as a challenge of
      software integration, 199
versatility, as an advantage of
      concise summaries, 174
Video Watermark Pro, 244
videos. See also media
   creating with AI, 168–169
   GenAI for transription of, 95
   optimization of, 148
   role of artificial intelligence (AI)
      in production of, 37–38
virtual assistants, GenAI compared
      with, 9–10
visual aids, as a factor influencing
      content readability, 228
visual arts, GenAI for, 19, 69–70
visual assists, using GenAI
      for, 69–72
visual concept generation,
      storyboarding and, 183
visual content, generating with AI
      tools, 70–71
visuals, engaging with, 128
vocabulary,180, 228
voice-activated personal
      assistant, 212
voiceovers, GenAI for, 96
voice-to-text transcription,
      GenAI for, 143

W

wall art, 42–43
Warning icon, 3
warnings, for content
      customization,
      128–131
Watermarkly, 244
webinars, 58
Whimsical AI, 231
white papers, creating using
      GenAI, 105–107
wit, injecting, 181
Wix ADI (Artificial Design
      Intelligence), 147
World Economic Forum's
      AI Governance Alliance,
      253
writing assistant, GenAI
      as a, 63–69

Y

Yewno Discover, 106
YouTube, 59, 153, 154

Z

ZoeroBib, 108
Zotero, 99, 111
Zyro, 147

About the Author

Pam Baker is a veteran analyst, freelance journalist, and author. Her previous book, *ChatGPT For Dummies*, is already in its 2nd edition. Some of her other books, such as *Decision Intelligence For Dummies*, are also on the topic of AI.

Baker writes for several mainstream and tech media outlets, including *Institutional Investor*, *Ars Technica*, CIO, CISO, *InformationWeek*, CNN, *The New York Times*, *PC magazine*, and *TechTarget*. She's the author of several books and a popular speaker at science and technology conferences. Her speech on mobile health data and analytics is published in the Annals of the New York Academy of Sciences. Former analyst engagements include research and reporting for ABI Research, VisionGain, and Evans Research.

Pam is a member of the National Press Club (NPC), the Society of Professional Journalists (SPJ), and the Internet Press Guild (IPG). For her LinkedIn bio, references, and clips, go to www.linkedin.com/in/pambaker/.

Dedication

Dedicated to Stephanie Baker Forston and David Forston, Ben Baker and Dr. Katherine Poruk Baker, and my all-inspiring and joy-infusing granddaughter crew: Mirabel, Coco, Poppy, and Charlotte. Special thanks to Ben for being my sounding board and adviser on all things tech, including AI. Thanks to Katherine for letting me use her office down by the sea — again! The two cats, Luna and Cinny, are always an extra nice touch, guys. Thanks to Stephanie for bringing your all every single time to every situation. To all of you, thanks for being my inspiration and support team through this and other writing marathons and for rocking my world.

Author's Acknowledgments

In the best of times, producing a book worthy of our readers is a huge undertaking. But blazing a trail to produce this book as a pilot project for using GenAI in publishing has been both an extraordinary and trying experience for me and the entire Wiley team. Together and apart, myself, and the editorial, technical, and AI departments worked in concert to figure out how to make this project work from the raw idea to a polished and useful book on shelves in bookstores around the world.

Each of us, together and individually, battled a growing list of unforeseen and vexing obstacles, pushed models not previously tested for this type of work, celebrated small and large victories, sweated unforgiving deadlines, and pushed our own skills and resilience to the limit.

I offer my deepest gratitude to the many people who made this book possible and made it far better than I could have ever done alone.

A special thanks to Steve Hayes, executive editor, for his fearless leadership in going where few publishers have ever gone before. Hayes is creative and logical, which is the perfect mix when you're chasing innovation that makes great business sense.

Also, many, many thanks to Chrissy Guthrie, development editor, without whom I may have never made it to the final deadline. That's the thing with blazing trails, you see. You go down a lot of wrong paths and have to circle back, you lose your way often, forget what you wrote three chapters back, and haggle with multiple GenAI tools simultaneously only to repeatedly lose your place, among dealing with other things like exhaustion and avoiding the virtual gators and mosquitoes in datasets and RAG limits. Chrissy kept us all on course and poked me to fix this and change that as needed to make the book a more informative and enjoyable read.

A special thanks to Guy Hart-Davis, technical editor, for double-checking my work and proactively guarding against AI hallucinations, all the while making me giggle at his quips and jokes. Kelly Henthorne, copy editor, guarded us all from my own errors. GenAI certainly doesn't own the market on mistakes and jumbled wording.

Shouting a big thanks to Etzer Botes, Nyo Maw, Sithira Weerabahu, Gary Spencer, and Andrew Jones who waded into the weeds to discover ways to make the various GenAI models work when their pre-packaged features fell far short of what was needed. They blew my mind in how well they pulled that off. And that's not easy to do, given that I've worked with various types of AI and AI teams for decades.

Another huge thanks to the rest of the very talented editorial and production staff at Wiley. If I overlooked anyone, please accept my profound apologies. And, of course and always, a heartfelt thanks to my agent, Carole Jelen.

We learned a lot. And while it took us longer than expected to produce this book, the next one will go much more quickly than normal because the path has been cleared and the way well marked.

Publisher's Acknowledgments

Executive Editor: Steven Hayes
Development Editor: Christina Guthrie
Copy Editor: Kelly D. Henthorne
Technical Editor: Guy Hart-Davis

Managing Editor: Kristie Pyles
Production Editor: Tamilmani Varadharaj
Cover Image: © IndiaPix/IndiaPicture/ Getty Images